The Holy Spirit and Worship

The Holy Spirit and Worship

Transformation and Truth in the Theologies
of John Owen and John Zizioulas

ELIZABETH A. WELCH

Foreword by Ben Quash

PICKWICK *Publications* · Eugene, Oregon

THE HOLY SPIRIT AND WORSHIP
Transformation and Truth in the Theologies of John Owen and John Zizioulas

Pickwick Publications
An Imprint of Wipf and Stock Publishers
199 W. 8th Ave., Suite 3
Eugene, OR 97401

www.wipfandstock.com

PAPERBACK ISBN: 978-1-7252-6111-2
HARDCOVER ISBN: 978-1-7252-6110-5
EBOOK ISBN: 978-1-7252-6112-9

Cataloguing-in-Publication data:

Names: Welch, Elizabeth A.

Title: The Holy Spirit and worship : transformation and truth in the theologies of John Owen and John Zizioulas / Elizabeth A. Welch.

Description: Eugene, OR: Pickwick Publications, 2021 | Includes bibliographical references and index.

Identifiers: ISBN 978-1-7252-6111-2 (paperback) | ISBN 978-1-7252-6110-5 (hardcover) | ISBN 978-1-7252-6112-9 (ebook)

Subjects: LCSH: Holy Spirit. | Public worship. | Worship. | Owen, John, 1616–1683. | Zizioulas, Jean, 1931–. | Theology—History

Classification: BT121.2 2021 (paperback) | BT121.2 (ebook)

12/08/20

This work is dedicated to my beloved husband, Peter Skerratt, for his support and encouragement, and to the many faithful people of God I have been privileged to encounter over the years, across different traditions of the church, who have stimulated my thinking about the Holy Spirit and worship, both theoretically and in practice.

Contents

Foreword

It is in the worship of God that human beings realize themselves most completely. In worship, they fulfil their vocation as creatures. The worshipping vocation is a vocation shared with all other creatures, non-human ones included (which is why the Bible talks of trees, mountains, deserts, and seas giving glory to God). But there are distinctive ways in which worship works as human vocation. It provides the context in which humans grasp themselves in their deepest truth and potential, precisely as they find themselves grasped by God. Worship is the medium—best characterized using the language of *relationship*—in which full human personhood emerges. In worship, inward dispositions and outward actions are reciprocally related as part of a formative orientation to God by which we are shaped together for holiness.

There are plenty of ways in which Christian worship can be characterized and described using the tools of the human sciences: sociological, anthropological, historical, psychological, and more. Christian worship can be placed in a baggy common category entitled "ritual practices," and the artefacts associated with it examined as forms of "material culture." But from a Christian theological perspective, however illuminating these studies may be, the one thing needful for an adequate characterization of worship is a good doctrine of the Holy Spirit.

Ultimately, it is only the Holy Spirit who allows worship to be worship. Without the Holy Spirit, it is something less (a personal habit, a vehicle for the expression of spiritual aspirations, a mechanism of collective socialization, a solace-giving retreat from the demands of the world). Under the inspiration of the Holy Spirit worship becomes more than any of these, and is protected from becoming what all of them could easily become: idolatry.

It is only the Holy Spirit who allows worship to be worship. When this affirmation is allowed the centrality that the Christian faith insists that it should have, then other things (which have at times seemed of huge importance to the churches) are put in a better context. The specifics of worship—the details of what is and isn't done—are properly secondary to this one thing needful.

It is only the Holy Spirit who allows worship to be worship. Elizabeth Welch's book is a sustained exploration of that central truth, and is the fruit both of careful scholarship and of a lifetime of dedicated service to ecumenical conversation. *The Holy Spirit and Worship* has all the hallmarks of a book by a seasoned ecumenist. The author is careful in the best sense: attentive, measured, hospitable to many perspectives, and generous-spirited in seeking points of connection rather than laboring differences. She cares deeply about this subject, and that care is evident on each page of the book, as well as in the fact that the book exists at all.

Moreover, her ecumenist's desire, and ability, to make connections is manifested in the multiple connections that the book's pneumatological approach allows her to make. These connections are at the center of this book's achievements.

First of all, she connects the Church past and present by her sustained comparison of one of the great (though often neglected) divines of the seventeenth century, John Owen, with one of the foremost theologians of the modern period, John Zizioulas. It is a bold connection to make, but it shows far more effectively than a series of generalized but free-floating claims could ever do that it is not a fantasy to claim that the Church (in the power of the Spirit) is one, in all times and places. The commonality of concerns across the centuries is one of the great revelations in the pages that follow.

In a similar vein, Welch explores with insight how the local is connected with the universal: universal claims about the Church are never adequate unless they are also locally evidenced and grounded. The Church is like the sacraments of which it is custodian in always being concrete. This book is alert to particular contexts and to how they are windows onto enduring truths.

Next, this is a book that connects head and heart. It astutely unveils the ways that the doctrines that shape and articulate what is going on in worship ought not to be divorced from the experiences and emotions that are at play in worship, but also that such affective and felt aspects of worship are "proved" by doctrine (in the traditional sense of tested, established, and demonstrated). The Spirit is one who both teaches the mind and warms the affections. In particular, Welch gives the lie to caricatures of Puritanism as resolutely intellectualist—focused on the saving power of right doctrines, conceptually distilled from divine revelation in Scripture. She shows Owen, the Puritan, to be someone who has ample room for what she describes as experiential and relational knowledge, and here too finds profound affinities with Zizioulas's theology.

Zizioulas's is a theology of "persons in communion." Only in relationship with others are human beings persons at all, and only in relation with others are we participants in the eternal life of the Trinity. This allows Welch's comparative engagement with Owen and Zizioulas to make another connection: that between the individual and the community. She gives a pneumatological account of how worship makes a "we" out of many "I"s. It is in the power of the Spirit that the Body of Christ is bound together and all its parts coordinated. The gifts of the Spirit are for the sanctification of individuals only because they bestow social virtues. The fruits of these virtues are collectively known and held: love, joy, peace, patience, kindness, goodness, faithfulness, gentleness, and self-control (Gal 5:22–23). The supreme context in which these gifts of the Spirit are given is worship.

Past and present; local and universal; head and heart; individual and community: these connections are reestablished and renewed every time Christians worship. This book explores those connections as the work of the Holy Spirit, the divine connector, who binds all things.

And the final connection the book makes is between East and West—across a Christian denominational difference that on the face of it looks about as extreme as you could imagine: Reformed Protestantism and Greek Orthodoxy. In Welch's hands, the divide looks far more like a rich field of reciprocities, many of them being realized for the very first time in the groundbreaking chapters that follow. If these two church traditions can be brought so productively into dialogue, there is surely hope for a great many other divided traditions too. The human vocation will be fulfilled in such convergences. The wisdom needed to accomplish them is the wisdom that the Holy Spirit imparts when human beings worship in spirit and in truth.

BEN QUASH
Professor of Arts and Christianity at King's College, London.

Preface

My reflections on the Holy Spirit and Worship have been greatly helped by my lived experience of leading worship and my engagement with both lay and ordained people in reflecting on the meaning and nature of worship, as inspired by the Holy Spirit.

In this book, I look at the significance of the relationship between the Holy Spirit and worship as seen in two theologians from different parts of the church, and from different centuries. I comment on the unexpected congruities within their thinking, and categorise these in terms of a quadrilateral, with the four sides being personhood, immediacy, truth and transformation.

These two theologians are John Owen, seventeenth-century English Puritan Divine, who wrote extensively on pneumatology and saw the regenerating and sanctifying work of the Holy Spirit as having a particular focus in worship; and John Zizioulas, contemporary Orthodox theologian, for whom the Holy Spirit embodies communion, particularly in worship as focussed in the Eucharist.

I argue that in worship there is an immediacy of encounter with the triune God through the particular mediation of the Holy Spirit; that this encounter draws the person into relationship with the God who is known within the Trinity as being in relationship, and who draws people into a relationship that brings about the fulfilment of personhood; that this encounter leads into a truth that is relational, thus expanding the nature and understanding of the role of doctrine; and that this encounter is transformational, in terms of the person and creation.

I build on perspectives from theologians from two different centuries and traditions of the church for whom pneumatology and worship are significant areas of their thinking. I do this in order to argue that one part of the activity of the Holy Spirit is the flourishing of diversity, a diversity which is held relationally within the source of divine life within the Trinity. I conclude by looking at the ecumenical challenges offered in the coming together of these two perspectives.

Acknowledgments

I have been grateful for the care and attention, wisdom and insight of my PhD supervisor at Kings College, Ben Quash. I am appreciative of the range of insights offered by John Burgess, Paul Avis, Julian Templeton, John Webster, and others who have offered comments on my doctoral research.

The Dr. Williams Library has been like a second home and I have valued the support of the director, Dr. Wykes, and help of the staff.

The works of Colin Gunton, Geoffrey Nuttall, and John Zizioulas have been inspirational in the thinking that led to my doctoral thesis.

John de Jong has offered his time generously on the re-formatting for the book, Joanna Frew has helped with the details for the footnotes and the bibliography for the PhD, and Peter Skerratt helped with the formatting of the PhD.

1

The Holy Spirit and Worship

Setting the Scene

THE HOLY SPIRIT AND THE RENEWAL OF WORSHIP

The purpose of this book is to contribute to a deepening of contemporary ecumenical thinking about the Holy Spirit and the relationship of the Holy Spirit to worship. While much has been written about both the Holy Spirit and worship, this work argues that a theological approach centered on the transformative work of the Holy Spirit, understood in the context of the doctrine of the triune God and drawing together doctrine and experience, deserves to be given more weight in contemporary approaches to the understanding and development of Christian worship.

This chapter introduces the book, starting by looking at contemporary factors with regard to the Holy Spirit and worship which form the setting for the research. The chapter continues by offering a summary of the aim of this work, which is to look at the development of what will be called a "quadrilateral" approach to the nature of the Holy Spirit as manifest in worship. This aim will be pursued by examining the writings of two theologians—John Owen (an English nonconformist Reformed theologian from the seventeenth century) and John Zizioulas (a contemporary Eastern Orthodox theologian)—who offer a particular focus on the Holy Spirit and

1

worship from their radically different contexts.[1] The interesting and unexpected congruities between these different theologians form the basis for the arguments that are being developed, within what is being referred to as a "quadrilateral framework"—a fourfold integrated approach to the Holy Spirit and worship.

A summary of this quadrilateral framework is offered in this chapter and at the end of this chapter an outline is offered of the way the argument is taken forward.

CONTEMPORARY CONTEXTS REGARDING THE HOLY SPIRIT AND WORSHIP

In order to set the backdrop to the discussion of the nature and work of the Holy Spirit in worship this chapter refers to some contemporary Christian contexts in relation to the understanding and activity of the Holy Spirit, particularly with regard to worship.

Taking a broad ecumenical sweep, it is significant to note that the World Council of Churches, in its themes for its Assembly over the past sixty years, has moved on from what had been suggested verged on a Christomonist position—"Christ—the Hope of the World" (Evanston, 1954), "Jesus Christ—the Light of the World" (New Delhi, 1961), "Jesus Christ Frees and Unites" (Nairobi, 1975), and "Jesus Christ—the Life of the World" (Vancouver, 1983)—to the pneumatological theme of the Canberra Assembly in 1991, "Come Holy Spirit," echoed in the eschatological perspective of Harare in 1998, "Turn to God—Rejoice in Hope." My concluding chapter will return to the ecumenical implications of pursuing the perspective on the Holy Spirit in relation to worship that this volume advances.

Moving to a more local perspective, that of the United Kingdom, a key contemporary factor with regard to worship is the decline in the numbers of people participating in worship in the "historic" churches.[2] Much has been written about the changing nature of the Christian faith in Britain and the way in which people in the United Kingdom still hold some form of Christian

1. Owen's writing equally balances his references to "Holy Spirit" and "Holy Ghost." For the sake of coherence in this book, I will be using "Holy Spirit," apart from when directly quoting Owen's references to "Holy Ghost."

2. At one time in the UK, it could be argued that the "historic" churches were the mainstream churches. However, with the growth of new evangelical and Pentecostal churches, there is now a greater range of churches that could be described as "mainstream." I am using the word "historic" to refer to pre- and post-Reformation churches rather than the new churches of the twentieth and twenty-first centuries.

faith but do not see the need to live out this faith within the context of a wor-shipping Christian community.[3] There is a range of factors involved in this. Worship is not necessarily seen as an encounter with the living, transform-ing God who changes people's lives. Even among those who are churchgo-ers in many of the "historic" churches, there is diffidence about articulating the nature of the presence of God in worship. It is interesting to note that, despite Grace Davie's influential writing on "Believing but not Belonging" in her helpful analysis of religion in Britain, traditional Christian believing, as associated with regular churchgoing in the historic churches, has also been gently declining, although nowhere near as rapidly as churchgoing.[4] As the focus on the self increases, so the need for the development of a stable com-munity life and community events diminishes, especially events in which there is a mutual and ongoing commitment across diverse communities of age, gender, and ethnicity.[5] Worship becomes privatized and is an activity that a person can undertake on his or her own. As faith in God diminishes, so the desire to worship diminishes. There is a further issue for the churches in Britain today as to whether the sense of encounter with God through the power of the Holy Spirit has diminished, and whether in fact this has led to a decline in churchgoing.

Reclaiming the Holiness of God in Worship

There has been a range of responses to decline, including the development of initiatives across a spectrum of perspectives, from Fresh Expressions to those who offer a critique of some contemporary expressions of worship. Chapter 4 will offer an analysis of current writings on worship and the range of perspectives from which these come.[6]

Some contemporary approaches look at worship primarily from a human experiential perspective, often helpfully developing lively,

3. For example, Brown, *Death of Christian Britain*; Murray, *Church after Christen-dom*; MacLaren, *Mission Implausible*; Brierley, *Pulling Out*; *Mission-Shaped Church*.

4. Davie, *Religion in Britain*.

5. "Expressive individuation has become one of the cornerstones of modern cul-ture" (Taylor, *Sources of the Self*, 376). This book helpfully offers a significant contri-bution to the history and background of the "turn to the self" as well as setting this within the framework of contemporary issues.

6. Fresh Expressions is a Church of England/Methodist initiative which defines itself as follows: "A fresh expression of church is a new gathering or network that en-gages mainly with people who have never been to church. There is no single model, but the emphasis is on starting something which is appropriate to its context" (Fresh Expressions, "Starting Our Journey").

culturally-rooted expressions of worship.[7] A growing number of twenty-first-century approaches to worship seek to redress what is perceived to be an empty ritualizing of worship by including a focus on the need for innovation, relevance, and the development of an experiential approach.[8] These developments relate well to the intricacies and vagaries of human experience but can neglect the awe and wonder of the reality of the divine. A contemporary American Lutheran liturgical theologian, Gordon Lathrop, comments critically on a range of perspectives, referring at one end of the spectrum to the danger of the over-ritualizing of worship which can lead to a present sense of emptiness of worship and, at the other end of the spectrum, to the search for excitement in worship which neglects the reality of the divine:

> When, in practice, the symbols have shriveled and the ritual has ceased to draw or to surprise us, when the meaning of the meeting has been hidden or forgotten, when the manner of the gathering's leaders has become the manner of entertainers and when the assembly itself has come to be regarded as largely a privately chosen and purchased exercise of individual religious taste, it is difficult to see the application of word and sacraments to the universe we currently know and to the aching and complex needs of the end of the twentieth century and the beginning of the twenty-first.[9]

Another contemporary approach to worship focuses on worship as primarily the place for community-building, emphasizing again the human dimension of worship to the diminishment of the encounter with the divine. Lathrop's critical approach to some of the ways in which worship is developed was taken further by the American born but largely English-based Anglican theologian, Daniel Hardy, when he commented: "The occupational hazard is to treat worship as a routine ritual practice of community-formation unmotivated by—and inert in the presence of—the holiness of God."[10] Hardy continues by stressing the reality of the divine in the link between worship and participation in the holiness of God:

> Yet if we see worship as the situation in which the relational and directive propriety of the holiness of God is intrinsically present

7. Chapter 4 offers more detailed references on worship.

8. The development of the strands of "Alternative Worship" and "Fresh Expressions" are examples of approaches to contemporary worship with a more experiential focus. See, for example, Baker and Gay, *Alternative Worship*.

9. Lathrop, *Holy Things*, 4.

10. Hardy, *Finding the Church*, 20.

in social enactment, there is a direct connection between the contingent human attempt to "worship" and in the inner dynamic of the holiness of God.[11]

This book argues that this "inner dynamic of the holiness of God" is particularly found in the nature and activity of the Holy Spirit. The "direct connection" to which Hardy refers is what is unpacked in the third part of the quadrilateral argument under the concept of "immediacy."

Growth in Churches with an Emphasis on the Holy Spirit

The decline of churchgoing in the UK has been helpfully analyzed by the Christian Research Association. This Association, in its wide-ranging research into trends in churchgoing, has examined the way in which the years since the Second World War in the UK have seen a marked decline in church attendance, firstly in England and Wales and then more recently in Scotland and Ireland.[12] The Christian Research Association has also identified churches that have reversed this trend and have been marked by a rise in churchgoing often formed through immigration.[13] While Pentecostal and charismatic churches are at the forefront of church growth, the research done by Brierley in 2005 notes that another of the traditions of the church to show growth in the UK is that of the Orthodox churches, with one interpretation of this rise being a link with the particular pneumatological orientation of Orthodoxy.[14]

Orthodox churches, and many of the Pentecostal churches, have their origins in parent churches in different parts of the world, largely external to Western Europe. Both Orthodox and Pentecostal churches have an emphasis—albeit held in very different ways from different traditions and backgrounds—on the Holy Spirit. This ongoing centrality of the Spirit in churches outside the West is pointed to by Eugene Rogers. In his helpful book, *After the Spirit: A Constructive Pneumatology from Resources outside the Modern West*, Rogers takes as a theme through the book the way in which the Eastern Church has a greater continuity with the early church in

---

11. Hardy, *Finding the Church*, 20.

12. Brierley, *Religious Trends*. More recent research can be found online at Christian Research (www.christian-research.org).

13. "The Pentecostal and the Orthodox saw considerable proportions growing quickly, both partly because of planting new churches and through growing larger congregations" (Brierley, *Pulling Out of the Nosedive*, 194).

14. Brierley, *Religious Trends*, 5.

its stronger emphasis on the Holy Spirit than has been found in the church in the West.[15]

The debate about the role of the Holy Spirit can be seen in the contention with regard to the inclusion of the "filioque" clause in the Creed. The discussion with regard to the role of the Spirit and of the Son during the early centuries of the church was one of several factors which contributed to the gradual separation of churches of East and West, symbolized in 1054 by the action of papal legates, led by Cardinal Humbert, placing a Bull of Excommunication on the altar of the Hagia Sophia Church in Constantinople.[16] The debate about "filioque" and whether or not it should be present in the Creed was not simply a debate about a word but involved a theological discussion with regard to the triune nature of the divine. "The real issue behind the *filioque* concerns the question whether the ultimate ontological category in theology is the person or the substance."[17] It will be argued in this book that the Eastern Orthodox theologian, John Zizioulas, continues the tradition of Basil and the Cappadocian fathers by arguing "since the person in its identification with hypostasis is an ultimate—and not a secondary—ontological notion, it must be *a person*—and not a substance—that is the source of divine existence."[18] This argument and the issues it raises will be taken further in the body of this volume in terms of Zizioulas's particular articulation of the Holy Spirit and worship. The Eastern argument that the Spirit proceeds from the Father rather than from the Father and the Son emphasizes the greater role placed on the Spirit in the Eastern Church than in the Western Church. This emphasis on the Spirit is echoed in the Orthodox understanding of worship and the role that the Holy Spirit plays in worship.

While the outward practice in forms of worship is in marked variance between Pentecostal and Orthodox churches, there is a distinctive emphasis in each of these groups of churches on the Holy Spirit.

The Neglect of the Holy Spirit in the West

The attention to the Holy Spirit within Orthodoxy and Pentecostalism is particularly noteworthy as a contrast to the range of writing expressing a concern about the insufficient attention given to the Holy Spirit in Western

15. Rogers, *After the Spirit.*

16. Kallistos Ware gives an account of the event in 1054 and of the history that led up to the separation of East from West, a separation that continued to develop in the centuries after 1054. See Ware, *Orthodox Church.*

17. Zizioulas, *Communion and Otherness,* 196.

18. Zizioulas, *Communion and Otherness,* 186.

Christianity. There is a diverse cross-section of writing on the Holy Spirit over the second half of the twentieth century. Some writers on the Holy Spirit have seen the need for a revival of thinking about the Holy Spirit in the West, lamenting the lack of emphasis on the Holy Spirit. Hendry, in 1957, writes, "It has become almost a convention that those who undertake to write about the Holy Spirit should begin by deploring the neglect of this doctrine in the thought and life of the Church today";[19] and Berkhof, in 1964, refers to pneumatology as "a neglected field of systematic theology."[20] Other writers have looked at interpretations of the Holy Spirit which have become over-generalized in a way which takes from the Holy Spirit a sense of specificity within a trinitarian understanding. Carr, in 1975, writes, "The discussion of the Holy Spirit is becoming a ragbag—the Spirit is becoming whatever we like to make it. We need to look again at the Holy Spirit."[21] Yet other writers critique the way in which the neglect of the doctrine of the Holy Spirit does not allow for the Spirit to be seen as having particular power. Welker, in 1994, reflecting on the power of the Holy Spirit, asks the question, "Why is it impossible in the modern world to talk convincingly about God and God's action?"[22]

Kärkkäinen, in his helpful ecumenical survey of Pneumatology, *Pneumatology: The Holy Spirit in Ecumenical, International, and Contextual Perspective*, refers to the late twentieth century as a time of "pneumatological renaissance."[23] He quotes a range of theologians in evidence of this, from Barth to Congar, from Eastern Orthodoxy to Pentecostalism.

While the subject of this book is not the Pentecostal and charismatic traditions of the church, what is offered next is a brief look at Pentecostalism in order to reflect on the input on the Holy Spirit and worship from this particular tradition of the church, a tradition which carries a strong emphasis on Spirit-filled worship. The rise of Pentecostalism is the most predominant phenomenon over the past century with regard to the development of worship as rooted in the power of the Holy Spirit. This volume will be offering contrasting understandings of the Holy Spirit and worship, particularly from Reformed and Orthodox traditions, to hold alongside the helpful emphases from Pentecostal and charismatic traditions.

19. Hendry, *Holy Spirit*, 11.

20. Berkhof, *Doctrine of the Holy Spirit*, 10.

21. Carr, "Towards a Contemporary Theology," 501–16.

22. Welker, *God the Spirit*, 4.

23. Kärkkäinen, *Pneumatology*, 9.

The Rise of Pentecostalism

Alongside the issue of the diminishing role of the divine in worship in the West, the question has been raised as to whether the Holy Spirit has "moved" to the Pentecostal churches (in particular the Black and Minority Ethnic Pentecostal churches), both in the United Kingdom and across the world, because a developed understanding of the work of the Holy Spirit has been neglected in the mainstream traditions. While this way of thinking might seem to be anthropomorphic, it has been raised by those who have observed the growth of Pentecostalism and made comments about the evidence that arises from an experiential approach to the work of the Holy Spirit.

Joe Aldred, Bishop in the Church of God of Prophecy, and (in 2017) a full-time member of staff in Churches Together in England with responsibility for Pentecostal and Multicultural Relations, writes:

> The growth of Black Pentecostalism in England coincides with what appears to be an inexorable decline in White-majority mainstream churches. Attendance in Black Pentecostal churches as a percentage of the overall church-going population exceeds five-fold the Black presence as a percentage of the general population. According to Christian Research, between 1975 and 1989 African Caribbean church attendance remained a steady 5 percent of combined Free Church attendance.[24] By 1998, combined Black church attendance was put at 7.2 percent of the overall church attendance in England at a time when Black people represented 1.9 percent of the overall population of the country.[25] By this time also, Black Pentecostals in the country accounted for a third of all of Pentecostal church going. Between 1995 and 2005, Black-led churches had increased by half, and now represented 10 percent of the overall church-going population whilst being just 2 percent of the overall population in England.[26]
>
> By any measurement this is stupendous growth, and the reasons that occasion it may be manifold. This much can be said with some confidence, that anyone who attends Black Pentecostal worship will testify there is at the heart of the Black worship expression an impulse that is driven by dependence upon something other than human reality. There is an interaction with the Holy Spirit that connects the worshipper with a transcendent

24. Brierley, *Christian England*, 37.
25. Brierley, *Tide is Running Out*, 134.
26. Brierley, *Pulling Out*, 92.

and immanent God. This understanding of God's immanence is emphasized by such choral refrains as, "He is here, Holy Spirit, He is here right now." That Black Pentecostal worship is highly experiential and emotionally charged is indicative of the understanding that the reliance on the Holy Spirit is not just a matter for "within these walls" but is something that affects the entire life of the person and community.[27]

Aldred's analysis from the British context reflects the wider growth of Pentecostalism over the last century. Keith Warrington begins his work *Pentecostal Theology* by writing, "Just over one hundred years ago, Pentecostalism was born. Since then, it has grown to be one of the biggest and fastest growing components of Christianity. Its inception in the West is generally identified as being in Azusa Street, Los Angeles, in 1906."[28] Other writers, as for example, Anderson, Dayton, Hollenweger, and Kay have traced the longer origins of this movement.[29] However, the Azusa Street revival is generally regarded as a key moment in the development of modern Pentecostalism. Since this revival, Pentecostal churches have grown rapidly across the world. While there are a number of significant streams of Pentecostalism, this strand of the church is marked by a range of independent churches, particularly in the Americas, Africa, and Asia.

Pentecostal churches, as seen in many of their parent churches in their countries of origin in Africa and the West Indies and also widely across South America and Asia, have had a full-bodied emphasis on the encounter with the Holy Spirit. In Pentecostal and charismatic churches there is both a key emphasis on the work of the Holy Spirit in the teaching and worship of the church, and also claims made for the effective power of the Holy Spirit at work in such areas as healing and miracles.

The growth of Pentecostalism alongside the slow decline of churchgoing in Europe over the last hundred years raises the pneumatological issue of what the rise of the emphasis on the particular work of the Holy Spirit in Pentecostalism has to say to mainstream churches across Europe. Alongside the growth of Pentecostal churches needs to be held the growth of charismatic movements in mainstream churches across Europe in more recent years, and the range of complicated factors which have led to radically

27. Aldred, *Holy Spirit in the Pentecostal Tradition*.

28. Warrington, *Pentecostal Theology*, 1. The many footnotes in the first chapter provide a comprehensive overview of publications on Pentecostalism.

29. Anderson and Hollenweger, *Pentecostals after a Century*; Kay, *Pentecostalism*; Dayton, *Theological Roots*. These writers offer a broader outline of the movement including referring to John Wesley and the development of the Holiness Movement in the USA and the role of revivals in various parts of the church.

changed patterns in churchgoing and the variety of patterns by which the
presence of the Holy Spirit is understood in different parts of the church
(for example, in the way in which the Holy Spirit shapes the tradition of the
Church, the way the Holy Spirit guides the councils of the church, the way
in which the Holy Spirit shapes ecclesiology, or the prayer to the Holy Spirit
in the "*epiklesis*" during Holy Communion).

Some writers have seen the contribution given by the Pentecostal
churches and charismatic renewal movement as a sign of the renewal in
the Holy Spirit after a time of what might be termed a deficit of the Holy
Spirit. In 1987 Dayton made this point when looking at the origins and
growth of contemporary Pentecostalism: "Some Pentecostals do not want
a history—because the Spirit descended again after nineteen relatively
quiet centuries."[30] In 2002, Kärkkäinen referred to "The Holy Spirit as the
'Cinderella' of Theology." He then went on to indicate the way in which he
understands there to be a twenty-first-century revival of interest in the Holy
Spirit after the lack of attention given in the early church and the West: "This
is no longer the case [that the Holy Spirit is the Cinderella] . . . but it has
been the case . . . in the early centuries; and in the Western church." He continues by reflecting that there is "not so much a forgetting of the Holy Spirit
as a pneumatological deficit."[31] In 2006, Rogers laments the lack of attention
given to the Holy Spirit. He refers to his writing as treating "the continual
lip service and equally continual lack of substance accorded the Holy Spirit
in modern Christian thought. Committed to talk of the Spirit by multiple
traditions, modern Christian thought has less and less to say about it."[32]

During the twentieth century there has been an outpouring of Pentecostal writings on the Holy Spirit and on worship. These Pentecostal writings have, until the latter part of the century, focused more on the particular
bodily manifestations of the Holy Spirit in worship and in the development
of the life of the local church, but are now being undergirded by a more developed systematic theological perspective on the Holy Spirit and worship.[33]

The drawing together of the Holy Spirit and worship in Pentecostalism
offers helpful insights into the theological significance of the Holy Spirit in
relation to worship and points to a dynamic recovery of the understanding

---

30. Dayton, *Theological Roots*, 10.

31. Kärkkäinen, *Pneumatology*, 16–17.

32. Rogers, *After the Spirit*, 1.

33. Allen, *Unfailing Stream*; Anderson and Hollenweger, *Pentecostals after a Century*; Chan, *Liturgical Theology*; Cox, *Fire from Heaven*; Dayton, *Theological Roots*;
Vondey, *Beyond Pentecostalism*. See also Amos Yong's range of books, including *Who
is the Holy Spirit?*; *Spirit Poured Out*; *Spirit of Love*; *Beyond the Impasse*; *Missiological
Spirit*.

of God in the context of a transformative encounter with God. Kärkkäinen highlights this in his survey of developments in writing about the Holy Spirit when he makes the point, "we live in a pneumatological renaissance," a subject he takes forward in his first chapter.[34]

Challenges Arising out of a Pentecostal Perspective

Aldred's analysis of the rise of Pentecostalism raises some thought-provoking questions about the Holy Spirit and the activity of the Spirit. Is the seemingly greater activity of the Holy Spirit in these churches a reflection of the Spirit "choosing" to work in more fruitful fields? Or is it an indication of insufficient attention given to the Spirit in the mainstream churches in the United Kingdom? Even to ask this question is to raise the issue as to whether it is possible for people to block the working of the Spirit. Can a neglect of attention given to the Holy Spirit restrict the work of the Holy Spirit? Shults and Hollingsworth in their helpful Eerdmans Guide Series *The Holy Spirit* refer to "the waxing and waning of the tide of pneumatological interest throughout church history."[35] The pointer to the transformative activity of the Holy Spirit that the rise of Pentecostalism across the twentieth century gives is of assistance in renewing an interest in pneumatology across the range of mainstream churches. The rise of Pentecostalism goes some small way to illustrate the possibility that the Holy Spirit also might find other possibilities of activity amongst people and churches that have different approaches—possibly less dynamic and full-bodied approaches—to the Holy Spirit.

Shults and Hollingsworth point to the rise of interest in pneumatology over this period:

> Most treatments of the doctrine of the Holy Spirit in the middle of the twentieth century began with a complaint about the inadequacy of the Christian tradition's treatment of the "third person" of the Trinity (e.g., Hendry, 1956; Come, 1959). In the last few decades, however, reflection on the Spirit has come to the forefront of discussions within and across theological disciplines (e.g., systematic, biblical and practical theology). Moreover, Pneumatology has increasingly become a generative theme

---

34. Kärkkäinen, *Pneumatology*, 9.

35. Shults and Hollingsworth, *Holy Spirit*. This book, from the Eerdmans Guide to Theology series, is particularly helpful for its extensive annotated bibliography of English-language resources on the Holy Spirit (see 99–150).

around which creative dialogue across religious traditions has
flourished (e.g., ecumenism and interreligious dialogue)."[36]

Later in the book, Shults and Hollingsworth also refer to the pneumatological development seen in new developments such as feminist, liberationist,
and ecological theologies.

Both the visibility and the growth of Pentecostalism raise questions
about the activity of the Holy Spirit. However, the rise of Pentecostalism is
only one aspect of renewed interest in the Holy Spirit. It is also possible to
look at the rise of interest in the Trinity and in trinitarian theology, as seen
in the growing number of books and articles written on the Trinity in the
last sixty years, and see that this reflects, in part, a desire to re-emphasize
the person of the Holy Spirit. This trinitarian emphasis, by focusing on
the nature of God in three persons, counterbalances the more experiential
Pentecostal approach with its emphasis on the third person of the Trinity.
Chapter 2 will look further at the discussion with regard to the Trinity that
underlies the renewal of thinking about the Holy Spirit.

The growth of Pentecostalism brings to the fore the way in which the
Holy Spirit is seen as transformative and the way in which this transformation is focused in corporate worship. This book addresses theological issues
with regard to the Holy Spirit and worship in order to build a constructive pneumatological approach to worship which can be held alongside the
Pentecostal approach but which offers a different shape to pneumatology
and worship, building on the renewed emphasis on the Holy Spirit that has
emerged in the second half of the twentieth century.

This volume argues that a significant part of the activity of the Holy
Spirit is encountered in the trusting relationship to God that is found in
personal and corporate worship, a relationship that opens up knowledge
of God and brings about holy living. The discussion considers the connection between the Trinity and the human person, arguing that the nature
of the relationship between humanity and the Holy Spirit that is uniquely
encountered in worship is personal because it is an encounter between the
triune God, a community of three in one, and persons in relationship in a
worshipping community.

An interpretation of the nature and role of the Holy Spirit in the Trinity is outlined as key to the offering of worship in the community of believers. The goal is to draw out theological reflection on the knowledge of God
in the relationship and activity of worship, drawing together theology and
practice, doctrine and worship. The focus is on the nature and understanding of the Holy Spirit in relation to worship, looking at the particular role

36. Shults and Hollingsworth, *Holy Spirit*, 1.

of the Holy Spirit in drawing people to worship the one triune God and in inspiring people in that worship.

The particular focus in this book is the consideration of pneumatology and worship through the eyes of a Reformed (John Owen) and an Orthodox (John Zizioulas) theologian. While Pentecostalism has provided one of the starting points for this thinking, this work turns to two theologians who are deeply rooted in their own traditions of the church and who have each given attention in different ways to the Holy Spirit. The aim is to develop the ways in which the work of the Holy Spirit can be reclaimed and re-articulated in the twenty-first century. While Owen and Zizioulas come from different eras, different philosophical frameworks, and different traditions of the church, we consider here the way in which their insights complement each other, as well as their contrasting ideas, and how this contributes to the enrichment of a contemporary understanding of the Holy Spirit and worship. This volume deliberately compares two theologians from two different traditions of the church. These two theologians are representative in significant ways of their two traditions as will be seen throughout this book. The wider comparison of these two traditions as a whole would require an overview of a number of theologians from each tradition alongside the examination of agreed church statements and dialogues from the traditions. Such work would be a fruitful subject for a separate volume.

OWEN, ZIZIOULAS, AND THE
QUADRILATERAL FRAMEWORK

This book seeks to bridge the gap that can sometimes be perceived as arising between theology and worship. It does so by examining the approaches of John Owen, a theologian writing in the seventeenth century at what has been argued to be a critical moment in terms of the loosening of the bond between a trinitarian theology and the offering of worship, and John Zizioulas, a contemporary Orthodox theologian who is at times critical of a stronger Western Christological approach to the Christian faith, which can be seen to neglect the role and activity of the Holy Spirit.[37] Significant congruities are identified, particularly with regard to the Holy Spirit and the significance of worship, for the development of theology.

Both Owen and Zizioulas give weight to the nature and work of the Holy Spirit with an understanding of the Holy Spirit in personal terms as

---

37. Owen references Lim, *Mystery Unveiled*; Vickers, *Invocation and Assent*; Dixon, *Nice and Hot Disputes*; Zizioulas, *Being as Communion*; *Communion and Otherness*; *Lectures*; *Eucharistic Communion*.

the third person of the Trinity. Arising out of their emphasis on the personal language in relation to God, they place an emphasis on the language of personhood, drawing in part upon the writings of the early fathers. Both—albeit in different ways, with Owen emphasizing sanctification and Zizioulas emphasizing communion—see theology as bringing people into a living relationship with God, which relationship is most clearly embodied in the worshipping life of the church.[38]

We look through the lens of Owen's and Zizioulas's writings at the activity of the Holy Spirit with a focus on the conceptualization of the Holy Spirit's presence in worship in order to develop the pneumatological dimension of a theology of worship. These two theologians, from their very different contexts, place a key emphasis on the role of the Holy Spirit in relation to worship, looking at the way in which theological thinking itself is rooted in the relationship with God that is shaped in worship. Owen, from his seventeenth-century dissenting context, favored the political and ecclesial independency of the local church and was therefore opposed to the imposition of liturgies by the wider church. He also desired to reclaim the centrality of the Trinity in the midst of the voices which were arguing against this centrality, leading to a stronger focus on the significance of the Holy Spirit in local church worship and life. He wrote:

> In our worship of and obedience to God, in our own consolation, sanctification and ministerial employment, the Spirit is the principle, the life, soul, the all of the whole.[39]

Zizioulas, from his twentieth- and twenty-first-century liturgically orientated Eastern Orthodox perspective, wrote:

> For the East, Pneumatology will always occupy an important place given the fact that a liturgical meta-historical approach to Christian existence seems to mark the Eastern ethos.[40]

I argue that these two theologians have a particular contribution to make to the understanding of the knowledge of God through examining the relationship between the Holy Spirit and worship. This approach is offered to complement the outpouring of writing on contemporary practical approaches to worship in order to draw out again the theological significance

38. The areas of personhood and relationship will be looked at more fully in chapter 5.

39. Owen, *Works*, 2:254. I am using Goold's twenty-four volume *Works of John Owen* (1856), following Rehnman, *Divine Discourse*, 17n3. These volumes are increasingly available both in hard copy and electronically. Appendix 1 gives the full outline of the contents, volume by volume.

40. Zizioulas, *Being as Communion*, 129.

THE HOLY SPIRIT AND WORSHIP 15

of worship in its leading to a greater understanding and knowledge of God.[41] Comparing and contrasting these two diverse theologians reveals their unexpected similarities of argument, the way in which, it is suggested, their arguments mutually critique each other, and the way in which their insights offer a renewed ecumenical approach to the basis of Christian theology and worship. Nicholas Lash, in *The Beginning and the End of "Religion,"* comments on the discernment of a shared approach, seeking "some glimmer of understanding of the mystery of God," from a different set of theologians representing a range of different approaches:

> Notwithstanding the dizzying differences—in spirit and structure, economy and imagination—which separate the worlds of Anselm, Luther, Schleiermacher and Barth, they were, as Christian theologians, bound together in a common project: that of the quest, within the practice of discipleship, for some glimmer of understanding of the mystery of God.[42]

Owen, in introducing *Pneumatologia*, points to the mystery of the Holy Spirit, and continues by asking the question: "But what value is there in that name or title, where the whole mystery of the gospel is excluded out of our religion?"[43] The balance between the mystery that is reflected in the "otherness" of the Holy Spirit, the embodiment that is seen in the "presence" of the Holy Spirit, and the way in which this is explicated between two different theologians provides a key theme in this book.

I argue that Owen and Zizioulas, two theologians radically separated by many different factors (which will be offered in mutual critique chapter by chapter) are bound together by a common search for articulating the mystery of Christian theology in the setting of the personal encounter with God that worship offers. The argument is made that the exploration of the commonality of understanding of Owen and Zizioulas in relation to the Trinity (chapter 2), the Holy Spirit (chapter 3), and worship (chapter 4)—in the midst of their many differences—offers a helpful ecumenical model for drawing together contentious issues which have at times in the past led to separation of churches from one another. This commonality of understanding forms the basis for the development of what is being referred to as a "quadrilateral framework."

---

41. These approaches will be referred to in more detail in chapter 4.

42. Lash, *Beginning and the End*, 157.

43. Owen, *Works*, 4:8.

The Development of a "Quadrilateral" Approach to the Holy Spirit and Worship

This "quadrilateral framework" is drawn out of the writings of Owen and Zizioulas in order to deepen an understanding of the nature of the relationship between the Holy Spirit and worship. The specific argument that is being developed in this book arises out of the way in which the thinking of Owen and Zizioulas, in their similarities and differences, points to four characteristics of the Holy Spirit embodied in worship—personhood, the immediacy of the personal encounter in worship, the relationality of truth, and transformation. These, alongside the interrelationship between them, are grounded in Owen's and Zizioulas's understanding of the Trinity, foregrounded in their thinking about the Holy Spirit, and lead to a particular articulation about the nature of worship. These four characteristics are summarized as follows:

1. the personal and relational understanding of the Trinity and the way in which God, through the Holy Spirit, draws people into relationship—with God and with other people (chapter 5);

2. the way in which the Holy Spirit can be encountered as the immediate presence of God in worship (chapter 6);

3. the Holy Spirit opening up truth as relational, as seen in the way in which knowing God can be interpreted through an understanding of the nature of relationality as developed in worship (chapter 7); and

4. the transformative nature of the Holy Spirit, for the person, the world, and creation, as particularly experienced in worship (chapter 8).

The final chapter (chapter 9) looks at ecumenical implications of this argument.

"THE LINGERING SHADOW OF JOHN OWEN"—INTRODUCING OWEN'S WRITINGS AND HISTORICAL BACKGROUND

In the seventeenth century, the political ferment around the Civil War, with its overturning of the established monarchical pattern of governance, brought with it a renewed theological understanding of authority and the location of authority. For Puritans, emphasizing the authority of the Holy Spirit, both reduced the authority of the establishment, politically and religiously, and increased the sense of the local nature of authority—in each person and in each place. John Owen played a significant role in the public life of the country during the Commonwealth period. His fortunes waxed and waned with those of Oliver Cromwell, to whom he was friend and chaplain. He preached to Parliament on several key occasions, including the day after the beheading of King Charles. In 1651 he was made Dean of Christ Church, Oxford's largest college, an office he held until 1660. From 1652 to 1657 he was Vice-Chancellor of Oxford University "which he then reorganized with conspicuous success."[44] After the Restoration, Owen's role in public life disappeared. In the years after this until his death, he focused on his writing and on the support of Independent ministers and congregations.

Owen was a prolific writer and preacher. Owen's academic and intellectual character was evident from an early age. He was at university by the age of twelve and took his MA by the time he was nineteen. His "Works" were of significance in his day and had a revival in the nineteenth century and late twentieth centuries. In 1826, Thomas Russell edited a twenty-eight-volume edition of Owen's "Works" (although only the first twenty-one volumes bear his name as editor). In 1856, Rev. William H. Goold brought out a twenty-four volume edition of Owen's "Works." In the late twentieth century and early twenty-first century there has been a resurgence of interest in Owen, as will be evidenced by the range of writings referred to in this book. The ongoing interest in Owen is reflected in the publishing of fourteen books and numerous articles in the last two decades of the twentieth century and the first decade of the twenty-first century, with nearly one a year being published since 2000.[45] During this period there has been a re-issue of a selection of Owen's *Works* as well as the various books and articles about Owen, both electronically and in hard copy, alongside a complete bibliography of Owen's writings.[46]

Owen has been seen as one of the most influential of the English Puritan divines. J. I. Packer, who has written extensively on Puritanism, declares that "Owen was by common consent the weightiest Puritan theologian, and many would bracket him with Jonathan Edwards as one of the greatest Reformed theologians of all time."[47] Kelly Kapic, in his recent book on John Owen, *Communion with God*, begins by quoting James Moffatt (*The Golden*

44. Packer, "Quest for Godliness."

45. Daniels, *Christology of John Owen*; Lee, *John Owen Represbyterianized*; Kay, *Trinitarian Spirituality*; Kapic, *Communion with God*; Kapic and Taylor, *Overcoming Sin and Temptation*; Oliver, *John Owen*; Payne, *John Owen on the Lord's Supper*; Rehnman, *Divine Discourse*, 38; Trueman, *John Owen*.

46. This complete bibliography has been compiled electronically by Mark Burden. See Burden, "John Owen."

47. Packer, "About John Owen."

Book of John Owen, 1904): "Some writer in the last century (Dr. James Hamilton, if I mistake not) declared that evangelical theology had been hitherto alluvial for the most part, and that its main element was a detritus from mount Owen."[48]

Kapic proceeds with an extensive and helpful survey of the "lingering shadow of John Owen" across the centuries since his life, including referring to the way in which in the nineteenth century a book was published on Owen on average once every year between 1800 and 1860.[49] He also refers to the range of other languages in which translations of John Owen's works have appeared and the revival of interest in Owen over the past thirty years as seen by the growing number of articles and books. However, these works, and articles have focused more on Owen's Christology, his strong trinitarian approach, his theological method, and the development of personal devotion than on his Pneumatology and his approach to worship. Kapic comments: "Although several studies have more recently focused on the topics of Christology and the Trinity in Owen, there are surprisingly few extended discussions on his Pneumatology."[50] In 2014, published writing on Owen's approach to worship was analyzed by Ryan M. McGraw in *A Heavenly Directory: Trinitarian Piety, Public Worship and a Reassessment of John Owen's Theology*.[51]

Carl Trueman, in his book *John Owen: Reformed Catholic, Renaissance Man*, explains the later lack of Owen's popularity by arguing that his political and theological views were characteristic of the side that lost, and so he was written out of history: "It was his misfortune to be on the losing side—as a Puritan and allied to the Independent Party." He continues by maintaining that "John Owen was without doubt the most significant theological intellect in England in the third quarter of the seventeenth century, and one of the two or three most impressive Protestant theologians in Europe at the time."[52]

The writing of John Owen has a relevance for Christian faith in the twenty-first century for a range of reasons. He wrote at a time of unparalleled political change and ferment in England when issues about Republicanism came to the fore in a way not seen since, in terms of the outcomes of these issues leading to a Civil War. He lived at the cusp of philosophical change when the great "modernist" enterprise was beginning to grow. The development of

48. Kapic, *Communion with God*.

49. Kapic, *Communion with God*, 5. This phrase is the title of chapter one in Kapic's survey of Owen and his writing.

50. See Kapic and Jones, *Ashgate Research Companion*, 113–84 (for an overview of this discussion, see 114n4).

51. McGraw, *Heavenly Directory*.

52. Trueman, *John Owen*, 1.

"post-modernism" has opened up a questioning of this "modernist" enterprise and a searching for different ways of thinking. Owen held human experience as significant in his theological framework in a way that has resonance when approaching late twentieth- and early twenty-first-century desires for an experiential theological approach. However, he kept the significance of human experience within a strong trinitarian framework, offering a helpful model for contemporary theological work. The movement in his writings between doctrine, faith, and life, holding together the knowledge of God within the framework of the transformative experience of God as found in the relationship with God in worship, gives a fruitful paradigm for the questioning and experientially-focused twenty-first century in the United Kingdom.

INTRODUCING JOHN ZIZIOULAS— HISTORICAL BACKGROUND

Theologian John Zizioulas is deeply rooted within his Orthodox tradition. However, his background and academic career reflect the broad ecumenical foundation for his writing, bridging as they do both Eastern and Western academic establishments. His studies took him from the University of Thessaloniki and the University of Athens to Harvard Divinity School, where he studied patristics with Father George Florovsky, subsequently receiving his PhD from the University of Athens. His PhD included a critique of the writing of Afanasiev, *The Church of the Holy Spirit*, which Zizioulas concluded had too strong a congregational focus and needed to be balanced by a strengthening of the significance of episcopacy. During his early studies, he spent a year at the Ecumenical Institute at Bossey, laying the foundations for a lifelong interest in and involvement with the World Council of Churches (WCC), often as a critical friend. His teaching pathway began at the University of Athens, then continued with three years at the University of Edinburgh, followed by fourteen years holding a chair of systematic theology at the University of Glasgow. He has been a visiting professor at Kings College London, the University of Geneva, and the Gregorian University. In 1986 he became Metropolitan of Pergamon within the Ecumenical Patriarchate. He develops the thinking of the Ecumenical Patriarch, Bartholomew, in writing and speaking on ecological and environmental issues from a theological perspective. More recently Zizioulas's ecumenical interest was illustrated by his agreeing in 2012 to be one of a panel of ten editorial consultants for a new WCC Orthodox book series, *Doxa and Praxis: Exploring Orthodox Theology*.

Zizioulas's Writings and Theological Approach

Zizioulas's books are primarily compilations of articles and lectures rather than the development of an extended systematic theology. Most of them were initially published in languages other than English.[53] Until the twenty-first century, Zizioulas's main publication in English language book form was *Being as Communion*, a compilation of essays, lectures, and articles from the years 1971 to 1981, the majority of which were first published in French, German, Italian, or Greek. Since 2000, his PhD thesis (from the mid-sixties) and three further compilations have been published. These draw together and make readily available a number of articles, essays, and lectures which are referred to in the literature on Zizioulas but which previously have not been so readily accessible in English. However, a number of his articles and essays are still only available in journals published in languages other than English. The year 2001 saw the publication of his PhD thesis, *Eucharist, Bishop, Church: The Unity of the Church in the Divine Eucharist and the Bishop during the First Three Centuries*.[54] In 2006 *Communion and Otherness* (with three chapters in this volume published for the first time and five chapters having already appeared in various books and journals) was published;[55] 2008 (with a reprint in 2010) saw the publication of *Lectures in Christian Dogmatics* (based on a series of lectures given in Edinburgh, Glasgow, London, and Thessalonica and primarily adapted from tape recordings made in Thessalonica); and in 2011 *The Eucharistic Communion and the World* (a collection of articles and addresses) was published.[56] In 2013 a further book on eschatology, *Remembering the Future*, was published.[57] The range of chapters across these volumes develops the themes characteristic of Zizioulas of an ontology of the Trinity seen in personal and relational terms, a personal understanding of the nature and work of the Holy Spirit, the church as instituted by Christ, constituted by the Spirit, and embodied in the Eucharist, and a redefinition of personhood countering what Zizioulas sees as a Western over-emphasis on individualism. Zizioulas returns to these themes in each publication.

---

53. I can speculate that what might seem like a lack of systematic theology is in fact a tribute to the Holy Spirit, who takes people beyond systematizing. Similarly, the breadth of languages used by Zizioulas gives a small reflection of Pentecost, with the Spirit's ability to transcend the human boundaries erected by language.

54. Zizioulas, *Eucharist, Bishop, Church*.

55. Zizioulas, *Communion and Otherness*.

56. Zizioulas, *Lectures; Eucharistic Communion*.

57. Zizioulas, *Remembering the Future*.

THE HOLY SPIRIT AND WORSHIP 21

The complexity of Zizioulas's ideas and some of the controversies that surround them is well summarized by Luke Ben Tallon in his introduction to *The Eucharistic Communion and the World*, where he writes about *Being as Communion*: "Not surprisingly, this dense and difficult work has been interpreted in a variety of ways by both admirers and detractors from across the ecumenical spectrum, with Zizioulas emerging variously as a true teacher of the Orthodox church, an existentialist in theologian's garb, or a despiser of the natural world."[58]

It is interesting to note that the main English language books published on Zizioulas's writing develop his thinking comparatively, primarily with theologians of other traditions of the church. For example, Collins, in *Trinitarian Theology: West and East: Karl Barth, the Cappadocian Fathers and John Zizioulas* seeks to interpret Barth in terms of Zizioulas's language of "an event of communion," noting as he does so, in a way that supports the arguments in this book, the influence of the Cappadocian Fathers on both Barth and Calvin.[59] McPartlan and Areeplackal set Zizioulas alongside the Roman Catholic theologians Henri de Lubac and Yves Congar in McPartlan's influential work *The Eucharist makes the Church* and Areeplackal's work from an Indian setting, *Spirit and Ministries*.[60] McCall, in *Which Trinity? Whose Monotheism?* sets Zizioulas alongside Jenson, Moltmann, and a range of Evangelical theologians in order to look comparatively at a range of contemporary interpretations of the Trinity.[61]

Papanikolaou offers an inner-Orthodox critique of Zizioulas by setting him alongside Lossky and drawing out Lossky's apophatic understanding in relation to Zizioulas's ontological thinking in *Being with God*.[62] The ecumenical cross-section of articles and essays published on Zizioulas is reflected in the work edited by Knight, *The Theology of John Zizioulas, Personhood and the Church*.[63] In this work, Brown, in his essay "On the Criticism of *Being as Communion* in Anglophone Orthodox Theology," gives an overview of some of the critiques of Zizioulas both from within and from outside the Orthodox tradition, for example, by Behr, Turcescu, Louth, and Coakley.[64] These critiques are echoed in Loudovikos's essay "Christian Life and Institutional Church" in which he raises issues about Zizioulas's

58. Zizioulas, *Remembering the Future*, viii.
59. Collins, *Trinitarian Theology*.
60. McPartlan, *Eucharist Makes the Church*; Areeplackal, *Spirit and Ministries*.
61. McCall, *Which Trinity?*
62. Papanikolaou, *Being with God*.
63. Knight, *Theology of John Zizioulas*.
64. See Brown, "On the Criticism of *Being as Communion*."

"abstract structural models,"[65] critiques that are taken further in his article "Person instead of Grace and Dictated Otherness: John Zizioulas's Final Theological Position."[66] Brown offers a robust defense of Zizioulas against what he defines as Anglophone Orthodoxy as well as particular Anglican traditions of patristic scholarship and postliberal theology. The influence of Zizioulas from within a survey of Orthodox perspectives is clearly seen in *The Cambridge Companion to Orthodox Christian Theology*.[67] In terms of shorter articles from the combination of a Reformed and an Orthodox perspective, Gunton contributes a chapter in *Theology through the Theologians* on a comparison of Owen and Zizioulas, looking in particular at the role of the Holy Spirit in shaping the church and the influence of Cappadocian theology on both theologians.[68]

Zizioulas's theological method arises out of his understanding of the link between worship and theology. He writes: "Theology starts in the worship of God and in the Church's experience of communion with God. . . . The Church articulates its theology, not simply to add to our knowledge of God or the world, but so that we may gain the life which can never be brought to an end."[69] He expands this methodological understanding when he writes:

> Christian theology is the expression of the experience of the living Church, rather than of intellectual perception of the logical arrangement of propositions. Theology affirms truths which come, not from the intellect alone, but from the whole relationship of man with God. . . .
>
> A theologian must be familiar with the intellectual climate of his or her own time. But he or she must also be a philosopher in the sense of being a truly enquiring mind, and in the wider sense of being sensitive to the deepest needs of human beings. The theologian must also be familiar with the liturgical

---

65. See Loudovikos, "Christian Life and Institutional Church."

66. Loudovikos, "Person Instead of Grace," 684–99.

67. Cunningham and Theokritoff, *Cambridge Companion to Orthodox Christian Theology*. In this book, Zizioulas is referred to—at times extensively—in eight of the eighteen chapters. It is also interesting to note the number of references to Zizioulas in the index in comparison with other Orthodox theologians, both from the early Fathers and from the twentieth century. Zizioulas is referred to fifteen times, compared with the Cappadocian Fathers, individually and corporately, who receive fifty-one mentions, followed by Maximus the Confessor (twenty-seven references), Georges Florovsky (twenty-one references), Gregory Palamas (seventeen references), Vladimir Lossky (sixteen references) and Athanasius (fifteen references); John Meyendorff, Origen, and Alexander Schmemann have ten references each.

68. Gunton, *Theology Through the Theologians*, 187–206.

69. Zizioulas, *Lectures*, 1.

experience and the life of the Church, including the institutional forms established by the canons of the Church.[70]

Part of the interest in Zizioulas in this book is his serious intellectual wrestling with ideas about the eternal reality of God which are rooted in the present reality of the Eucharist. While it could be argued that he is being overly "meta-historical," this volume argues that the rootedness of his theology in the present ecclesial reality of the Eucharist opens up a deep perspective on God and God's action in history, which is a valuable offering from the Eastern to the Western church.

An example of Zizioulas's engagement with the intellectual climate of his time is seen in his interaction with Heidegger, as noted in *Being as Communion* and *Communion and Otherness* and referenced in the doctoral work of Norris and Robinson and in the writing of McCall.[71] In *Being as Communion* Zizioulas offers an extensive footnote both acknowledging and critiquing Heidegger's influence.[72] Norris continues Zizioulas's critique in relation to the notion of God and time, and McCall raises the affinity of Zizioulas to Heidegger's notion of "thrownness" while at the same time pointing to Zizioulas's critique of this idea. This brief note here serves to highlight Zizioulas's wider philosophical engagement.

SIMILARITIES AND DIFFERENCES

Three areas of similarities and differences between Owen and Zizioulas are noted at this point and will be addressed more fully over the course of this book.

Theological Settings

Owen and Zizioulas come out of different theological and philosophical traditions, with many of Owen's influences coming from the Reformation period and Zizioulas being rooted in the early church and the Cappadocian Fathers. Owen wrote at an early point in the Modern period, while Zizioulas responded to more contemporary philosophers such as Heidegger and to the onset of postmodernism. Owen's writing took place at a time of turmoil in the English church, while Zizioulas bridged the contemporary international ecumenical world. This volume argues that the congruity of

70. Zizioulas, *Lectures*, 3, 5.

71. Norris, "Pneumatology, Existentialism, and Personal Encounter," 162, 165, 178; Robinson, "Towards a Definition"; McCall, *Which Trinity?* 194–95.

72. Zizioulas, *Being as Communion*, 44–46.

their thinking in the midst of this diversity points in itself to the work of the Holy Spirit, that Spirit who opens up a breadth of interpretation within the one triune God.

Scripture and Tradition

Both Owen and Zizioulas hold fast to the shared starting points of scripture and tradition in determining their theological understanding. However, they have different approaches to scripture and tradition, with Owen's approach being to quote scripture with great frequency throughout his work while Zizioulas references scripture more occasionally. Owen draws broadly on a cross-section of the early Fathers together with a focus on Augustine in terms of sin and sanctification. Zizioulas draws upon the Cappadocian Fathers in particular. The comparison of their approaches to those of the early Fathers will be taken further in chapter 5 on the personal and relational aspects of the quadrilateral; the epistemological issues with regard to the weight given to scripture and tradition will be developed in chapter 6 on the nature of relational truth.

Ecclesiological Differences

The differing understanding of the reception of the Holy Spirit in shaping worship is seen in Owen's emphasis on the local people gathered in worship and Zizioulas's emphasis on the bishop as the focus of communion.

TAKING THE ARGUMENT FORWARD

Each chapter will start with a separate analysis of Owen's and Zizioulas's writings on the particular theme of the chapter and conclude with an analysis of their similarities and differences in order to draw out their surprising congruities.

- Chapter 2 outlines the factors relating to the context, background, and thinking of Owen and Zizioulas with regard to the Trinity in terms of a personal and relational understanding to lay the foundation for the unexpected similarities of two theologians who write from very different contexts and times.
- Chapter 3 looks at Owen's and Zizioulas's particular emphases on the Holy Spirit.

- Chapter 4 analyzes their understanding of worship.

- Chapter 5 turns to the first part of the quadrilateral framework, looking at the meaning of personal relationality in terms of the Trinity and the human community.

- Chapter 6 looks at the second part of the quadrilateral framework, focusing on the nature of the immediacy of the Holy Spirit in worship.

- Chapter 7 takes up the third part of the quadrilateral framework, examining an understanding of the Holy Spirit's guiding into truth.

- Chapter 8 finishes with the final part of the quadrilateral framework, outlining the way in which the work of the Holy Spirit in worship can be seen as transformational.

The final chapter draws out ecumenical conclusions from this fourfold argument with regard to the possibilities that this particular comparative theological approach to the Holy Spirit and worship opens up for ecumenical dialogue. The implications of the pneumatological theology of worship for an understanding of ecclesiology and a renewal of the churches' ecumenical journey are drawn out. The strands from the seventeenth-century Reformed tradition and the contemporary Orthodox tradition are drawn together in order to see the possibility of the ways in which the Holy Spirit can still enliven and refresh worship across the mainstream churches in the West, looking in particular at the way in which it is possible to have a common understanding of the Holy Spirit in worship which undergirds differing manifestations of worship.

2

Owen's and Zizioulas's
Trinitarian Foundations

THIS CHAPTER LAYS THE foundation for the development of a quadrilateral
approach to the Holy Spirit, the primary subject of this book, by outlining
the rootedness of Owen's and Zizioulas's theological approaches in their
trinitarian thinking.

John Zizioulas represents a different perspective from John Owen in,
seemingly, almost every aspect. Owen was a leader of a minority English
Independent tradition in seventeenth-century Britain whose personal experience was primarily in England. Zizioulas is a theologian of the widespread and deep-rooted Orthodox tradition which spans the world and
whose personal experience has crossed East and West. Owen, out of his
Christian convictions, was caught up in the political ferment surrounding
the English Civil War. Zizioulas, out of his understanding of the church, has
been at a distance from political involvement. Owen's writing was rooted in
the Augustinian and Calvinist tradition that predominated in many parts
of Puritanism. Zizioulas's writing is rooted in the early Fathers. Yet here
the thought-provoking parallels begin. While Owen's theological roots lie in
Augustine and Calvin, his theological understanding was also shaped by his
wide reading in the early Fathers. Both Owen and Zizioulas are concerned
to re-emphasize the trinitarian nature of the Christian faith, Owen against

the backdrop of anti-trinitarian writing and thinking that was prevalent in certain quarters in the seventeenth century (for example among the Socinians) and Zizioulas against the perceived neglect of trinitarian thinking in the nineteenth and twentieth centuries, particularly in the West. In the theological setting of England, both Owen and Zizioulas are minority ecclesial voices in comparison with the predominance of the Church of England and with the renewal of Roman Catholicism during the nineteenth and twentieth centuries.

Owen and Zizioulas inhabit different worlds in terms of their century, their country and their confessional allegiance. Nevertheless, this book points to an unexpected degree of overlap in their theological orientation, an overlap that can helpfully feed into contemporary twenty-first-century ecumenical and theological discourse, or rather, discourses, as the range of contemporary theological understanding and interpretation has broadened, by confession, country, and theological orientation.[1] The contribution that both Owen and Zizioulas make is in the area of a personalist trinitarian theology, with an emphasis on the particular role and activity of the Holy Spirit in relation to worship, within a confessional understanding. In this emphasis they draw together both theology and experience, and worship and doctrine. In the midst of the many different angles from which theologians write about theology and practice, Owen and Zizioulas share a common orientation in keeping the starting point of their theological understanding rooted in the life of the Trinity, and seeing that starting point as embedded in worship.

CONTEMPORARY CHALLENGES TO TRINITARIAN THINKING

The second half of the twentieth century and the early years of the twenty-first century have seen a revival of writing on the Trinity. However, it is significant to note, in the recent outpouring of books and theses on various aspects of the Trinity, the limited attention given in many of these to the connection between trinitarian faith and worship.[2]

1. This can be seen in a comparison of the range of "Companions" to various fields of theology from Oxford, Cambridge, and Blackwell, covering natural, philosophical, systematic, evangelical, feminist, postmodern, and Reformation theology, amongst others.

2. Some of the more recent books include Anatolios, *Retrieving Nicaea*; Ayres, *Nicaea and its Legacy*; *Augustine and the Trinity*; Collins *Trinity*; Grenz, *Social God*; Gunton, *Promise of Trinitarian Theology*; Holmes, *Holy Trinity*; LaCugna, *God for Us*;

The British Council of Churches study guide, *The Forgotten Trinity*, first published in 1989, with a new expanded study edition in 2011 illustrates both a concern about the decline in the doctrine of the Trinity and the significance of its recovery. The introduction to the 2011 edition begins by saying that:

> There is a feeling abroad that the doctrine of the Trinity is an irrelevance. Once the center of fierce debate, it now seems to belong to our religious past and to have little to say about the great issues of the day. It appears to be a mere abstraction, a playing with mathematical conundrums, of interest simply to those engaged in the higher reaches of theological speculation but of little moment for the worship of the church and the life of the world.[3]

The introduction then continues: "It has become clear to us that, on the question of the Trinity, center numerous matters of great moment." The study guide goes on to unpack some of these, for example, worship, creation and salvation, and the nature of the human person.

In Kay's stimulating book on John Owen, *Trinitarian Spirituality*, looking at the relationship of Christian doctrine and Christian spirituality, he writes about the late twentieth-century rediscovery of the Trinity.

> The doctrine of the Trinity itself, as perhaps Christianity's most nuanced and irresolvably mysterious belief, has all the makings of a doctrine that should have been destined for permanent streamlining. And yet, not only has Liberal rationalism and even Evangelical pragmatism failed to entirely extinguish the old doctrine, Trinitarian studies seems now to be enjoying a renaissance across the theological spectrum—Roman Catholic, Protestant, and Eastern Orthodox theologians have all made notable contributions to the present revival.[4]

McCall, *Which Trinity?*; Peters, *God as Trinity*; Schwobel, *Trinitarian Theology*; Torrance, *Christian Doctrine of God*; Wozniak and Maspero, *Rethinking Trinitarian Theology*; Tibbs, "East Meets West"; Horrell, "Toward a Biblical Model."

3. CTBI, *Forgotten Trinity*, 3. (The expanded edition includes the original text, "Part 2: A Study Guide," and "Part 3: A Selection of Papers presented to the BCC Study Commission on Trinitarian Doctrine Today.")

4. Kay, *Trinitarian Spirituality*, 8. Kay goes on to reference some of these theologians when he writes, "The initial theological work, especially of Karl Barth and Karl Rahner, has been seized on and creatively expanded by later writers such as Jurgen Moltmann, Robert Jensen, John Zizioulas, Colin Gunton, Alan Torrance, James Torrance, David Cunningham, and Catherine Mowry LaCugna, to name a few" (9).

The seventeenth century in England saw a particular separation of trinitarian doctrine from trinitarian worship, a separation which led to a reduced emphasis on trinitarian doctrine in the West until the twentieth century. Grenz, in *The Social God and the Relational Self* points to the way in which this separation continued over the next two centuries:

> As Peters and Cunningham suggest, the current flowering of trinitarian thought forms a remarkable contrast to the paltry interest evident in much of nineteenth-century theology, which in turn was deeply influenced by the challenge Enlightenment rationalism posed to all speculative dogmas of the Christian faith. The situation was exacerbated when Kant limited human cognition to the phenomenal real, thereby placing knowledge of God—and of course, the inner working of the divine life—beyond the pale of "pure" (i.e., scientific or empirical) reason. . . . Daunted by either the seeming impossibility of trinitarian speculation or the superfluity of the doctrine, many theologians relegated it to at best second-rank status.[5]

The late twentieth- and early twenty-first-century revival of interest in the Trinity is given weight by revisiting the writings of those for whom this doctrine has been significant over many centuries. While attention naturally turns to the early Fathers, an examination of the writings of those such as John Owen who have been more on the sidelines of church history can also cast a new light on the development of this doctrine and the way it is understood in relation to the world, the church, and the believer. The writings of John Zizioulas, from an Eastern Orthodox perspective, help to complement the Western approaches to the Trinity, and to raise up the significance of rooting these approaches in worship.

An understanding of God as trinitarian has been central to the Christian faith since the early days of the Christian church, although a full doctrinal formulation took the early Councils several centuries to develop and agree.[6] Explicating an understanding of the Trinity has led theologians to a variety of interpretations, the divergence of interpretation being most clearly seen in the argument over the "filioque," one of many factors that culminated in the split of the Eastern and Western churches in 1054.[7] Both

---

5. Grenz, *Social God*, 24.

6. Hanson, in *Search for the Christian Doctrine of God*, focusing on the Arian controversy, offers a helpful analysis of the issues around this particular controversy in terms of the development of an understanding about the nature of God in the early centuries of the church.

7. The ecumenical consequences of this split and the more recent ecumenical

Owen, from his English seventeenth-century setting rooted in a Western Reformation understanding, and Zizioulas, from his contemporary position in the Eastern church, argue for a trinitarian framework that is foundational for the knowledge and experience of God, a framework that arises out of a particular emphasis on the Trinity in terms of the language of persons in relationship.[8] The setting for both Owen and Zizioulas of their conceptualizations of the Trinity is laid out here in order to indicate the contribution they have to offer to contemporary trinitarian thinking, and to lay the foundations for the explication of their understanding of the Holy Spirit and the relationship of the Holy Spirit to worship. This discussion leads on to the development of the quadrilateral framework.

In order to develop further the relationship between the Holy Spirit and worship, building the foundations for the quadrilateral approach, I turn now to look at the way in which Owen's and Zizioulas's explication of the Holy Spirit is grounded in their understanding of the Trinity. The emphasis here is not on an extended analysis of their trinitarian thinking (which would require a separate book) but on an overview of the nature of their trinitarian understanding and the similarities and differences of their trinitarian setting in order to focus on the trinitarian origins of their arguments in relation to the Holy Spirit and worship. Their emphasis on the personal and relational conceptualizing of the Trinity is of particular significance. It is interesting to note the coherence between Owen's scripturally-based understanding of God as trinitarian and of the personal nature of the three persons of the Trinity alluded to in Scripture alongside Zizioulas's more philosophical approach with regard to the nature of being as personal and relational.

OWEN'S TRINITARIAN UNDERSTANDING

Owen's Theological Context Undergirding His Trinitarian Approach: The Trinity Drawing Together Doctrine and Experience

Owen wrote in a century during which, as Vickers has outlined, the Trinity moved from being a living focus of worship and of daily life to an abstract doctrine over which theologians argued, but which was seen as disconnected from the Christian life.[9] Owen's central trinitarian framework counters

---

developments in addressing this will be looked at further in the final chapter on the ecumenical implications of the arguments put forward in this book.

8. See chapter 5.

9. Vickers, *Invocation and Assent*. In his introduction, commenting on the revival

the disconnection by holding together doctrine and experience (experience as involving both reason and also the fullness of Christian living, including heart and spirit), through the activity of the Holy Spirit, focused in the relationship and activity of worship. This drawing together of doctrine and experience through a focus on the Holy Spirit in both the understanding of the Trinity and the life of the believer in the relationship and activity of worship is one of Owen's distinctive theological contributions and relates to the primary focus of this book.

The development of Owen's theological understanding is seen in his balancing the writings of those who have gone before him in the wider tradition of the church with his close scrutiny of scripture.[10] He holds these two aspects together alongside his emphasis on the lens of experience.[11] These three undergirding points which shape the theological methodology of Owen are seen in his introduction to *Pneumatologia*, "in the substance of what is delivered, I have the plain testimonies of the Scripture, the suffrage of the ancient church, and the experience of them who do sincerely believe, to rest upon"; a comment which Kapic reinforces when he writes "three principal sources guide Owen's reflections: the Scriptures, historical theology and experience."[12] Owen has a particular focus on scripture in terms of his historical context in his desire to present an alternative to the Roman Catholic Church's view of herself as the authority over the interpretation of scripture. He holds to an understanding of the Spirit helping to interpret the scriptures in the midst of the gathered believers and thus the local congregation having its own authority to interpret scripture.

The interest in Owen in this work lies in the way in which he holds together Christian doctrine, Christian believing, and Christian living. His writing weaves an intricate tapestry rather than being a systematic theological exposition. He writes from an apologetic and pastoral stance, but with a concern to be a theological interpreter, from a scriptural perspective, of core beliefs such as the Trinity. For Owen, the reality of God is known both objectively and subjectively, in particular through the activity of the

---

of trinitarian thinking in the twentieth century, he writes, "What is rarely discussed is how the Trinity came to need such a massive retrieval effort on the part of contemporary theologians in the first place" (x).

10. As in, for example, his pointing to, "When the Spirit of truth comes, he will guide you into all the truth; for he will not speak on his own, but will speak whatever he hears, and he will declare to you the things that are to come" (John 16:12 NRSV).

11. The relationship between these three areas and the way they shape an understanding of an approach to the nature of "truth," as discerned through the Holy Spirit "who guides into all truth," will be reflected on further in chapter 7.

12. Owen, *Works*, 3:10; Kapic, *Communion with God*, 22.

Holy Spirit who brings the knowledge of God to fruitfulness in human life through the transformative work of regeneration and sanctification. The Holy Spirit becomes the bridge between an object-subject divide, as seen in practice in Owen's writings where he travels back and forth in each part of his writing between object and subject, between God and the person, between the faith as it is held in scripture and the early church and the lived experience of the receiver of faith.

Engaging arguments are being made in twenty-first-century writings on the understanding of the Trinity in the seventeenth century. One example of these is Dixon's analysis, exploring the move from the sense of the Trinity being a lived reality in people's lives to the understanding of the Trinity as a doctrine to be understood (or not) intellectually, but not connected with everyday living.[13] Owen's somewhat prolix style and tendency to many sub-headings and sub-divisions can at first sight lead to a feeling of confusion. However, the breadth of the material he covers and the range of in-depth expositions from many different angles on the understanding of the triune God and the activity of the Holy Spirit are rewarding to follow.

Owen Countering Socinians: The Emphasis on the Three-Fold Personal Nature of the Triune God

Owen's emphasis on the Trinity needs to be seen against the particular theological controversies of his day. In response to these controversies, Owen's concern is to explicate traditional Christian teaching on the Trinity rather than to take the faith in directions that could be seen to be less than fully trinitarian. He was concerned to combat those he saw as heretics, both over the previous centuries and in his contemporary world. Of particular concern were Quakers and Socinians, whom Owen saw as interpreting the faith in ways which departed from a traditional trinitarian understanding of God and who did less than justice to the Holy Spirit, diminishing the divine identity and the personhood of the Holy Spirit.[14] He summarizes his argument as follows:

> Some grant his personality but deny his deity; others deny his personality and assert that, what is called the Spirit of God, is

---

13. Dixon, *Nice and Hot Disputes*.

14. Sarah Mortimer gives an interesting analysis of the development of Socinianism in England and of Owen's response. See Mortimer, *Reason and Religion*.

nothing but a quality in the divine nature, or the power that God exerts for particular purposes.[15]

The Socinians, with their unitarian approach—seeing Christ as created rather than pre-existent—frequently came under Owen's fiery attacks in his writings. One of the theological arguments that Owen had with them about the Trinity related to the biblical literalist position they adopted, which denied the possibility of the Trinity on the grounds of it not being a stated doctrine in scripture. He outlines the way in which his thinking on the Trinity arises out of both scripture and subsequent reflection on scripture in *A Brief Declaration and Vindication of the Doctrine of the Trinity*, summarizing his approach at the start of the work as follows:

> The doctrine of the blessed Trinity may be considered in two ways: First, in respect unto the revelation and proposal of it in the scriptures, to direct us unto the author, object, and end of our faith, in our worship and obedience. Secondly, as it is farther declared and explained, in terms, expressions and propositions, reduced from the original revelation of it, suited thereunto and meet to direct and keep the mind from undue apprehensions of the things it believes, and to declare them, unto farther edification.[16]

Owen places a significant emphasis on revelation, in both scripture and the "farther declaration and explanation" of scripture. For Owen, revelation points to the priority of God in the revealing of truth, putting the emphasis on the divine origin of truth while holding this emphasis within the setting of the capability of the human mind to receive and understand truth.[17] In

15. Owen, *Works*, 3:68.

16. Owen, *Works*, 3:377. From *Of Communion with God the Father, the Son, and Holy Ghost: A Brief Declaration and Vindication of the Doctrine of the Trinity* (1668–1669)—a later work by Owen, defending the Trinity against the attacks by Socinians, particularly in terms of their argument against the pre-existence of the Son of God.

17. In the introductory section to *Pneumatologia*, Owen writes, in the first of many of his references to revelation: "Now, all the concernments of the Holy Spirit are an eminent part of the 'mystery' or 'deep things of God'; for as the knowledge of them doth wholly depend on and is regulated by divine revelation, so are they in their own nature divine and heavenly. . . . The truth of things natural is made known from God by the exercise of reason, or the due application of the understanding that is in man unto their investigation; for 'the things of a man knoweth the spirit of a man that is in him.' Neither, ordinarily, is there anything more required unto that degree of certainty of knowledge in things of that nature whereof our minds are capable, but the diligent application of the faculties of our souls, in the due use of proper means, unto the attainment thereof" (Owen, *Works*, 3:6).

Pneumatologia Owen writes of revelation from a range of angles. His is not the systematic view of Karl Barth's "revealer, revelation and revealedness," but he shares Barth's concern for, as described by Ben Quash, "the priority, independence and autonomy of God's initiative in revealing himself."[18]

One of the key issues in relation to the Trinity is the conception of oneness and threeness and the way in which these are held together. Owen points to his understanding of the unity and distinctions within the doctrine of the Trinity when he writes:

> That God is one;—that this one God is Father, Son and Holy Ghost;—that the Father is the Father of the Son; and the Son, the Son of the Father; and the Holy Ghost, the Spirit of the Father and the Son; and that, in respect of this their mutual relation, they are distinct from each other.[19]

In the area of relation and distinction, Owen develops an understanding of the Trinity as personal which flows more out of the thinking of the East and the Cappadocian Fathers than the West with an at times over-emphasized reference to one part of the Augustinian understanding of the Spirit, focusing primarily on the Spirit as the bond of love.[20] Personal relationality signifies the way in which the Trinity is seen as persons in relationship, with all the promise and challenges that such an approach implies.

The Quakers, with what Owen saw as their lack of differentiation between the human spirit and the divine Spirit, as in their emphasis on the significance of the "light within," were also criticized by Owen as diminishing the presence of the Spirit as participating fully in the trinitarian life of God.[21]

The Relationship with the Trinity: The Lived Reality Encountered in Worship

Owen's distinctive trinitarian approach lies in the emphasis he places on the role of the Holy Spirit as the person within the Trinity who draws people

18. Quash, "Revelation," 333.

19. Owen, *Works*, 2:377.

20. This argument is taken further in chapter 5, looking at issues with regard to personal relationality and the work of the Holy Spirit.

21. Owen writes polemically about the distinction between the Spirit of God and the light within: "This is that which some men call 'the light within them,' though indeed it be nothing but a dark product of Satan upon their own imaginations, or at best the natural light of conscience; which some of the heathens also call 'a spirit.' But hereunto do they trust, as to that which doth all for them, leaving no room for the 'promise of the Spirit of God,' nor any thing for him to do" (Owen, *Works*, 3:33).

close to God and the way in which this "drawing close" to God is rooted in worship.[22] Brian Kay sees the writing of Owen making a positive contribution to the revival of interest in trinitarian theology in the late twentieth century in terms of developing a theology that is rooted in a living spiritual tradition. In *Trinitarian Spirituality* Kay makes an argument for the link between the doctrine of the Trinity and the life of the church and the believer, a link that arises out of Owen's writing. He summarizes his argument by writing, "The conclusion of this work is that Owen . . . comes closer than most other figures in Western spirituality to integrating a doctrinally rich trinitarianism into the heart of a spiritual method."[23] While the phrase "spiritual method" carries with it an understanding that is probably more precise than Owen had in mind, Kay points to Owen's holding together of doctrine and the spirituality of the believer. Owen refers to the relationship within God and with God as "communion" as is seen in *Of Communion with God the Father, the Son, and Holy Ghost.*[24] This line of thought is taken up and developed by Kapic in *Communion with God.*[25]

The particular significance of Owen's trinitarian perspective for this book is the way in which Owen sees the Trinity not as an abstract doctrine to be argued over, but as a lived reality to be encountered in worship through the power of the Holy Spirit. In *Pneumatologia*, he offers five principles which outline his thinking and the distinctiveness of his understanding.[26] These five principles[27] are outlined as follows:

- First, "The nature and being of God is the foundation of all true religion and holy religious worship in the world."[28]

22. The discussion about the language of person in relation to the Trinity will be looked at in chapter 4.

23. Kay, *Trinitarian Spirituality*, 28.

24. See Owen, *Works*, vol. 2.

25. Kapic comments about Owen's contribution to theology: "Looking back to John Owen's insistent application of trinitarian theology to the believer's life may prove of interest not only to historians but also to systematic theologians. Owen's description of communion with the Triune God offers insights into the relevance of trinitarian theology for the life of the church and human experience" (Kapic, *Communion with God*, 148).

26. Owen, *Works*, 3:64–68.

27. Owen develops these five principles in a short paragraph on each one. In this book, principles one and two will be further developed in chapter 4 on worship; principle two will be critically examined in chapter 6; principles three to five will be looked at in more depth in chapter 5 on personal relationality, with further attention being given to principle five in chapter 3 on the Holy Spirit.

28. Owen continues: "The great end for which we were made, for which we were brought forth by the power of God into this world, is to worship him and to give glory

- Second, "The revelation that God is pleased to make of himself unto us gives the rule and measure of all religious worship and obedience."[29]

- Third, "God hath revealed or manifested himself as three in one . . . that is, as three distinct persons, subsisting in the same infinitely holy, one, undivided essence."[30]

- Fourth, "These divine persons are so distinct in their peculiar subsistence, that distinct actings and operations are ascribed unto them."[31]

- Fifth, "This Spirit . . . is in himself, a distinct, living, powerful, intelligent, divine person; for none other can be the author of those internal and external divine acts and operations which are ascribed unto him."[32]

The first two of these five principles make clear the way in which Owen holds together his thinking about God within the setting of worship. God is the one not only to be studied and thought about but is to be encountered in the relationship that is experienced in worship. It is the interplay of thought and encounter that leads to the knowledge of God. The relationship with God that arises out of the participation in the act of worship is Owen's starting point for developing his trinitarian thinking. It is only by the third principle that Owen proceeds with the more doctrinal and intellectual issues with regard to the oneness and threeness of God. The first two principles make clear one of the arguments that lie at the heart of this book with regard to the relationship between God and humanity as particularly defined and experienced in worship: Owen sees God, not as an abstract principle about which many arguments can be made, but as the beginning and end of all things, the one to whom people are drawn in a particular relationship, encountered in worship.

Owen makes it clear that he is referring both to the "outward" activity of God in relation to the world and to the very nature and being of God. The balance between "activity" and "being" in God will provide a thread for the argument that is being developed in each part of the quadrilateral discussion.[33] Owen argues that worship is not only a human activity, giving praise

---

unto him; for he 'made all things for himself,' or his own glory, Prov 16:4 . . . and that which makes this worship indispensably necessary unto us, and from whence it is holy or religious, is the nature and being of God himself" (Owen, *Works*, 3:65).

29. Owen, *Works*, 3:66.

30. Owen, *Works*, 3:66.

31. Owen, *Works*, 3:67.

32. Owen, *Works*, 3:68.

33. The discussion about activity and being in God has been a focus for extensive

to God for what God has "done for us"; worship is drawn out of humanity by who God is. Worship is evoked by the encounter with the being of God, by what God is in terms of himself and God's inherent characteristics. He makes this clear as he continues with his first principle:

> There are, indeed, many parts or acts of religious worship which immediately respect (as their reason and motive) what God is unto us, or what he hath done and doth for us; but the principal and adequate reason of all divine worship, and that which makes it such, is what God is in himself. Because he is,—that is, an infinitely glorious, good, wise, holy, powerful, righteous, self-subsisting, self-sufficient, all-sufficient Being, the fountain, cause, and author of life and being to all things, and of all that is good in every kind, the first cause, last end, and absolutely sovereign Lord of all, the rest and all-satisfactory reward of all other beings,—therefore is he by us to be adored and worshipped with divine and religious worship.[34]

Having laid the grounds for holding together the nature and being of God with the response to God that is evoked in worship, Owen then proceeds with the principles three to five, which relate to the triune nature of God. Both the unity of God and the distinctiveness of the three persons of the Godhead are important for Owen, particularly as he focuses on the distinctive person and work of the Holy Spirit. For Owen, the activity of the Holy Spirit is not separated from the activity of God but it is distinctive. Owen uses the language of person to describe this distinctiveness. Under his fourth principle, Owen refers to the *"distinct actings and operations"* of the divine persons. In explaining what he means by this, he continues by identifying two sorts of "actings." He describes these in traditional language as *"ad intra"* and *"ad extra,"* internal and external "actings." The internal actings are

> natural and necessary, inseparable from the being and existence of God. So the Father knows the Son and loveth him, and the Son seeeth, knoweth and loveth the Father. In these mutual actings, one person is the object of the knowledge and love of the other: . . . So the Spirit is the mutual love of the Father and

---

twentieth-century discussion since Rahner's declaration that "the economic Trinity is the immanent Trinity, and the immanent Trinity is the economic Trinity" (Rahner, *Trinity*, 21–24).

34. Owen, *Works*, 3:65.

the Son, knowing them as he is known, and "searching the deep things of God."[35]

In describing the external actings, Owen holds the view that these "actings" are not a necessary part of God's existence but are in fulfilment of God's deliberate choice. These "actings" are

> voluntary, or effects of will and choice, and not natural or necessary. And these are of two sorts: 1. Such as respect one another; for there are external acts of one person towards another: but then the person that is the object of these actings is not considered absolutely as a divine person, but with respect unto some peculiar dispensation and condescension. So the Father gives, sends, commands the Son, as he had condescended to take our nature upon him, and to be the mediator between God and man. So the Father and the Son do send the Spirit, as he condescends in an especial manner to the office of being the sanctifier and comforter of the church. Now, these are free and voluntary acts, depending upon the sovereign will, counsel, and pleasure of God, and might not have been, without the least diminution of his eternal blessedness. 2. There are especial acts, ad extra, towards the creatures.[36]

Owen's fifth principle develops his trinitarian thinking by emphasizing the personal nature of the Spirit:

> Fifthly, the Spirit *is in himself, a distinct, living, powerful, intelligent, divine person*; for none other can be the author of those internal and external divine acts and operations which are ascribed unto him.[37]

While such a specific view of the Holy Spirit as personal might be seen as verging on a tritheistic view of the Trinity, it is important to hold together two aspects of Owen's thinking within his particular historical context of the seventeenth century. These have been referred to above in terms of the

35. Owen, *Works*, 3:67. "John 3:67. 'The Father loveth the Son, and hath given all things into his hand.' Chap. v. 'The Father loveth the Son.' Matt 11:27: 'No man knoweth the Son, but the Father; neither knoweth any man the Father, save the Son.' John 6:46: 'None hath seen the Father, save he which is of God, he hath seen the Father.' This mutual knowledge and love of Father and Son is expressed at large, Prov 8:22–31; which place I have opened and vindicated elsewhere. And they are absolute, infinite, natural, and necessary unto the being and blessedness of God" (Owen, *Works*, 3:66–67).

36. Owen, *Works*, 3:67.

37. Owen, *Works*, 3:67.

rise of unitarian thinking (with particular reference to the Socinians) and the rise of Quaker thinking focusing on the "inner light" and the inner spirit, thus, as Owen saw it, reducing the being of the Holy Spirit within the life the triune God. Alongside this, in response to the rise of rationalistic philosophical trends such as that of Descartes and Locke, which evoked arguments about the nature of the Trinity leading to the Trinity being seen by some as more of an abstract doctrine remote from human experience, Owen was concerned to hold together doctrine and personal experience of God.[38] Out of this historical context, Owen developed a view of the Holy Spirit that was concerned to point both the personal nature of the Holy Spirit and the experience of God in a person's life that is the outworking of the activity of the Holy Spirit.

This brief indication of Owen's understanding of the Trinity will be followed in subsequent chapters with an analysis of issues with regard to the Holy Spirit within the Trinity, the relationship between worship and the understanding of the Trinity, and epistemological arguments with regard to the use of scripture in developing Owen's trinitarian approach.

COMMUNION AS THE FOUNDATIONAL THEME IN ZIZIOULAS'S TRINITARIAN UNDERSTANDING

Zizioulas's trinitarian framework arises out of his rootedness in the tradition and experience of the early church as seen through the lens of the Cappadocian Fathers and in the liturgical experience of the Orthodox church. It is out of the particular relationship with God the Holy Trinity that an understanding of the role of human reason and experience is discerned in the shaping of theological understanding. His trinitarian thinking combines mind, body, and spirit in a way which points to God as known through both the reasoning of the attentive mind and the experience of encounter with God in the Eucharist. Zizioulas's trinitarian framework follows an ontological route concerned with the nature of being understood as communion, which is signified by the three persons of the Trinity in relation.

In looking at communion, four interrelated themes run through Zizioulas's writing and undergird what will be drawn out in terms of his approach to the Trinity, the Holy Spirit, and worship. Zizioulas draws together the characteristics of God the Holy Trinity with the embodiment of these characteristics in the church, particularly in the Eucharist. The theme of communion finds

---

38. These arguments are outlined in more detail by writers referred to in chapter 1, including Dixon, *Nice and Hot Disputes*; Lim, *Mystery Unveiled*; Grenz, *Social God*.

its focus in the Eucharist and its framework in the personal and relational ontology which Zizioulas argues arises out of the Cappadocian Fathers.

These interrelated themes are:

a. an ontological approach to communion;

b. communion—the personal and relational nature of God in the Trinity; and

c. the church as an embodiment of the relational characteristics of the trinitarian life of God.

Underlying these themes is the thought that the activity of the Holy Spirit in the Eucharist leads to an understanding of human personhood redefined in relational terms.

An Ontological Approach to Communion

In an age in which "contextual" approaches are much to the fore, Zizioulas's ontological approach comes as a striking contrast. He points to the range of meanings that ontology embraces when he writes of ontology as

> a word to which various meanings have been given, while for some people it indicates almost nothing at all. In this chapter, we take it to mean the area of philosophy (and theology) in which the question of being is raised more or less in the sense in which it was posed for the first time by ancient Greek philosophy, applied here to the specific problem of personal identity. It is all too often assumed that people "have" personhood rather than "being" persons, precisely because ontology is not operative enough in our thinking.[39]

---

39. Zizioulas, *Communion and Otherness*, 99. In his footnote at this point he adds: "This was more or less the sense in which the term *ontology* was employed for the first time in the seventeenth century by authors such as R. Goclenius (*Lexicon Philosophicum*, 1613) and, more explicitly, J. Glauberg (*Metaphysica de Ente*, 1656), who defines it as the part of philosophy which speculates on being *qua* being. The same definition is recovered and employed without change by Ch. Wolff (*Philosophia prima sive ontologia*, 1729, especially paragraphs 1 and 2) who is responsible for the establishment of this term in philosophy. Kant, in his *Critique of Pure Reason* (esp C. III) tried to give the term a different meaning, which however has not prevailed. Heidegger and the modern existentialist philosophers have also employed it with a different meaning in their attempt to take a critical view of classical philosophy, whereas authors such as E. Levinas in our time prefer not to attach to it the traditional metaphysical importance."

From this ontological approach, Zizioulas emphasizes the personal and relational nature of God the Holy Trinity. He summarizes his approach in the introduction to *Being as Communion*:

> The being of God is a relational being: without the concept of communion it would not be possible to speak of the being of God. . . . It would be unthinkable to speak of the "one God" before speaking of the God who is "communion," that is to say, of the Holy Trinity. The Holy Trinity is a primordial ontological concept and not a notion which is added to the divine substance or rather which follows it.[40]

Communion is a key category for Zizioulas.[41] An understanding of communion arises out of the influence on him of the Cappadocian Fathers in terms of the Trinity and of relational identity. His explication of communion or *koinonia* is rooted in particular in the writings of Basil. Zizioulas points to the way in which Basil developed the early understanding of ontology as signifying substance on its own, to one that signifies the relationality of persons that is the nature of communion.

> Basil . . . replaces the notion of substance as an ontological category with that of koinonia. Instead of speaking of the unity of God in terms of His one nature, he prefers to speak of it in terms of the communion of persons; communion is for Basil an ontological category. The nature of God is communion. This does not mean that the persons have an ontological priority over the one substance of God, but that the one substance of God coincides with the communion of the three persons.[42]

This analysis of substance as being coincident with communion is a key point in Zizioulas's thinking about relational identity.

It has been much discussed between East and West as to whether this emphasis on an ontology of communion is a factor in differentiating Eastern from Western thinking, or whether the contrasts between Eastern and Western thinking in this area have been exaggerated.[43] Weinandy writes of Zizioulas:

40. Zizioulas, *Being as Communion*, 17.

41. This is reflected in the titles of two of his significant writings, *Being as Communion* and *Communion and Otherness*, which expand on key aspects of the nature of Communion.

42. Zizioulas, *Being as Communion*, 134.

43. Ayres, *Nicaea*; Weinandy, "Zizioulas"; Loudovikos, "Person Instead of Grace"; McCall, *Which Trinity?*; Tibbs, "East Meets West."

> In contrast to Greek philosophy, which gave ontological priority to "nature" or "substance," Zizioulas consistently argues that Christian theology, specifically through the work of the Cappadocian Fathers, obtained the insight that "person" has true ontological priority. The catalyst for such an insight was the working out of a theological understanding of the Trinity, especially, Zizioulas argues, in the light of western Sabellianism, which denied the ontological distinctiveness of the persons."[44]

Weinandy continues, however, by arguing that Zizioulas is over-reliant on the Cappadocians and thus neglects Augustine and Aquinas. Ayres counter-argues by pointing to the way in which Augustine's "psychological" model of the Trinity has been taken out of context by being seen on its own as the primary means of understanding the Trinity. Ayres helpfully points to the psychological model as being secondary rather than primary, developed as a means of understanding the inner life of the Trinity in Augustine but not reducing the personal nature of Father, Son, and Spirit.[45]

For Zizioulas, worship, as seen in the Eucharist, is the point of coming to know God. This knowledge of God is not primarily focused in understanding but in relationship, relationship that is personal, both in terms of the communion of the persons of the Trinity and also in terms of the communion into which the human person is drawn thus becoming fully whom he or she is meant to be, a person in relationship. Communion and personhood are key ontological categories for Zizioulas (to which I will return in discussing the similarities and differences between Owen and Zizioulas). It is the Holy Spirit who constitutes the church in the liturgy.

Communion: The Personal and Relational Nature of God in the Trinity

Zizioulas develops his understanding of the persons within the Trinity and the particular influence of the Cappadocian Fathers on his thinking in *Communion and Otherness*.[46]

---

44. Weinandy, "Zizioulas," 407. A further interesting piece of research would be to compare Sabellianism with Socinianism, to assess how far the ideas promoted in two different eras of the church's life share similarities in terms of the way in which the counter-arguments have shaped the understanding of the Trinity, as well as to examine how far these arguments are still being made in the twenty-first century.

45. Ayres, *Augustine*.

46. Zizioulas, *Communion and Otherness*, esp. 155–205.

Zizioulas redefines personhood from a trinitarian perspective, moving away from an Enlightenment approach—with the definition of a person focused on self-consciousness—to seeing the definition of person in terms of participating in the relationality of the Trinity. He develops this thinking from a relational perspective on the Trinity, exemplified in *Being as Communion* and arising out of his reflection on patristic thought. He outlines this in two theses:

a. There is not true being without communion. Nothing exists as an "individual," conceivable in itself. Communion is an ontological category.

b. Communion which does not come from a "hypostasis," that is a concrete and free person, and which does not lead to "hypostases," that is concrete and free persons, is not an "image" of the being of God. The person cannot exist without communion; but every form of communion which denies or suppresses the person, is inadmissible.[47]

He reinforces his argument by writing "respect for man's 'personal identity' is perhaps the most important ideal of our time . . . historically as well as existentially the concept of the person is indissolubly bound up with theology . . . the person both as a concept and as a living reality is purely the product of patristic thought."[48]

Zizioulas draws together his thinking about seeing personhood in relationship, and points to this relationality as being rooted in God.

The Church as an Embodiment of the Relational Characteristics of the Trinitarian Life of God

Zizioulas points to the location of communion in the church:

All the observations we have made so far concerning faith in the Trinity, in Christ and in the Spirit take their concrete form in the Church. It is there that communion with the other fully reflects the relation between communion and otherness in the holy Trinity, in Christ and in the Spirit.[49]

47. Zizioulas, *Communion and Otherness*, 18.
48. Zizioulas, *Communion and Otherness*, 27.
49. Zizioulas, *Communion and Otherness*, 6.

Zizioulas refers to the church as "not simply an institution. She is a 'mode of existence,' a way of being. This way of being is rooted in the being of God."[50] He draws together in his thinking the nature of the triune God as embodied through the power of the Holy Spirit, in the Eucharist, which becomes constitutive of the church.

> How can we draw together ecclesial being and the being of God, history and eschatology, without destroying their dialectical relationship? To achieve this we need to find again the lost consciousness of the primitive Church concerning the decisive importance of the Eucharist in ecclesiology.[51]

Zizioulas holds together his understanding of God and the church with his focus on communion, which, for him, is both an ontological category and is embodied in the Eucharist:

> Ecclesiology in the Orthodox tradition has always been determined by the liturgy, the Eucharist; and for this reason, it is the first two aspects of Pneumatology, namely eschatology and communion that have determined Orthodox ecclesiology. Both eschatology and communion constitute fundamental elements of the Orthodox understanding of the Eucharist. The fact that these two things are also fundamental aspects of Pneumatology shows that if we want to understand Orthodox ecclesiology properly, and its relation to Pneumatology, it is mainly to these two aspects of Pneumatology that we must turn, namely to eschatology and communion.[52]

Zizioulas writes further on the Eucharist:

> The Eucharist was not the act of a pre-existing Church; it was an event constitutive of the being of the Church, enabling the Church to be. The Eucharist constituted the Church's being. Consequently, the Eucharist had the unique privilege of reuniting in one whole, in one unique experience, the work of Christ and that of the Holy Spirit. It expressed the eschatological vision through historical realities by combining in the ecclesial life the institutional with the charismatic elements.[53]

---

50. Zizioulas, *Being as Communion*, 15.

51. Zizioulas, *Being as Communion*, 20.

52. Zizioulas, *Being as Communion*, 131.

53. Zizioulas, *Being as Communion*, 21.

Zizioulas builds on the Cappadocian Fathers, and Basil in particular, in emphasizing the relationship between worship and trinitarian understanding. The church was both constituted at one point in time, at Pentecost, through the coming of the Holy Spirit, and is also constituted over and again in each present moment as the Eucharist is offered. In drawing together worship and trinitarian understanding, he locates the Trinity not only within the realm of human reason, but in the relationship between humanity and God that is experienced in worship. In this argument lies part of the counterbalancing of the emphasis on the priority of the Father:

> If . . . one speaks of God in terms of liturgical and especially Eucharistic experience, then, Basil argues, the proper doxology is that of *meta/syn-* and this makes the inter-trinitarian relations look entirely different. The three persons of the Trinity appear to be equal in honor and placed one next to the other without hierarchical distinction.[54]

This emphasis on the lack of hierarchical distinction is then followed by a reference to the Liturgy as revealing God in the act of communion, with a pointer to the element of mystery that pertains to an understanding of communion.

> The existence of God is revealed to us in the Liturgy as an event of communion. Basil, in agreement with the Fathers of both East and West, stresses the unity of divine operations *ad extra*,[55] and cannot see how else one can speak of God in his own being: "If one truly receives the Son, the Son will bring with him on either hand the presence of his Father and that of his own Holy Spirit; likewise he who receives the Father receives also in effect the Son and the Spirit. . . . So ineffable and so far beyond our understanding are both the communion (*koinonia*) and the distinctiveness (*diakrisis*) of the divine hypostases." From whatever end you begin in speaking of the holy Trinity, you end up with the co-presence and co-existence of all three persons at once. This is the deeper meaning—and the merit—of the *meta/syn-* doxology and, for that matter, of a theology inspired by the Liturgy. As Gregory of Nazianzus put it later, the worship of one

---

54. Zizioulas, *Communion and Otherness*, 189, quoting Basil, "Glory be to the Father with (*meta*) the Son, with (*syn*) the Holy Spirit" (Basil, *De Spiritus Sancti* 1:3f; 7:16).

55. Zizioulas refers in a footnote to the analysis given by John McIntyre, "where the entire question of the unity of divine operations ad extra (indivisible but not undifferentiated) received a profound and balanced analysis" (McIntyre, "Holy Spirit in Greek Patristic Thought," 357–58).

person in the Trinity implies the worship of the Three, for the
Three are one in honour and Godhead.[56]

Zizioulas takes the argument further in terms of the relationship between
worship and theology when he writes:

> This language, which is taken up by Constantinople, opens the
> way to an argument based on liturgical experience and worship
> and thus to a theology which does not rest merely upon histori-
> cal or "economical" experience.[57]

Zizioulas's approach to theology is connected to his ecclesial understanding in terms of the way in which the church arises out of the being of
God and embodies the communion that is the nature of the Trinity. In his
introduction to *Being as Communion*, Zizioulas writes:

> In the first place, ecclesial being is bound to the very being
> of God. From the fact that a human being is a member of the
> Church, he becomes an "image of God," he exists as God Him-
> self exists, he takes on God's "way of being." This way of being
> is not a moral attainment, something that man *accomplishes*. It
> is a way of *relationship* with the world, with other people and
> with God, an event of *communion*, and that is why it cannot
> be realized as the achievement of an *individual* but only as an
> *ecclesial* fact.[58]

Zizioulas responds to two areas that have been raised in terms of a
critique of his writing on the Trinity and the nature of communion.

1. Differentiation in the Trinity

One dilemma in terms of the concept of communion in relation to the
Trinity is that the opportunities for difference are narrowed, either in terms
of the distinctive identity of the Father, Son, and Spirit or in terms of the
particularity of human identity. However, Zizioulas addresses this issue in
Communion and Otherness, pointing both to the nature of the Trinity and
the consequent differentiation between individuality and personhood. The
first aspect that emerges from a study of the doctrine of the Trinity is that
otherness is constitutive of unity and not consequent upon it.

56. Zizioulas, *Communion as Otherness*, 189.
57. Zizioulas, *Communion as Otherness*, 190.
58. Zizioulas, *Being as Communion*, 15.

2. History and Particularity

He further argues for the particularity of each member of the Trinity in the economy. "Only the Son is incarnate. Both the Father and the Spirit are involved in history, but only the Son becomes history . . . if becoming history is the particularity of the Son in the economy, what is the contribution of the Spirit? Precisely the opposite: it is to liberate the Son and the economy from the bondage of history . . . when the Spirit acts in history he does so in order to bring into history the last days, the eschaton. Hence the first fundamental particularity of Pneumatology is its eschatological character."[59] The doctrine of the Trinity draws together the historical and embodied aspect of God in the life of the Son with an understanding of God that points to God's presence not only at one time, but in all time, and for eternity.

Monarchia

I move to look at a further key critical area of Zizioulas's thinking, that is his "monarchical" approach, which addresses the question: If the Father is the original cause within the Godhead, can the Son and the Spirit be equally constitutive of the Trinity? This raises the further issue of whether or not Zizioulas's relational thinking about God can be justified if it is asymmetrical between the three persons of the Trinity.

Monarchia is one of the more contentious issues to emerge out of Zizioulas's thinking—the argument from the early Fathers that the Father is the originator of the Trinity and that the Son and the Spirit, while coequal, have their origins in the Father. This raises the issue as to whether the "origin" of the nature of God lies in the Father, or the "substance" underlying the three persons of the Trinity or the three persons of the Trinity together.

Zizioulas summarizes the argument he makes in detail with regard to the priority of the Father[60] by referring to the new light cast by the Cappadocian Fathers after the Arian controversy and Athanasius's response to this:

> What was the importance of this stage in ontology, reached by the Cappadocians? Above all, it was that the being of God became placed on a new and more biblical foundation. By usurping, as it were, the ontological character of *ousia*, the word person/hypostasis became capable of signifying God's being in an ultimate sense. The subsequent developments of trinitarian theology, especially in the West with Augustine and the scholastics, have

59. Zizioulas, *Being as Communion*, 130
60. Zizioulas, *Being as Communion*, 39–42

led us to see the term *ousia*, not *hypostasis*, as the expression of the ultimate character and the causal principle (*arxe*) in God's being. The result has been that in textbooks on dogmatics, the Trinity gets placed after the chapter on the One God (the unique *ousia*) with all the difficulties which we still meet when trying to accommodate the Trinity to our doctrine of God. By contrast, the Cappadocians' position—characteristic of all the Greek Fathers—lay, as Karl Rahner observes, in that the final assertion of ontology in God has to be attached not to the unique *ousia* of God but to the Father, that is, to a *hypostasis* or person.[61]

Zizioulas's reference to the Cappadocians' emphasis on persons within the Trinity plays a significant role in his writing. However, the consequent focus on the Father as originator tends toward subordinationism and the downplaying of the role of the Son and the Spirit.

Tibbs puts the issue as follows:

A significant family of critiques levelled at Metropolitan Zizioulas's trinitarian theology comes in response to his insistence that the monarchy (*monarchia*) of the Father as the one cause (*aitia*) of the Trinity is absolutely necessary to preserve a correct understanding of the Trinity. One focus of criticism which affects both trinitarian theology and ecclesiology is whether Zizioulas's insistence on the monarchy of the person of the Father results in a subordinationist view of the Trinity.[62]

However, there is an issue as to where the balance in Zizioulas's thinking lies behind *monarchia* and communion. As already referred to above in his writing on communion, Zizioulas points to the way in which the "one substance of God coincides with the communion of the three persons." This would appear to open the door to a more nuanced approach to *monarchia*, counter-balancing Zizioulas's rigorous approach to the Father as origin. McCall in *Which Trinity? Whose Monotheism?* develops this line of thinking in his chapter on "Holy Love and Divine Aseity in the thinking of John Zizioulas,"[63] arguing for a combining of Zizioulas's argument nearer the beginning of *Being as Communion* with what McCall refers to (following Jay Wesley Richards and Alvin Plantinga) as the "Sovereignty-Aseity Conviction."[64] This conviction gives greater weight to the shared prior-

61. Zizioulas, *Being as Communion*, 88.

62. Tibbs, "East Meets West," 69.

63. McCall, *Which Trinity?* 189–215.

64. McCall, *Which Trinity?* 33–35, refers to Richards, *Untamed God*; Plantinga, *Does God Have a Nature?*

ity of the three persons of the Trinity together in loving relationship. N. J. Awad also points to the inner contradiction in Zizioulas with regard to communion and *monarchia*.[65]

The particular aspect of the nature of personhood in relationship, and the way in which this affects the understanding of the Trinity, will be looked at further in chapter 5. The argument will focus on the priority of all three persons of the Trinity together in relation if a concept of relationality is to be foundational to an understanding of God the Trinity.

OWEN AND ZIZIOULAS: SIMILARITIES AND DIFFERENCES

What is significant in looking at the thinking of Owen and Zizioulas is not so much the expected diversity of two theologians from their different contexts but the overlapping threads that run through both of their understandings.

A Shared Pneumatological Approach

The next two chapters move from the more general trinitarian understanding of Owen and Zizioulas to focus in particular on the nature and role of the Holy Spirit and the emphasis that they place on the Holy Spirit as drawing people into the worshipping relationship with God. Out of this relationship, the worshipping community is shaped.

Communion and Personal Relationality

The overlapping of titles of key works by Owen and Zizioulas has been noted earlier.[66] While titles themselves need to be unpacked in order to see the way in which they relate to the content of the work, the commonality of the titles between Owen and Zizioulas offers a pointer to the congruity of some of their key underlying arguments.

---

65. Awad, "Personhood as Particularity," 1–22.

66. Referred to in chapter 1. See *Of Communion with God* (Owen, *Works*, vol. 2); Zizioulas, *Being as Communion; Communion and Otherness*.

Communion

Communion is a primary concept for both Owen and Zizioulas, pointing to a particular understanding of the relational nature of the Trinity. An area of difference lies in the way in which communion is understood ecclesially. For Owen, the outcome of the trinitarian focus on communion is a focus on the individual's communion with God through the Holy Spirit in the work of sanctification. For Zizioulas, an understanding of communion leads to an emphasis on the Eucharist and the gathering of the community around the bread and the wine. There is a helpful interplay between Owen and Zizioulas with regard to the relationship between the individual and the community that leads to a deeper understanding of the nature of communion as it is received and lived out through the church.

Personal Relationality

The discussion about the nature of "person" in terms of the Trinity, and the consequent effect of this discussion on an understanding of the human person, will be looked at further in chapter 5, unpacking the first side of the quadrilateral argument. This chapter examines further the way in which the concept of Communion is developed in personal and relational terms, developing and critiquing the personal and relational understanding of the Trinity that Zizioulas explicates and taking forward the discussion about the "one and the three," the arguments with regard to social trinitarianism and the debate about the origin of the nature of person. It is noted how Zizioulas's emphasis on the equal significance of the Son and the Spirit in the Trinity echoes Owen's understanding of Son and Spirit equally conveying the fullness of the Gospel.

Philosophical and Theological Influences

While there is a wide range of diverse philosophical and theological influences upon Owen and Zizioulas there are overlaps in terms of the weight they give to the early Fathers. Chapter 5, explicating their focuses on the origins of a "personal" understanding of the Trinity, looks briefly at the similarities and contrasts between Owen and Zizioulas in terms of the influence of the Cappadocian Fathers, particularly in relation to the differing understandings of the Holy Spirit as "person."

   A contrast is seen between their approaches to scripture. In comparison to Owen's approach, which references a wide number of scriptural passages at each point, Zizioulas focuses in more depth on the arguments of the early church and in particular on the Cappadocian Fathers.

Regarding the epistemological setting of worship for the knowledge of God, chapter 6 looks at the way in which both Owen and Zizioulas understand worship as an immediate encounter with God made possible by the Holy Spirit, with chapter 7 looking at an understanding of truth in terms of the way in which the Holy Spirit in worship leads to knowledge of God.

Ecclesial Diversity

There are parallels and distinctives, developed over the course of this book, with Owen emphasizing the work of the Spirit in relation to Jesus Christ, focusing more on the personal particularity of Christ rather than on the church as the body of Christ. Here Zizioulas differs from Owen in his ecclesiological emphasis: Owen emphasizes the work of the Holy Spirit in sanctification as a personal event while Zizioulas holds this work more deliberately in an ecclesial setting.

Zizioulas refers to sanctification but maintains that this aspect has not become a decisive aspect of ecclesiology in the East. "Ecclesiology in the Orthodox tradition has been determined by the liturgy, the Eucharist; and for this reason it is the first two aspects of Pneumatology, namely eschatology and communion that have determined Orthodox ecclesiology."[67] However, the Orthodox emphasis—as seen for example in John Romanides's writing as outlined in Kelley's lectures on Romanides *A Realism of Glory*[68] on the participation in God's transforming glory—is also an emphasis in John Owen's writings.[69]

Regarding ecclesiological differences: there is a differing ecclesial understanding of the reception of the Holy Spirit in shaping worship, as seen in Owen's emphasis on the local people gathered in worship and Zizioulas's emphasis on the bishop as the focus of communion, which is looked at in chapter 4.

Scriptural Approach

Owen and Zizioulas hold different approaches with regard to Biblical hermeneutics. While there are similarities in their understanding of the

---

67. Zizioulas, *Communion and Otherness*, 131.

68. Kelley, *Realism of Glory*.

69. With eight references to this phrase in *Pneumatologia*.

role of scripture in shaping the church, there is a differing emphasis on the weight given to scripture throughout their writing, and the balance between the influence of scripture and that of tradition. Chapter 7 looks at this area in terms of the different sources of Owen and Zizioulas's theological understanding and in terms of the epistemological shaping of relational truth as a way into the knowledge of God.

The Nature of Transformation

Owen emphasizes the transforming work of the Holy Spirit taking place in personal sanctification. Zizioulas emphasizes the work of Spirit in constituting the church, in eschatology, and, more recently, in the transformation of creation. This area is developed in chapter 8 on the transformative nature of the Holy Spirit.

3

The "Dynamic Recovery" of the
Holy Spirit in Owen and Zizioulas

I MOVE NOW TO what I refer to as the "dynamic recovery" of the Holy Spirit in Owen and Zizioulas. I use this phrase to indicate the particular significance that each of these writers gives to an understanding of both the nature of the Holy Spirit within the Trinity and the activity of the Holy Spirit amongst God's people.

The themes of the Holy Spirit and of worship have been looked at from many different angles over the centuries and have been critical in determining certain aspects of the life and doctrine of the church.[1] The twentieth century has seen a well-documented rise in pneumatological and liturgical studies from a range of Christian perspectives.[2] However, the specific

1. A prime example is the argument over the *filioque* clause in the creed, one of a range of social, political, and religious factors culminating in the separation of the Eastern from the Western church in 1054, with reverberations and re-formulations of the creed still continuing to be felt in the life of the churches in the twentieth and twenty-first centuries. Zizioulas gives a helpful analysis of the issues with regard to the *filioque* in his *Lectures*, 75–77.

2. What follows are some examples of key writings from a range of perspectives on the Holy Spirit from the second half of the twentieth century onwards (a list of references to worship and liturgy will follow in the next chapter): Barr and Yocom, *Church*; Berkhof, *Doctrine of the Holy Spirit*; Buckley and Yeago, *Knowing the Triune God*; Carr,

theological holding together of the Holy Spirit and worship has been less evident. Berger and Spinks, in their introduction to *The Spirit in Worship—Worship in the Spirit,* a book published in 2009 as a result of a 2008 conference on the same theme at the Yale Institute of Sacred Music, write: "Sadly, in this theological turn to Pneumatology, the study of worship as a site of the Spirit's presence and work remains, for the most part, marginal."[3]

This chapter develops a response to the contemporary issues surrounding the Holy Spirit and worship previously outlined, builds on the understanding of the Trinity in Owen and Zizioulas, and goes more deeply into Owen's and Zizioulas's thinking about the Holy Spirit in order to take further the central argument of this book, the development of a "quadrilateral" approach to the Holy Spirit and worship.

I look at the connections between these two theologians of different traditions and backgrounds on the assumption that as there is one Holy Spirit, although manifest in a variety of ways, there will be connections to be discovered from theologians of apparently very diverse traditions. In the interplay between these connections comes a renewed understanding of the significance of the nature and work of the Holy Spirit and the understanding of the role of the Holy Spirit in worship as shaping the transformative encounter with God. This understanding of the Holy Spirit is significant both in looking at the re-vitalization of the mainstream churches in the West and in contributing to the dialogue with Pentecostalism. I proceed to examine in more detail the writing of Owen and Zizioulas with regard to the Holy Spirit before leading in to a focus on worship and then the outlining of the quadrilateral framework.

This volume seeks to draw out the way in which the role of the Holy Spirit in Owen and Zizioulas is seen as embodied in the relationship with God that is found in worship. In this relationship, the Holy Spirit is both part of the three-fold focus of worship, as the third person of the Holy

---

"Towards a Contemporary Theology"; Congar, *I Believe in the Holy Spirit*; Doctrine Commission of the Church of England, *We Believe in the Holy Spirit*; Fee, *God's Empowering Presence*; Gabriel, *Lord is the Spirit*; Hendry, *Holy Spirit in Christian Theology*; Heron, *Holy Spirit*; Jensen, *Triune Identity*; Kärkkäinen, *Pneumatology*; Losel, "Guidance from the Gaps"; McIntyre, *Shape of Pneumatology*; Moule, *Holy Spirit;* Quash, *Found Theology*; Rogers, *After the Spirit*; Stringer, "Lord and Giver of Life"; Welker, *God the Spirit.*

3. Berger and Spinks, *Spirit in Worship*, xv. I also note Ratzinger's *Spirit of the Liturgy*, building on the earlier work of the same name by Romana Guardini. However, these two works focus primarily on deepening the understanding the liturgy itself rather than entering into the pneumatological understanding of worship. Fletcher and Cocksworth, *Spirit and Liturgy*, offers a brief theological development of the role of the Holy Spirit in worship.

Trinity, and also the One who draws people into the worshipping relationship with God. In this relationship, God is known. This knowledge of God is made manifest in particular acts of worship. This chapter builds on the Trinitarian undergirding of this knowledge of God and develops the idea of the "quadrilateral framework" in order to develop a constructive theological approach to the Holy Spirit and worship.

It is out of a theological approach to the Holy Spirit and worship that the image of the quadrilateral is offered. This is not to exhaust all that Owen and Zizioulas write about the Holy Spirit and worship, but to draw out a distinctive pattern arising from the unexpected congruities between them.[4] The four sides of the quadrilateral framework are personal relationality, immediacy, truth, and transformation, each of which will be explored further throughout this book. Each side arises out of the nature and characteristics of the Holy Spirit and contributes to the overall worshipping relationship of the believer with God. As in a quadrilateral each side can vary in length, so the contribution of each of the points that Owen and Zizioulas makes varies in scale. However, what is significant as we compare these two theologians is the way in which all four sides are present, although in different ways, and, in being present, complete the argument and point to the fullness of the presence of the Holy Spirit in worship. The unfixed nature of the length of each side of the quadrilateral, yet the dependence on there being four sides, point to the particular and varied manifestation of the Holy Spirit who yet retains a unity and integrity of identity. This volume argues that it is possible to enter the quadrilateral from any one of the four sides but that it is important to continue from the point of entry into a discovery of the remaining sides in order to enter in to a living and transforming knowledge of God and for worship to be truly offered.

I move to look at Owen's extensive writing on the Holy Spirit, drawing out his understanding of the personal nature of the Holy Spirit within the Trinity and looking at the sanctifying role of the Holy Spirit within the life of the person. This is held alongside Zizioulas's understanding of the nature of the Holy Spirit in terms of his consideration of the Spirit's role in communion and eschatology. A particular focus is the similarity of approach between Owen and Zizioulas in terms of their re-balancing between Christology and Pneumatology.

---

4. A parallel image, "interweaving," is developed by Hardy, *God's Ways*. Hardy focuses on the relationship of the Holy Spirit to the world in terms of the interweaving role of the Holy Spirit in relation to culture. I argue that the quadrilateral image is another parallel image, indicating the way in which the Holy Spirit holds together a range of differing characteristics.

The similarities between Owen and Zizioulas are seen in terms of their understanding of the nature of the activity of the Holy Spirit in relation to worship. A common understanding in both writers is that in worship a relationship is opened up with the divine, and that in this relationship the Holy Spirit brings people into the likeness of Christ in a way which involves personal inner transformation, described by Owen as sanctification; and the drawing of people into communion, described by Zizioulas as constituting the church.

OWEN'S DYNAMIC RECOVERY OF THE HOLY SPIRIT

Perspectives From Owen's Historical Setting and Theological Context

Why, in the twenty-first century, go to a seventeenth-century English Puritan theologian to look at the theology of worship through the transformative activity of the Holy Spirit? Because there is a rich vein of connection between Puritanism, its emphasis on Pneumatology, and the piety embedded in the experience of the regenerating and sanctifying work of the Holy Spirit in worship.

Geoffrey Nuttall, focusing in the mid-twentieth century on Puritan history, writes in the preface to his book, *The Holy Spirit in Puritan Faith and Experience*: "The doctrine of the Holy Spirit received a more thorough and detailed consideration from the Puritans of seventeenth-century England than it has received at any other time in Christian history."[5] This comment might owe something to the affection of the aficionado. It also predates the resurgence of systematic theological interest in the Holy Spirit across the second half of the twentieth century. However, it does illustrate the underdeveloped nature of systematic emphasis on the Holy Spirit in Christian writing in the West.

In looking at the longer history of theology in relation to the Holy Spirit, McIntyre comments on the different approaches to Christology and Pneumatology in the early years of the church's life:

> (a) The comparative brevity of the Spirit debates, the narrower lines of interpretation followed in the formative centuries, as well as the lack of any comprehensive metaphysical apparatus to extend these lines—there was not to be a "chalcedonian

---

5. Nuttall, *Holy Spirit in Puritan Faith*, 8. In his writing, Nuttall is focusing in particular on the Western church.

pneumatology"—ensure that the doctrine entered the modern period having been less intensively debated than Christology, and without the canonical authority of a full creed.[6]

He further reflects on the way in which Pneumatology remained undeveloped in succeeding centuries in contrast to Christology:

> (b) It was not just in the great formative centuries of doctrine that the person of Jesus Christ received detailed, if at times also very controversial treatment, for in the last century and in this, there has been enormous continuing Christological debate relating to the nature of the humanity of Christ, the historicity of the stories about him . . . and so on. Once again, there have been no comparably profound disagreements about the person of the Holy Spirit in the same period. There have been many optional accounts of his nature and work, but these have been, on the whole, alternatives to one another, not in any sense competitively vying with one another or attempting to be exclusive of one another as has been the case in the modern Christological debates.[7]

There is a variety of factors in play in the development of seventeenth-century Puritan interest in the Holy Spirit ranging across the spectrum from political to cultural to philosophical to theological. This book focuses on the theological factors. (Developing an understanding of the political, cultural, and philosophical aspects will need to wait for further work in a different piece of research.)

I point to the way in which Owen's writings offer insights that are extensive but not necessarily fully developed in contemporary writing in order to see the contribution that Owen's pneumatological perspectives on worship can make. I reference Owen's historical context as providing the setting for the development of his own Trinitarian and pneumatological outlook. Owen's writings are formulated within the context of Calvin and the Reformed tradition, with Owen's emphasis on the Holy Spirit within the triune God leading to the weight he gives to sanctification and a personal relationship with God. B. B. Warfield describes Calvin as the "theologian of the Spirit," a reference that has been taken up widely subsequently.[8] While Owen does not himself use this phrase about Calvin, it could be considered that the same title be applied to Owen as to Calvin. Owen's writings on the Holy Spirit, from the latter part of his life, indicate the way in which he was at

6. McIntyre, *Shape of Pneumatology*, 18.

7. McIntyre, *Shape of Pneumatology*, 19.

8. Warfield, *Calvin and Calvinism*.

that time influenced by the early Fathers, with references in *Pneumatologia* including many more early church theologians than references to Calvin.[9]

While writing about Owen's Pneumatology has been on the increase, it is worth noting that the most extensive exploration of Owen's Pneumatology is to be found in Dale Stover's 1967 unpublished PhD thesis looking at Owen's theological method in relation to his Pneumatology and in comparison with Calvin.[10] Stover's work makes a helpful link with Calvin and Owen and places Owen in Calvin's footsteps while also being critical of Owen's approach in comparison with that of Calvin. For example, Stover argues that Calvin's is a fundamentally different handling of the relation between Christ and the Spirit from Owen's, with Calvin only seeing the Spirit as Christ's Spirit and Owen cutting the Spirit off from the incarnation, an argument which this book holds to be an exaggeration of Owen's position.[11] Stover emphasizes both Owen's rootedness in Puritanism, pointing to the particular emphasis that the Puritans placed on the Holy Spirit, and in the European Reformed tradition, and his contribution from these perspectives to succeeding generations.[12]

This chapter seeks to balance the more Christological emphasis of Owen's early writings with his later more pneumatological emphases and to contribute this more detailed pneumatological focus to the growing number of twentieth- and twenty-first-century writings on Owen. This volume also seeks to contribute to the growing number of theological rather than historical writings on Owen.

9. In the citations in *Pneumatologia* there is a much more extensive list of references to the early Fathers than citations of the Reformers, indicating Owen's engagement, both favorably and critically, with the writers of the early church. There are six or more references to each of the following: Ambrose, Augustine, Basil, Chrysostom, Didymus, Jerome, Origen, and Pelagius; Calvin receives two citations; the only near contemporaries to Owen to receive six or more citations are John Crell (twelve), Samuel Parker (six), and Schlichtingius (seven).

10. Stover, "Pneumatology of John Owen."

11. Stover, "Pneumatology of John Owen," 304.

12. Stover, "Pneumatology of John Owen," 23, 24. Stover quotes, for example, Jerald Brauer: "The personal or experiential nature of Puritanism resulted in a concern with the doctrine of the Holy Spirit which is unparalleled in Christian history. At some point, almost every Puritan preached about the Spirit or attempted to place this doctrine at the center of his religious life" (Brauer, "Reflections," 102).

Owen's Writings on the Holy Spirit

Owen wrote significantly on the Holy Spirit (at greater length than either on God the Father or God the Son, on both of which areas he wrote extensively), particularly with regard to the transformative work of the Holy Spirit in regeneration and sanctification.[13] The extensive nature of these writings is a reflection of the Puritan concern with the Holy Spirit. It also serves to highlight Owen's experiential approach to the Christian faith, with emphasis given to the way in which the Spirit is seen as transforming the life of the believer. The diversity of Owen's writing highlights the diversity of the ways of thinking about the Holy Spirit, in itself a pointer in the direction of the range of ways in which the Holy Spirit is manifest.

Goold, in his 1852 edition of Owen's *Works*, explains the background to *Pneumatologia* and the way in which he, Goold, has brought the variety of different writings of Owen on the Holy Spirit together.[14] He starts with his own summary of Owen's writings and his reasons for drawing them together:

> The year 1674 saw issuing from the press some of the most elaborate productions of our author. Besides his own share in the Communion controversy, he published in the course of that year the second volume of his Exposition of the Epistle to the Hebrews, and another folio of equal extent and importance, the first part of his work on the Holy Spirit; for what is generally known under the title of "Owen on the Holy Spirit," is but the first half of a treatise on that subject. The treatise was completed in successive publications:—*The Reason of Faith*, in 1677; *The Causes, Ways, and Means of Understanding the Mind of God*, etc., in 1678; *The Work of the Holy Spirit in Prayer*, in 1682; and, in 1693, two posthumous discourses appeared, *On the Work*

13. Amongst his many theological writings, lies Owen's lengthy work, *Pneumatologia*. Goold, in his 1852 edition of Owen's works, groups together (vols. 3–4) under the overall title of *Pneumatologia*, Owen's original work with a series of Owen's shorter writings on the Holy Spirit—"The Reason of Faith," "Causes, Ways and Means of Understanding the Mind of God," and the three Discourses concerning the Holy Spirit and his work: "Of the Holy Spirit in Prayer"; "On the Holy Spirit as a Comforter"; and "A Discourse of Spiritual Gifts." In these writings, Owen sought to expand his original work. The themes in these works are echoed in *Of Communion with God the Father, Son, and Holy Ghost*. There are also various references to the Holy Spirit during the course of his other writings and in the texts of sermons Owen preached on the Holy Spirit.

14. Goold's edition of Owen's *Works* is widely referenced in twentieth- and twenty-first-century writings on Owen and is a major source for the online referencing of Owen.

of the Spirit as a Comforter, and as he is the Author of Spiritual Gifts. From the statements of Owen himself, in various parts of these works, as well as on the authority of Nathaniel Mather, who wrote the preface to the last of them, we learn that they were all included in one design, and must be regarded as one entire and uniform work.[15]

Goold continues by quoting Owen in support of the line he, Goold, is taking in terms of the organization of Owen's writings. The quotation summarizes Owen's thinking with regard to the development of his Pneumatology and makes clear the extensive and diverse range of Owen's thinking with regard to the Holy Spirit:

In Owen's preface to the *Reason of Faith*, he expressly states, "About three years since I published a book about the dispensation and operations of the Spirit of God. That book was one part only of what I designed on that subject. The consideration of the Holy Spirit as the Spirit of illumination, of supplication, of consolation, and as the immediate author of all spiritual offices and gifts, extraordinary and ordinary, is designed unto the second part of it." . . . Owen was induced to issue separately the treatises belonging to the second part, according as he was able, under the pressure of other duties, to overtake the preparation and completion of them.[16]

There is a gentle movement back and forth in the writings drawn together under the heading of *Pneumatologia* between Owen's reflections on God in his own life and his understanding of the Holy Spirit as defined through scripture and experience. This movement begins in the five chapters of the first book of *Pneumatologia*. Owen's interplay of doctrinal understanding and the effects of the Holy Spirit in human life begin to emerge. Owen's focus on the significance of the early Fathers is seen in chapter 2 when he describes the "names" by which the Holy Spirit has been known, both in the Spirit's essence and the Spirit's effects, as seen in the writings of, for example, Ambrose, Didymus, and Jerome, as well as in scripture. The concluding two chapters unpack the sequence of the relationship of the Father to the Spirit, followed by the work of the Spirit both breathing life into creation and being poured out on people, like water on a barren land.

Volume 4 of Goold's edition of Owen's *Works* contains the writings which complete *Pneumatologia*, beginning with book 6, parts 1 and 2,[17]

15. Owen, *Works*, 3:1.

16. Owen *Works*, 3:2.

17. See part 1, "The Reason of Faith" (Owen, *Works*, 4:4–118) and part 2, "Causes,

which raises issues with regard to the way in which it is possible to know God, focusing in particular on revelation and scripture and arguments about the way in which each of these contributes to the knowledge of God. Owen also roots his thinking on aspects of the Spirit which relate pastorally to people's experience. Books 7 to 9 focus on pastoral dimensions, holding these alongside the movement in and out of doctrinal considerations as Owen looks at prayer, the work of the Spirit as Comforter, and the gifts that the Spirit offers.

Owen developed his writing on the person and work of the Holy Spirit within his concern to combat what he saw as heresy. He maintained the underlying unity of the Trinity while at the same time emphasizing the particular activity of each person of the Trinity.

Owen's consideration of the Holy Spirit arises out of his desire to interpret the Trinity in such a way as to make clear the connection between the triune God and human experience. In Owen's extensive focus on the Holy Spirit can be seen his concern to draw together an understanding of the nature of the triune God and the revelation and encounter with God in everyday human experience. Owen also wrote widely on the Christological aspects of the Trinity, aspects which have been well covered in contemporary scholarship, as seen, for example, in Alan Spence's *Incarnation and Inspiration* and Kelly Kapic's *Communion with God*.[18] This book seeks to supplement the writing that has taken place on Owen's Christology and his trinitarian framework by drawing out further insights from Owen's extensive pneumatological writing, and by looking in particular at worship as both the descriptor and the setting in which communion with God through the Holy Spirit takes place.

The comprehensive nature of Owen's writings on the Holy Spirit offer a wealth of themes. I move now to look at five underlying themes that emerge

---

Ways, and Means of Understanding the Mind of God" (Owen, *Works*, 4:118–236).

18. Spence, *Incarnation and Inspiration*. Spence addresses issues of the human and divine in Jesus by looking at the debates amongst the early Fathers and arguing for a Christology that is both incarnational and inspirational, arising out of Owen's addressing of seventeenth-century issues with regard to the Trinity. Kapic follows up on Owen's emphasis on the relationship between Christian doctrine and Christian living with what Kapic describes as Owen's "anthroposensitive theology," focused in particular on the Son. "Owen's anthroposensitive theology operates as a dialogue between truths discovered about the Son and how believers should respond to these discoveries." Kapic refers to three particular themes around which Owen structures his Christocentric framework within a trinitarian approach: "First, the character of the Son, his excellencies and 'personal grace'; second, the Son's affections for believers; and third, communion with the Son through 'purchased grace'" (Kapic, *Communion with God*, 176).

out of his writings in order to give an overview of Owen's thinking on the Holy Spirit and to lay the foundation for the four specific aspects that are developed more fully with regard to the quadrilateral on the Holy Spirit and worship. These themes are: re-balancing the emphasis between Spirit and Son, the personal nature of the Spirit, the Holy Spirit and human experience—including sanctification and pastoral outcomes, a developmental understanding of the Spirit, and revelation and mystery.

The Relationship between the Spirit and the Son

Owen's writings include a doctrinal reflection on the indivisible nature of the work of the Trinity alongside the distinction that can be made in terms of the effects of each member of the Trinity. He gives particular attention to re-balancing the understanding of relationship between the Spirit and the Son, holding together Christology and Pneumatology in a way which emphasizes the Spirit's incarnational role. This is particularly seen in *Pneumatologia* where he outlines ten theses demonstrating the efficacy of the Spirit in the life of the Son.[19] He addresses the main points of Jesus's life, his death, and his resurrection in order to show the impact of the Spirit in supporting and sustaining Jesus Christ's redeeming work. Owen makes clear the relationship of the Holy Spirit to Jesus, drawing out the prior work of the Holy Spirit in the life of Jesus rather than placing the weight of emphasis on the Son sending the Spirit. In his argument, Owen's scriptural grounding is made clear as at each point he supports his argument with scriptural

---

19. Owen, *Works*, 3:162–83. "Firstly, the framing, forming and miraculous conception of the body of Christ in the womb of the blessed Virgin was the peculiar and especial work of the Holy Ghost" (162); "Secondly, the human nature of Christ being thus formed in the womb by a creating act of the Holy Spirit was in the instant of its conception sanctified and filled with grace according to the measure of its receptivity" (168); "Thirdly, the Spirit *carried on that work* whose foundation he had thus laid" (169); "Fourthly, the Holy Spirit, in a peculiar manner, anointed him with those extraordinary powers and gifts which were necessary for the exercise and discharging of his office on the earth" (171); "Fifthly, it was in an especial manner by the power of the Holy Spirit he wrought those great and *miraculous works* whereby his ministry was attested unto and confirmed" (174); "Sixthly, by him was he *guided, directed, comforted, supported*, in the whole course of his ministry, temptations, obedience and suffering" (174); "Seventhly, He offered himself to God through the eternal Spirit" (176); "Eighthly, there was a peculiar work of the Holy Spirit towards the Lord Christ when he was in the *state of the dead*"(180); "Ninthly, there was a peculiar work of the Holy Spirit in his *resurrection*, this being the completing act in laying the foundation of the church, whereby Christ entered into his rest" (181); "Tenthly, it was the Holy Spirit that *glorified* the human nature [of Christ] and made it every way meet for its eternal residence at the right hand of God" (183).

reference and justification. Chapter 1 of *Pneumatologia* begins with a summary of scriptural references to the Holy Spirit and an indication of the way in which the Son and the Spirit are held equally together as Gospel truths.

Owen indicates a further dimension of the relationship between the Holy Spirit and Jesus Christ in the new creation by referring to the Spirit as the one "supplying the bodily absence of Christ." "It is the Holy Spirit who supplies the bodily absence of Christ, and by him doth he accomplish all his promises to the church."[20] He continues this strong emphasis by commenting "And this he doth by his Spirit alone; for, 'Know ye not that ye are the temple of God, and that the Spirit of God dwelleth in you?' [1 Cor 3:16]. He, therefore, so far represents the person, and supplies the bodily absence of Christ, that on his presence the being of the church, the success of the ministry, and the edification of the whole, do absolutely depend."[21]

Owen holds together his doctrinal understanding of the Trinity, including the nature of the three persons of the Trinity, with his scriptural explication of the relationship between the Son and the Spirit and his sense of the embodiment of the Spirit in the life of the church.

The Personal Nature of the Spirit

This book refers to the Trinitarian nature of God using the primary language of persons. Relevant to this is the reference that Owen makes to the Spirit as "in himself, a distinct, living, powerful, intelligent, divine person."[22] Owen continues with an analysis of the personal properties of the Spirit, such as wisdom and understanding, and the works which the Spirit effects, such as teaching and calling people to ministry, which point to the nature of the Spirit as personal. The issues of the nature of "person" and "personal" and how Owen defines these both in relation to the Spirit and to the human person are looked at in more depth in chapter 5 of this book, which focuses on this first aspect of the quadrilateral framework.

The Holy Spirit and Human Experience

Owen is concerned to overcome the divide which he sees as having been put between doctrine and holy living. His unfolding of his understanding of the Holy Spirit helpfully holds together his thinking about the nature of

---

20. Owen, *Works*, 3:167.
21. Owen, *Works*, 3:168.
22. Owen, *Works*, 3:67.

the triune God with his reflection on the effects of the Holy Spirit in human experience. Book 4 (comprising eight chapters) of *Pneumatologia* goes into detail about the work of the Holy Spirit in sanctification including the Spirit's role in creating the natural body of the Son and the mystical body of the church, and emphasizing the real effects of the Spirit's work in terms of such aspects as the increase of love and joy within a person. Owen unpacks the immediate but gradual nature of sanctification using the extended image of the growing of a tree, analyzes the way sanctification takes effect in the human soul, and reinforces the need to live a holy life. In order to explain the need for sanctification, Owen devotes two chapters to the nature of human sinfulness and human incapacity to achieve spiritual renewal and fullness of life. He addresses a range of psychological dynamics and opens up the shape of the real change that God can effect through the Holy Spirit in the life of the person.

He has a strong focus on the role of the Holy Spirit in the sanctification of the person and combines this with the use of dynamic metaphors to describe the activity of the Holy Spirit. In the earlier part of *Pneumatologia*, he comments:

> There shall be such a plentiful communication of the Spirit as that he and his work shall be made open, revealed, and plain. "I will pour my Spirit upon thy seed, and my blessing upon thine offspring." Isaiah 44:3. The word here [for pour] is so to pour a thing out as that it cleaveth unto and abideth on that which it is poured out upon; as the Spirit of God abides with them unto whom he is communicated.[23]

Owen holds together his understanding of the nature of the Spirit, in and of the Spirit's self, as the one who pours out blessing, with his interpretation of the way in which that blessing is received in the life of the human person.

Welker, in his book *God the Spirit*, expands the meaning of the "pouring out" of the Spirit:

> The pouring out of the Spirit means that the Spirit not only comes upon individual persons and groups of people in a surprising manner in order to become effective in and through them as well as to influence both their proximate and their distant environments. The Spirit also influences people by coming from both their proximate and their distant environments, inasmuch as the Spirit at the same time enlists the services of other people with them. . . .

---

23. Owen, *Works*, 3:114.

> The talk of the pouring out of the Spirit articulates the in-
> fluence that persons seized by the Spirit exercise in their own
> proper person on both their proximate and their distant envi-
> ronments, whether those persons are directly conscious of that
> influence or not.[24]

This "pouring out" will be looked at further in chapter 4 in terms of the particular location of the pouring out of the Spirit in the offering of worship and in chapter 8 in terms of the nature of the transformation that is effected by the Spirit.

A Developmental Understanding of the Spirit

The five chapters of book 2 of *Pneumatologia* cover the work of the Holy Spirit as seen through the Old Testament and the gradually developing role of the Spirit leading in to the new creation. I will return to the issue of the developmental role of the Holy Spirit, arguing that Owen makes a construc-tive point about the developing revelation of the Holy Spirit from the Old Testament to the New Testament, but disagreeing with Owen as to the need to halt this development after the New Testament. The issue about the con-cept of "sola scriptura" will be touched when I come to look at the nature of truth in terms of knowing God.

Revelation and Mystery

In Owen's earlier writings, with his stronger emphasis on Christology, the area of revelation is very much to the fore. However, in his discussions of the Holy Spirit, while continuing with his emphasis on revelation, he balances this out with a desire to see more of the "mystery" of God. In his opening preface to *Pneumatologia* he begins by acknowledging the desire to hold together thinking about the Holy Spirit as part of the "mystery" or "deep things of God" with the way in which the mystery might be known through the revelation that is found in Scripture.[25] These themes of "mystery" and "deep things of God" run through *Pneumatologia*. Holding together differ-ent approaches to the Spirit, Owen used a two-fold language when he wrote that the Spirit is both "a pure, spiritual or immaterial substance" and also fully personal.[26] This is an interpretation with elements of paradox, which,

24. Welker, *God the Spirit*, 228–29.

25. Owen, *Works*, 3:5.

26. Owen, *Works*, 3:54. The use of "substance" carried a particular meaning in the

in holding together different understandings, could be argued to point to the way in which the Holy Spirit cannot be straightforwardly categorized, thus pointing further to the mystery of the Spirit.

Owen's Contemporary Relevance

Owen's interest in the human psyche predates the development of more modern psychological understanding and links with the historical mystical tradition within Christianity.[27] His emphasis on experience, under the influence of the Holy Spirit, leads him to an exploration of the interiority of the human condition rather than in the direction of the more exterior manifestations of the Holy Spirit as, for example, in the development of some aspects of the worship offered in the Pentecostalist tradition of the church.

I draw out two particular approaches in Owen's thinking about the Holy Spirit, in order to draw out the significance of Owen for the church in the twenty-first century. The first is the way in which Owen articulates the encounter with the Holy Spirit in relation to human experience, seeing the working together of the Spirit and the person. I refer to this description of the divine/human encounter under the heading of "synchronicity"—the coming together at one moment of the Holy Spirit and the human spirit (which will be developed when looking at the notion of immediacy in terms of the personal encounter with God). This coming together is not a description of an activity between equal partners but refers to the moment of encounter between the giving Spirit and the receiving person. There is a groundedness and rootedness of the activity of the Spirit in human life, which is made clear in looking through the lens of immediacy. By focusing on particular moments of encounter between the Spirit and the person, the Spirit is seen as being evident and known in the work of human history.

The second is the way in which Owen sees the Holy Spirit as making present the origins of the Gospel, as seen in the incarnation of the historical Jesus, in the church's contemporary experience in the way in which people are transformed and made new. I refer to this under the headings of origins and originality—the way in which the Holy Spirit, in each generation, connects the origins of the Christian faith (as, for example, seen in scripture,

---

seventeenth century, as seen in the writings of Descartes and Hobbes. This meaning, arising out of the debates with scholastic-Aristotelianism, focused more on a concept of "being" or "reality" than on that of a particular material entity, as is more common usage in the twenty-first century.

27. Kay, *Trinitarian Spirituality*.

Jesus Christ, and the early church) with the encounter with God in the present moment that brings new life. From Owen's writing, I draw out an understanding of the Holy Spirit at work in the intersections within and between immediacy and transformation as played out in worship.

The Puritan emphasis on the Holy Spirit, which was diminished by the weight of the resurgent political establishment in the second half of the seventeenth century, has subsequently been seen in such developments as the Holiness Movement flowing out of John Wesley's teaching and writing. While the more rational approach of Puritanism to the Holy Spirit stands in contrast to the more emotional approach of Pentecostalism, a line has been traced from the Puritans to Pentecostalism through the route of the influence of Puritanism on John Wesley.[28] This Holiness movement, influenced by the writing and teaching of John Wesley, spread to the United States and is seen in the growth of American Methodism in the nineteenth century. This in turn laid the foundations for the development of American Pentecostalism at the beginning of the twentieth century. While Owen's contribution to the origins of this direction is noted, this book emphasizes Owen's wider contribution to an understanding of the Holy Spirit across churches.

ZIZIOULAS'S FOCUS ON THE SIGNIFICANCE OF PNEUMATOLOGY

Zizioulas's Context within the Orthodox Tradition and in the East-West Divide of the Church

Zizioulas, coming from the Eastern Orthodox Church, brings a perspective which gives weight both to the early Fathers and to the subsequent separation of theological thinking between East and West. His perspective emphasizes pneumatological thinking in relation to Trinitarian understanding and to the embodiment of the Spirit, with the Spirit being constitutive of the Body of Christ, as will be further outlined in this chapter.

---

28. Lorna Lock-Nah Khoo, *Wesleyan Eucharistic Spirituality*, 139, refers to John Wesley's reading Puritan writers and publishing John Owen, amongst others, in his *Christian Library*. Both Khoo and Torpy, *Prevenient Piety*, 27, refer to the influence on John Wesley of his mother and her strong Puritan background, with her husband even having received financial support from John Owen. Joel R. Beeke at the end of his chapter on Owen in *The Quest for Full Assurance* writes, quoting Jon Zens, "John Wesley appealed to Owen to support his own emphasis on the Holy Spirit's testimony in assurance" (Beeke, "John Owen on Assurance," 212).

I now focus on issues in relation to Pneumatology, and in particular the differing relationship between Pneumatology and Christology that Zizioulas identifies as characteristic of the Eastern and the Western churches. In referring to the "West" Zizioulas broadly refers to both Roman Catholic and Protestant understandings, making the argument for the differentiation between the Eastern Church and the Western Church in relation to Pneumatology, building on the difference he has identified between East and West in terms of an understanding of the nature of the relationship between the three and the one in the Trinity. He argues that the Western church, with its stronger Christological focus, neglected the area of Pneumatology, while this area was more to the fore in the Eastern Church. Although the early church balanced Christology and Pneumatology, this holding together was subsequently neglected in the West:

> It seems, therefore, that the question of priority between Christology and Pneumatology does not *necessarily* constitute a problem, and the Church could see no problem in this diversity of approach either liturgically or theologically for a long time. . . . The problem arose only when these two aspects were *in fact* separated from each other both liturgically and theologically. It was at this point in history that East and West started to follow their separate ways leading finally to total estrangement and division. Not only baptism and confirmation were separated liturgically in the West but Christology tended little by little to dominate Pneumatology, the *filioque* being only part of the new development.[29]

While Zizioulas's thinking can appear contentious to Western eyes, it has also won some favor in the West. Folsom comments on Zizioulas's significant contribution on Pneumatology:

> Barth may have developed his pneumatology had he lived, but we owe thanks to Zizioulas for an outstanding contribution to our understanding of pneumatology based on the theology of the patristic fathers. His emphasis on the pneumatological dimension of the church is a much-needed answer to the imbalance of western rationalistic, often pietistic, Christianity. Zizioulas, despite his allowance of ecclesial capacities, clearly affirms the necessity of the Spirit for the church's existence—an emphasis often neglected in western Christianity.[30]

29. Zizioulas, *Being as Communion*, 128.
30. Folsom, "Comparative Assessment," 165.

Zizioulas's interest lies not just in critiquing the West on pneumatological grounds, but in trying to re-balance what he sees as an overly Christological Western perspective in order to open up new ecumenical horizons between East and West. Weinandy concludes his article on "Zizioulas, the Trinity and Ecumenism" by commenting:

> Too often today, I believe, Western and Eastern theologians read and study the Fathers as if the Fathers had the same theological hang-ups among themselves as we do today. In so doing the Fathers are never read as they are, but merely as weapons to be used against either the East or the West, and so Christian theology never entirely reaps the abundant harvest of what they taught. By reading the Fathers in such a manner, Western theologians are disloyal to their heritage and Eastern theologians are false to theirs, and together they are unfaithful to the one Gospel. Only when the West and the East truly strive to live together, as Zizioulas has laboured so long to teach us, in communion with the Father, the Son and the Holy Spirit will the Church once more breathe with both lungs.[31]

The conclusion of this book looks further at the ecumenical perspectives opened up by the comparison between Zizioulas and Owen on the Holy Spirit and the possibilities that this approach addresses.

I now move to outline Zizioulas's approach to the Holy Spirit in order to lay the grounds for the development of the quadrilateral framework.

Zizioulas's Writings on the Holy Spirit

Zizioulas's writings on the Holy Spirit run as a thread through his published works. It is noteworthy that his thinking developed over the years so that he gave more priority to Pneumatology in his later writings. In his 1965 PhD thesis, first published in English in 2001, his primary focus is on the role of the bishop and the Eucharist in the first three centuries of the church in bringing unity to the church.[32] The introduction emphasizes the primary role of Christology and is more critical of a pneumatological ecclesiology:

> What is paramount in ecclesiology is not this or that doctrine, idea or value revealed by the Lord, but *the very person of Christ* and man's union with Him. . . . This Christological view of the mystery of the Church makes it equally impossible to study the

31. Weinandy, "Zizioulas," 407–15.
32. Zizioulas, *Eucharist, Bishop, Church.*

unity of the Church within a pneumatocentric ecclesiology, in which there is a risk of ecclesiology being made into "charismatic sociology." . . . This observation is not to deny that in ecclesiology a fundamental position is occupied by the Holy Spirit, and indeed by the Holy Trinity as a whole, Who undoubtedly constitutes the supreme principle of the church.

Zizioulas goes on to critique the idea of a pneumatocentric ecclesiology on the grounds that it focuses more sociologically on "'the body of Christians united in the Holy Spirit" than on an ontological understanding which focuses first on Christ and the unity of people in Christ.[33]

However, in his later work he develops his emphasis on the role of the Holy Spirit, particularly in terms of communion, as is seen initially in *Being as Communion*, his earliest book published in English.[34] This pneumatological development in Zizioulas's thinking is followed through in two of the later collections of his writings, *Communion and Otherness* and *Lectures in Christian Dogmatics*, in which the Holy Spirit plays a more integral role in his development of his thinking about Communion.[35] Alongside "Communion" the Holy Spirit forms a strong and consistent thread throughout Zizioulas's writings. It is also worth noting the attention given to the examination of Zizioulas's thinking on Pneumatology in some recent doctorates on Zizioulas's thought.[36] While Pneumatology is not necessarily the focus of each book, the role of the Holy Spirit in Zizioulas's thinking forms a key part of the development of the writing. Folsom, in his comparison of MacMurray, Zizioulas, and Barth on freedom, comments: "It is in his doctrine of the Holy Spirit that Zizioulas contributes the most significantly."[37]

I move to look at five underlying themes that arise out of Zizioulas's writing on the Holy Spirit, themes that flow into each other: re-balancing the relationship between Christology and Pneumatology, the Holy Spirit and the body of Christ, communion, eschatology, and the Eucharist. It is out of these underlying themes that the quadrilateral framework in relation to the Holy Spirit and worship emerges.

33. Zizioulas, *Eucharist, Bishop, Church*, 16, 17.

34. Zizioulas, *Being as Communion*.

35. Zizioulas, *Communion and Otherness*.

36. Folsom, "Comparative Assessment"; Tingcui, "Critical Study on Zizioulas"; Norris, "Pneumatology, Existentialism and Personal Encounter"; Robinson, "Towards a Definition."

37. Folsom, "Comparative Assessment," 90.

Re-balancing the Relationship between Christology and Pneumatology

I have referred to the way in which Zizioulas identifies the separation be-tween Christology and Pneumatology as a key issue of difference between churches of the East and of the West. I turn now to look in more detail at the issues Zizioulas raises about the relationship between Christology and Pneumatology.

Zizioulas succinctly summarizes the issues about the relation between Christology and Pneumatology from two directions, that of the priority of the one over the other and that of the content of Christian doctrine in rela-tion to both of these areas:

> The problem is not whether one accepts the importance of Pneumatology in Christology and vice versa: it arises in con-nection with the following two questions: i. The question of *pri-ority*: should Christology be made dependent on Pneumatology or should the order be the other way around? ii. The question of *content*: when we speak of Christology and Pneumatology, what *particular* aspects of Christian doctrine—and Christian existence—do we have in mind?

He continues by pointing to the way in which in the New Testament there is not a single response to the issue with regard to priority and highlights the way in which the New Testament writings point in both directions:

> In the New Testament writings themselves we come across both the view that the Spirit is given *by* Christ, particularly the risen and ascended Christ ("*there was no Spirit yet,* for Christ had not yet been glorified" John 7:39); and the view that there is, so to say, *no Christ* until the Spirit is at work, not only as *a forerunner* announcing his coming, but also as the one who *constitutes his very identity as Christ,* either at his baptism (Mark) or at his very biological conception (Matthew and Luke).[38]

On the basis of this scriptural understanding, Zizioulas points to the way in which the co-existence of these two views could be a helpful starting point for looking at possible theological and liturgical diversity in terms of the balance between Christology and Pneumatology in East and West. He raises the question of formulating a synthesis between Christology and Pneumatology which avoids the over-emphasis of the West on Christology

---

38. Zizioulas, *Being as Communion*, 127. Zizioulas summarizes the historical dif-ferences between the church in the East and the West in *Being as Communion*, 123–42.

and the East on Pneumatology. He goes on to argue for holding together an unbreakable unity between Christology and Pneumatology, even while at times there might be different practical emphases. He quotes as an example the way in which confirmation preceded baptism in Syria and Palestine until the fourth century AD.[39]

Zizioulas develops his thinking about the relationship between Christology and Pneumatology by analyzing two kinds of relationship between the Holy Spirit and Christ.[40] The first understands "Christ as an individual, seen objectively and historically, presenting Himself thereby for us as the truth." In this way of thinking, the gap between Christ and us is bridged "by the aid of certain means . . . being realised by the assistance or under the guidance of the Holy Spirit."[41] The second way of thinking focuses on Christ not as an individual but in relationship with his body, the church. "Here the Holy Spirit is not one who *aids* us in bridging the distance between Christ and ourselves but he is the person of the Trinity who actually realises in history that which we call Christ." In this second way of thinking, "Christ does not exist first as truth and then as communion, he is both at once. All separation between Christology and ecclesiology vanishes in the Spirit."[42] The weight of Zizioulas's thinking on this point comes when he emphasizes: "So we can say without risk of exaggeration that Christ exists only pneumatologically, whether in his distinct personal particularity or in his capacity as the body of the church and the recapitulation of all things."[43]

Zizioulas's emphasis on reuniting in one whole the work of Christ and that of the Holy Spirit draws us back to the contentions surrounding the *filioque*, emphasizing the Eastern perspective of the similarity of understanding of the role of Christ and the Holy Spirit in relation to the Father rather than seeing the Holy Spirit in a procession from the Father through the Son.

It is interesting to note the support for Zizioulas's approach from a Roman Catholic perspective from Kilian McDonnell in his book *The Other Hand of God: The Holy Spirit as the Universal Touch and Goal.*[44] McDonnell points to the same discussion that Zizioulas highlights about the influence of the early Fathers and the balance between Christology and Pneumatology. He draws attention to Zizioulas's writing: "John Zizioulas correctly lays out two New Testament models for the relationship between Christology

---

39. Zizioulas, *Being as Communion*, 128.

40. Zizioulas, *Being as Communion*, 67–122.

41. Zizioulas, *Being as Communion,* 110.

42. Zizioulas, *Being as Communion*, 111.

43. Zizioulas, *Being as Communion*, 111.

44. McDonnell, *Other Hand of God.*

and Pneumatology." After briefly analyzing these, McDonnell concludes: "At this moment in history I choose a Christology dependent on Pneumatology as an antidote to the imbalance arising from the dominance in the West of Pneumatology dependent on Christology."[45]

This re-balancing of the relationship between Pneumatology and Christology flows into an ecclesial re-balancing of the role of the Holy Spirit in relation to the body of Christ.

The Holy Spirit Shaping the Body of Christ

Out of his thinking on the relationship between Pneumatology and Christology, Zizioulas develops his emphasis on the role of the Holy Spirit in ecclesiology, holding that the church is instituted by Christ, but constituted by the Spirit. This two-fold approach leads Zizioulas to comment on the way in which Christ is understood not only as an individual but as "the body of Christ" in ecclesial terms:

> Another important contribution of the Holy Spirit to the Christ event is that, because of the involvement of the Holy Spirit in the economy, Christ is not just an individual, not "one" but "many." This "corporate personality" of Christ is impossible to conceive without Pneumatology.[46]

This aspect of "corporate personality" is linked to an understanding of the nature of the human person as being defined by being in relation.[47] Folsom comments of Zizioulas that "his is the most constructive description of the work of the Spirit in constituting the church and the person."[48]

Zizioulas writes that "pneumatology must be constitutive of Christology and ecclesiology, i.e., condition the very being of Christ and the church." He maintains that this can happen only if two particular ingredients of Pneumatology are introduced into the ontology of Christ and the church—eschatology and communion. Zizioulas shows the weight and seriousness of his approach when he writes, "It is not enough to speak of eschatology and communion as necessary aspects of Pneumatology and ecclesiology; it is necessary to make these aspects of Pneumatology

45. McDonnell, *Other Hand of God*, 193–94.

46. Zizioulas, *Being as Communion*, 130.

47. Chapter 5 will look further at the nature of "person" in arguing for the first side of the quadrilateral framework.

48. Folsom, "Comparative Assessment," 165.

constitutive of ecclesiology."[49] He continues to amplify the significance of his understanding:

> What I mean by "constitutive" is that these aspects of Pneumatology must qualify the very ontology of the Church. The Spirit is not something that "animates" a Church which already somehow exists. The Spirit makes the Church *be*. Pneumatology does not refer to the well-being but to the very being of the Church. It is not about a dynamism which is added to the essence of the Church. It is the very essence of the Church. The Church is constituted in and through eschatology and communion.[50]

He further amplifies his understanding by writing that when these are held together, "then the 'one' and the 'many' co-exist as two aspects of the same being."

McPartlan expands Zizioulas's argument, emphasizing the implications of the two different ways in which the relationship between Spirit and Son can be understood for the church and interprets the two different aspects of these ways of understanding by identifying, on the one hand, an approach which emphasizes mission in history and distance between the head and the body, and, on the other hand, gathering, communion, and eschatology.

> Let us see in a little more detail how Zizioulas analyses the data from the early Church. He actually considers that the scriptures and early Fathers show *two types* of pneumatology, resulting in two kinds of ecclesiology. In the first type, the Spirit is given by Christ to the Church for mission in history, and the Church is obedient, as the body of Christ, to its head. There is a "dialectic between the head and the body" in this perspective, he says, and "a certain *distance* between the head and the body in terms of ecclesiology," with an awareness of the Church's weakness and sin.

This interpretation can be seen to undergird not only certain Western understandings of the priority of Christology but also those approaches which give a high priority to the role of the church in history, with a more activist emphasis on mission. McPartlan goes on to interpret the second approach in a way that introduces Zizioulas's distinctive ecclesial thinking dependent on the priority of the Holy Spirit:

> In the second type, Christ is constituted by the Spirit, who overshadows his conception and ultimately brings about his

49. Zizioulas, *Being as Communion*, 131.
50. Zizioulas, *Being as Communion*, 132.

resurrection. The Church, likewise constituted by the Spirit, does not follow Christ in this picture but surrounds him. The accent is not on dispersion but on gathering and communion, not on history but on eschatology, not on distinction from Christ but on identity with him, not on obedience but on *mysticism*, not on sin but on holiness. The head and the body are unbreakably united, Christ is present not just *with* his Church but *as* his Church, and the "I" of the Church is Christ.[51]

McPartlan's analysis, in expanding Zizioulas's two types of pneumatological approach to ecclesiology, points to the debates that have continued over the centuries in the church about the nature of the church's identity. This is in particular with regard to the historical locatedness of the church versus the eschatological reality of the church, and to the debate about the church as a gathering of Spirit-filled individuals or a body of people in relationship with the Triune God.

Communion

Zizioulas places great significance in his thinking upon an understanding of communion, taking issue with what he sees as a Western "individualizing" approach to the Spirit:

> The Holy Spirit is associated, among other things, with *koinonia* (2 Cor 13:13) and the entrance of the last days into history (Acts 2:17–18), that is *eschatology*. When the Holy Spirit blows, he creates not good individual Christians, individual "saints," but an event of communion, which transforms everything the Spirit touches into a *relational* being. In that case the other becomes an ontological part of one's own identity. The Spirit de-individualises and personalises beings wherever he operates.[52]

Zizioulas points to the particular role of the Holy Spirit in the development of *koinonia* in terms of the way in which *koinonia* involves relationality and the way in which relationality transforms individuals into persons. Individuals are seen as having a focus on human autonomy while persons become persons by being in relation—to God and to one another.[53] It is the Spirit who draws people into this relation. Zizioulas comments, echoing the

---

51. McPartlan, "Who Is the Church?" 280.

52. Zizioulas, *Communion as Otherness*, 5–6.

53. This area of discussion will be taken further in chapter 5, on persons and relationality, as part of the development of the first part of the quadrilateral framework.

Nicene-Constantinopolitan Creed, "the Spirit is 'life-giving' because He is 'communion.'"[54]

Folsom interprets the significance for Zizioulas in this area by commenting that for Zizioulas, "the Spirit creates communion in the church and enables mutual interaction between God and humanity, thus renewing personhood."[55]

Eschatology

The eschatological dimension of Zizioulas's pneumatological approach to ecclesiology opens up ecclesial institutions from having a too concrete and historical sense of the institution. One of the issues with the extensive church in the West, and its strong Christological orientation, he maintains, is that there is too much historicity attached to the ecclesial institutions and there is not enough openness to the Spirit or to the future. On the other hand, he also sees that the Orthodox churches can be insufficiently rooted in history and thus could benefit from ecumenical dialogue with the Western church.[56] Zizioulas outlines the way in which the eschatological dimension of the Spirit affects the understanding of the human person:

> On the other hand, the eschatological dimension of the presence and activity of the Spirit deeply affects the identity of the other: it is on the basis not of someone's past or present that we should identify and accept him or her, but on the basis of their *future*. And since the future lies only in the hands of God, our approach to the other must be free from passing judgement on him or her.[57]

This eschatological reality is not other-worldly but has a present reality in terms of an ethical stance towards the other person. A further significant aspect of the present reality of Zizioulas's eschatological understanding arises out of the relation of the eschaton to the Eucharist:

---

54. Zizioulas, *Being as Communion*, 49.

55. Folsom, "Comparative Assessment," 90.

56. The argument with regard to the differences in pneumatological understanding in relation to Christology in East and West is outlined by Zizioulas in *Being as Communion*, 127–29. He also takes forward the argument with regard to eschatology, in relation to the Eucharist, in *Lectures*, 153–61. The aspect of the argument in relation to the Eucharist will be looked at further in chapter 4 of this book, on worship.

57. Zizioulas, *Communion and Otherness*, 6.

> For the Orthodox, the historical reality of the Church relates to
> the Eucharist and so to that reality which comes to us from the
> eschaton. This eschatological reality reveals itself to us by means
> of sacraments and icons, which must be described in terms of an
> eschatological and iconological ontology. These sacraments and
> images are created as the Holy Spirit draws us and all our history
> into relationship with the end time, the reconciliation of all par-
> tial kingdoms in the true history of the kingdom of God. To ask
> whether the true Church is the historical or the eschatological
> Church is to fail to grasp that the eschaton is the reconciliation
> and integration of all history and therefore the truth of history.[58]

Zizioulas's emphasis on the link between eschatology and history helps to
free the church from an over-dependence on historicity while affirming the
historical presence of the Spirit in the formation of persons and in the worship offered in the Eucharist.

The Eucharist

The Eucharist is the fifth significant area in the writings of Zizioulas on
which I am drawing as indicated by Zizioulas when he writes:

> Ecclesiology in the Orthodox tradition has always been deter-
> mined by the liturgy, the Eucharist; and for this reason it is the
> first two aspects of Pneumatology, namely *eschatology* and *com-
> munion* that have determined Orthodox ecclesiology.[59]

The way in which the theme of the inter-relatedness of the five areas is
opened up is noticeable in Zizioulas referring to these as significant in different parts of his writing. In *Communion and Otherness,* he writes:

> *Eucharist.* This is the heart of the church, where communion
> and otherness are realised par excellence. If the Eucharist is not
> celebrated properly, the Church ceases to be the Church. It is
> not by accident that the Church has given to the Eucharist the
> name of "Communion." For in the Eucharist we can find all the
> dimensions of communion: God communicates himself to us,
> we enter into communion with him, the participants of the sac-
> rament enter into communion with one another, and creation
> as a whole enters through man into communion with God. All

---

58. Zizioulas, *Lectures,* 153.
59. Zizioulas, *Being as Communion,* 131.

this takes place in Christ and the Spirit, who brings the last days into history and offers to the world a foretaste of the kingdom.[60]

He takes the argument further in *Christian Dogmatics*:

> The Eucharist is the inaugural event of freedom and the moment in which eschatological reality becomes the actual presence of this assembly brought together by the Holy Spirit. This is the work of the Holy Spirit, which is why the invocation (*epiclesis*) of the Holy Spirit is fundamental. The gifts that bear the body and blood of Christ bring us into increasing participation in that body. This event of person-to-person relationship takes place in the Spirit, between each of us and Christ. These eschatological events are seen, felt and tasted in the gathering of the Church. This gathering is the event in which the Holy Spirit opens us to life together in freedom.[61]

Papanikolaou draws out the key role that Zizioulas has played in developing the concept of personhood when he looks at communion and the Eucharist:

> For Zizioulas, theology begins with the experience of God in Christ, by the Holy Spirit, in the Eucharist. . . . The Pauline expression "Body of Christ" is not metaphorical for Zizioulas: the Eucharist is quite literally the event of the resurrected Body of Christ. It is such an event because of the presence of the Holy Spirit, who constitutes the faithful as the Body of Christ. The Holy Spirit does not simply inspire or empower individual Christians, but completes the work of Christ by making present the divine-human communion accomplished in the person of the resurrected Christ. The Holy Spirit's role is thus primarily communal and eschatological, in that it constitutes the Eucharist as the eschatological unity of all in Christ.[62]

These introductory references to Zizioulas's understanding of the Holy Spirit and the Eucharist give an indication of the weight that Zizioulas gives to this area and will be developed further when looking in more detail at the Holy Spirit and worship in the next chapter.

---

60. Zizioulas, *Communion and Otherness*, 7.

61. Zizioulas, *Christian Dogmatics*, 161.

62. Papanikolaou, "Personhood and Its Exponents," 238.

CONGRUITIES AND CHALLENGES ARISING OUT OF OWEN'S AND ZIZIOULAS'S THINKING ON THE HOLY SPIRIT

I move to look briefly at some of the similarities and differences of the thinking of Owen and Zizioulas in relation to the Holy Spirit, in order to draw out both congruities and challenges between these two theologians, before moving on to a more specific look at Owen's and Zizioulas's understanding of worship.

Congruities

Owen and Zizioulas share a common characteristic in that they come later in their writings to a full understanding of the nature, work, and significance of the Holy Spirit. They each build on their earlier Christological insights and then take the step of developing these insights to take on board a fuller pneumatological approach. In Owen's earlier writings, pre-dating *Pneumatologia*, he offered a stronger Christological focus, reflecting the more evident trend in the Western church. In *Pneumatologia* and in his writings on the Trinity and on the Holy Spirit, Owen develops a greater emphasis on the Spirit, balancing out the understanding of the work of the Son. Zizioulas argues that the Western Church was overly Christological and needed a certain amount of re-balancing pneumatologically.

This book, by drawing out the thinking of one particular Reformed theologian and contrasting it with this particular Orthodox theologian, seeks to point towards a greater diversity of view in the West with regard to Pneumatology than Zizioulas outlines. In looking at the strong pneumatological approach of John Owen this work seeks to counterbalance the Orthodox view of the Western dominance of Christology, as well as offering a constructive way forward in ecumenical discourse between Orthodox and Reformed churches. However, it is also interesting to note the neglect of Owen's pneumatological thinking, symptomatic of the more general neglect of Pneumatology in the West since Owen's time, outside the charismatic and Pentecostal movements, until the later part of the twentieth century. This volume argues that the re-balancing between Christology and Pneumatology that occurs in the later writings of Owen and of Zizioulas is a helpful contribution to developing a broader ecumenical understanding of the nature and work of the Holy Spirit.

I move to look briefly in more detail at the congruities between Owen and Zizioulas before moving to look at the challenges of the ways in which they differ in their understanding of the nature and work of the Holy Spirit.

Christology and Pneumatology in Balance

Both Owen and Zizioulas draw out in different ways the re-balancing between Christology and Pneumatology, giving greater weight to the life of the Spirit in an understanding of the Trinity and the life of the church. Owen outlines ten theses arising out of his scriptural analysis in order to illustrate his thinking.[63] Zizioulas develops his argument out of a comparison between the Eastern and the Western Churches' treatment of the relation between the Spirit and the Son.

The Personal and Relational Nature of the Holy Spirit

Both Owen and Zizioulas emphasize, out of their consideration of the nature of the Trinity, the personal nature of the Holy Spirit. They see the Holy Spirit as the person of the Trinity who draws human persons into relationship with God.

Worship as the Key Point of Encounter with the Holy Spirit

Both Owen and Zizioulas focus on the encounter that takes place with the Holy Spirit in the setting of worship. However, they have a varied understanding of the nature of worship, as will be referred to under challenges below and looked at in more depth when the nature of worship is more fully considered.

The Church as the Primary Focus For the Activity of the Holy Spirit

Both Owen and Zizioulas give weight to an ecclesial understanding of the Holy Spirit, seeing the Spirit as shaping the church and present to be discovered in the life of the church. However, the nature of their ecclesial understanding differs.

63. As outlined in footnote 88 in this chapter.

Challenges

The balance between the personal encounter with the Holy Spirit and the *koinonia* into which the Holy Spirit draws people is an area in which Owen and Zizioulas offer different perspectives. Owen puts a greater weight on a personal understanding of sanctification as the point of encounter with the Holy Spirit while Zizioulas downplays the individual in terms of the communion into which the Holy Spirit draws persons in relation to God and to one another. It could be argued that there is a dilemma in Owen's thinking in terms of him being too individualizing, and a dilemma on Zizioulas's side in terms of having too strong an emphasis on the community, leaving not enough emphasis on the individual and the indwelling of the Holy Spirit in the individual. This tension between the individual and the church is one that has been held in different ways in the church over the centuries, both within and between churches. I am suggesting that the diversity of views between Owen and Zizioulas, and the need to hold this diversity together as seen in the quadrilateral framework, is a helpful way to hold both views in balance.

The Holy Spirit and the Church

There is a range of differences between Owen and Zizioulas regarding their conceptualization of the church in relation to the presence and activity of the Spirit. Owen places greater emphasis on the local congregation as gathered in the power of the Spirit and embodying Christ in each place, without the need for wider oversight, whether conciliar or personal. For Owen, the Spirit is both local and universal in being the same experience of the Spirit which can be found in a multitude of different places. However, Owen focuses more specifically on the role of the Holy Spirit apart from structures of conciliarity in Episcopal oversight. While Zizioulas sees significance in the idea of local embodiment, he is critical of an understanding of local embodiment in detachment from a connection with conciliar and episcopal oversight. This is seen in his critique of Afanasiev who in *The Church of the Holy Spirit* makes a strong argument for local embodiment in a way which could be seen to be diminishing the oversight role of the bishop.[64] Zizioulas suggests Afanasiev has taken such an idea too far in a Congregationalist

---

64. Afanasiev, *Church of the Holy Spirit*, 1, with reference to Tertullian, followed by extensive analysis throughout the book with regard to the role of bishops in the church and the significance of the Holy Spirit forming and shaping the whole people of God.

direction and diminished a sense of wider connectedness. So also Zizioulas might critique Owen.

The Holy Spirit and the Nature of Worship

Zizioulas's focus on worship is centered on the Eucharist with an emphasis on the Spirit giving life to the Eucharist in each time and place that the Eucharist is celebrated. For Owen, worship has a stronger focus in the preaching of the Word, through which the Holy Spirit is heard to speak.

I move on to look at the context, content, implications, and mutual critique of Owen's and Zizioulas's understanding of worship in order to develop their understanding of the relationship between the Holy Spirit and worship. The language of "quadrilateral" arises from this examination and refers in particular to the four previously identified characteristics of the Holy Spirit. Out of the discussion on the Holy Spirit and worship, ten theses are also drawn out more specifically on the nature of worship and the role of the Holy Spirit in worship. The four characteristics and the ten theses are expanded in the succeeding chapters explicating the different aspects of the quadrilateral argument and drawing attention to the interlinking between each aspect and the quadrilateral as a whole. The final chapter draws out the ecumenical significance of the argument.

4

The Significance of Worship
for Owen and Zizioulas

INTRODUCTION

Considerable attention has been given to the theology of worship in both
the Eastern and Western churches. This theological approach to worship
has traditionally been developed as liturgical theology (as it is referred to
more from a Catholic or Orthodox perspective) or as the theology of worship (as it is referred to more from a Reformed perspective). However, these
approaches have not necessarily been reflected in mainstream theological
writing or taken up widely in the theological aspects of the development
of an understanding about the nature of worship and the way in which in
worship God is encountered and known. The more rationalist approach to
theology in the West since the Enlightenment has seen a separation between
theological reflection and worship. A more contemporary activist approach
to the Christian faith has seen an emphasis on living out the Christian life in
a way which has not always been rooted in worship. The growth of Western
secularizing approaches has led to a theological wrestling with philosophical
issues which also have at times taken theology out of the context of worship.
The Eastern churches, however, have continued with a greater emphasis on
the rooting of theology in worship leading to further debate between East

and West as to the relationship between theology and history. There have been thinkers from a range of Christian traditions who have sought to raise up the connection between theology and worship.

While specific attention to the Holy Spirit and worship has been more predominant in charismatic and Pentecostal traditions of the church, there have been writings on worship which have addressed these issues. Some writers have focused on the opening up of the history and development of worship, pointing to the issues which the church has faced over the centuries.[1] Other writers have dug deeply into the theological aspects of worship in order to integrate a doctrinal understanding of the nature of the Trinity with the awareness of God that is received in the act of worship.[2] Other writers have tackled directly the issues about worship and the changing context and culture in order to look at new ways of approaching worship.[3] There has been an outpouring of writings which seek to respond practically in terms of the development of worship in the congregation or the connection of worship to the engagement of the church in the life of the world.[4] Some writers have sought to draw together spirituality and worship, looking at the different aspects of meaning that each of these words convey.[5] A range of study guides has been written, some of which have had a focus on the

1. Abba, *Principles of Christian Worship*; Davies, *Worship and Theology*; Fenwick and Spinks, *Worship in Transition*; Dix: *Shape of the Liturgy*; Jones et al., *Study of Liturgy*; Old, *Reading and Preaching*; *Worship Reformed*; Rice and Huffstutler, *Reformed Worship*; Thompson, *Liturgies*; Templeton and Riglin, *Reforming Worship*; Vischer, *Christian Worship*; White, *Protestant Worship*.

2. Boulton, *God against Religion*; Caldwell, *Liturgy as Revelation*; Chan, *Liturgical Theology*; Earey, *Liturgical Worship*; Empereur, *Models of Liturgical Theology*; Fagerberg, *Theologia Prima*; Florenksy, *Iconostasis*; Ford and Hardy, *Living in Praise*; Guardini, *Spirit of the Liturgy*; Hughes, *Worship as Meaning*; Kavanagh, *On Liturgical Theology*; Lathrop, *Holy Things*; Lathrop, *Holy People*; Louth, *Introducing Eastern Orthodox Theology*; Otto, *Idea of the Holy*; Philibert, *At the Heart of Christian Worship*; Ratzinger, *Spirit of the Liturgy*; Schmemann, *Introduction to Liturgical Theology*; Schmemann, *Eucharist*; Underhill, *Worship*; Vogel, *Primary Sources*; Allmen, *Worship*; Wainwright, *Doxology*.

3. Benoit, *Liturgical Renewal*; David, *Sacrament and Struggle*; Burns et al., *Edge of God*; Dawn, *Reaching Out*; Forrester and Gay, *Worship and Liturgy*; Guiver, *Vision upon Vision*; Kreider and Kreider, *Worship and Mission*.

4. Baker and Gay, *Alternative Worship*; Bredin, *Praxis and Praise*; Bria, *Liturgy after the Liturgy*; Carson, *Worship, Adoration, and Action*; Cooper, *Glory in the Church*; Craig-Wild, *Tools for Transformation*; Giles, *Creating Uncommon Worship*; *Times and Seasons*; *Re-Pitching the Tent*; Green, *Only Connect*; Holtam, *Art of Worship*; Marvin, *Shaping Up*; Lomax and Moynagh, *Liquid Worship*; Parry, *Worshipping Trinity*.

5. Bernstein, *Liturgy and Spirituality*; George, *Silent Roots*; Guiver, *Pursuing the Mystery*; Nataraja, *Journey to the Heart*; White, *Spirit of Worship*.

theological connection with worship.[6] I have sought to keep the focus on those who have taken theological perspectives on worship from a contemporary context. It would also be possible to look at service and prayer books from the different Christian traditions, as well as biblical interpretations of worship. However, these aspects are beyond the scope of this book.

The development of a liturgical theology or a theology of worship takes a variety of forms. For example, Gordon Lathrop (a Lutheran theologian) develops a perspective on liturgical theology arising from an emphasis on the centrality of the gathering of the worshipping community in his approach to the theology of worship. He argues, "the liturgy itself is primary theology."[7] He refers to building on the work of the Roman Catholic Benedictine monk, Aidan Kavanagh in *On Liturgical Theology*.[8] Kavanagh draws out the varied nature of the discussion about liturgical theology, drawing attention to some of the uncertainties of understanding this area: "Both Liturgy and theology are highly equivocal terms today."[9] However, he also makes clear his own starting point: "[Kavanagh] regards liturgical tradition, in whatever Christian idiom, as the dynamic condition within which theological reflection is done, within which the Word of God is appropriately understood."[10]

Over the centuries liturgical theology has begun with a focus on the gathered worshipping congregation and the practices that have constituted worship for that congregation as the starting point for the development of theology, in contrast to approaches to theology that have as their starting point the encounter with God in reason, experience, tradition, and/or scripture in order to draw out the theology that undergirds worship. Lathrop points to approaches to worship from which theology has emerged out of an understanding of the nature of the practices involved. For example, Lathrop writes that "liturgical theology inquires into the meaning of the liturgy—by asking how the Christian meeting, in all its signs and words, says something authentic and reliable about God, and so says something true about ourselves and about our world as they are understood before God."[11]

Khaled Anatolios (from the Melkite Greek Catholic Church, a church which holds together the practice of the Byzantine rite of the Eastern

6. Burns, *Liturgy*; White, *Introduction to Christian Worship*; *Groundwork of Christian Worship*.

7. Lathrop, *Holy Things*, 5.

8. Kavanagh, *Liturgical Theology*, 74–75, 89.

9. Kavanagh, *Liturgical Theology*, 73.

10. Kavanagh, *Liturgical Theology*, 7, 8.

11. Lathrop, *Holy Things*, 3.

Orthodox Church with membership of the Roman Catholic Church) help-fully points to the multiplicity of ways in which it is possible to know God in worship:

> We have access to divine self-manifestation only through the multiplicity of scriptural language and narrative and the mani-fold variety of creation. Our knowing of God can never compre-hend the divine essence as if it were an inert object; our knowing succeeds in being in touch with the reality of God only when it reacts to the divine self-manifestation in wonder and worship.[12]

This book argues for the significance of holding together both theo-logical exploration and the encounter with God in worship in terms of the ways in which God is known. At this point, Anatolios's reference—arising out of the early Fathers—to multiplicity in knowing God and the way in which this multiplicity is set within wonder and worship is a pointer to the way in which holding together the thinking of Owen and Zizioulas can be fruitful for an enlarged understanding of worship within the diversity of the Christian traditions rather than a point of division between two particular traditions. Flowing out from the Trinity is a great richness of multiplicity in terms of God's self-manifestation amongst people and creation. While Anatolios is referring at this point to the Holy Trinity rather than the Holy Spirit, his reference to multiplicity develops the thinking in this volume about the quadrilateral framework.

THE NATURE AND UNDERSTANDING OF WORSHIP IN OWEN AND ZIZIOULAS AND THE RELATIONSHIP OF WORSHIP TO THE HOLY SPIRIT

Introduction

The approach to worship which is now taken, in terms of the development of a pneumatological understanding, arises out of the contrasting pneuma-tological writings of Owen and Zizioulas who both, from their different his-torical, philosophical and cultural perspectives, emphasize the significance of the relationship between the Holy Spirit and worship. Secondary litera-ture on Owen and Zizioulas reflects their different contexts and perspec-tives, with writers on Owen having a strong historical orientation from the seventeenth century and writers on Zizioulas including a greater reflection

---

12. Anatolios, *Retrieving Nicaea*, 194.

on his philosophical background.[13] Their different understandings are also seen in the way in which Owen's writings are characterized by his many references to scripture, while Zizioulas's writings are characterized by his range of references to the early Fathers. These different approaches make the comparison of Owen and Zizioulas all the more engaging.

This chapter draws out what Owen and Zizioulas have to offer in terms of an understanding of the role of the Holy Spirit in relation to worship. I look at Zizioulas's focus on the Eucharist and Owen's emphasis on the Word, drawing out the role of the Holy Spirit in both the shaping of the Eucharist and the opening up of scripture, as offered in worship.

The argument that is being pursued relates to developing an understanding of the Holy Spirit in worship, arising out of a comparison of Owen and Zizioulas, as being multi-vocal rather than univocal. There is one Holy Spirit but many ways in which the Holy Spirit is manifest, as is made visible in the varied patterns of worship across different traditions of the church. The Holy Spirit is manifest both in the simplicity of the encounter with God that a range of different patterns opens up within each of the differing traditions of the Christian Church, and in the multiplicity and variety of ways of worshipping within each strand of the Christian tradition. An examination of worship as it is offered in two different traditions of the Christian church points both to the reality of the activity of the Holy Spirit within those traditions and the way in which the Holy Spirit can be present in a range of ways. (There is a further piece of research to be undertaken in the comparative examination of the understanding of the activity of the Holy Spirit in the specific acts of worship offered across a wider spectrum of different traditions of the church.)

Within both Owen's and Zizioulas's writing it is clear that there is a range of ways in which it is possible to look at worship. The focus of this book is to take the four convergent themes, outlined in the quadrilateral framework, that emerge from Owen and Zizioulas with reference to the activity of the Holy Spirit in worship. These four themes do not exhaust the ways in which it is possible to look at either worship or the Holy Spirit. These themes are highlighted because they overlap areas of Owen's and Zizioulas's thought with regard to the role of the Holy Spirit in relation to worship, leading to knowledge of God. A shared concern of both Owen and Zizioulas, alongside their emphasis on the link between worship and

---

13. For example, writers on Owen such as Carl R. Trueman, Kelly M. Kapic, Brian Kay, and Sebastian Rehnman; and writers on Zizioulas such as Nicholas Loudovikos, Aristotle Papanikalaou, Eve M. Tibbs, and Thomas Weinandy.

theology, is to see worship as response to God's initiative rather than initiated by human activity.

I have two reasons for exploring such contrasting theologians. The first is that each of these theologians has a strong personal and relational Trinitarian orientation, with a particular emphasis on the Holy Spirit and the role of the Holy Spirit in relation to worship. It is on this basis that the arguments are developed that are core to this research. The second reason is that the similarities in the face of apparently radical difference point in a small way to the multi-vocal character of the Holy Spirit and lead to the hope of a greater ecumenical rapprochement as different traditions of the church can be seen to be drawn to the one Holy Spirit.

This approach complements the extensive contemporary writing on practical approaches to worship in order to draw out again the theological significance of worship. Chapter 1 referred briefly to the diminished connection between doctrine and worship, as seen in the seventeenth century and in the development of modernism and postmodernism. I turn now to focus on the origins and cause of worship in the triune God in order to look at the significance and the centrality of worship for knowing God. The particular focus that is being developed is on the role of the Holy Spirit in drawing people into worship.

Towards the end of this chapter the "embodiment" of the Holy Spirit in worship is considered before moving to ten theses with regard to worship that summarize the approach being taken here. I conclude with a reference to the way in which the quadrilateral framework is being developed.

I turn now to look in particular at the approaches to worship offered by Owen and Zizioulas, firstly introducing their thinking and then continuing the analysis under the following headings: theological, practical, pastoral, and critical. This will be followed by a consideration of their similarities and differences.

OWEN AND WORSHIP

The Influence of Owen's Historical Setting on His Theology of Worship

Horton Davies's two works, *The Worship of the English Puritans* and *Worship and Theology in England From Andrewes to Baxter and Fox, 1603–1690*, helpfully describe the Puritan and Reformed context that gave rise to some of Owen's more polemical writings.[14] It is intriguing to note that in parallel to the rise of later twentieth- and early twenty-first-century writing on Owen, there has been an increasing number of books drawing attention to the demise of Trinitarian thinking in the seventeenth century and the disconnect between the Trinity and worship.[15]

Vickers, in *Invocation and Assent*, refers to the changing focus on the Trinity in the West "as a shift from *invocation*, or prayer, to intellectual *assent*, or from *doxological* to *epistemological* activity."[16] He outlines the debate about the role of Scripture as an epistemological source, arguing that too much weight was given to the epistemic nature of scripture. While not referring to Owen specifically, he summarizes the seventeenth-century position:

> Late seventeenth-century Protestant theologians understood the theological task as having primarily to do with demonstrating the clarity and intelligibility of Christian beliefs. On this understanding, theology was first and foremost a matter of logical consistency or rationality and only secondarily, if at all, a matter of the re-formation of the human soul through the incorporation into the praying and worshipping community of the faithful. To put it another way, second-order theological reflection lost its moorings in the first-order liturgical tasks of baptism, prayer and worship. The aim of theology was not so much to assist humans to come to know and love God as it was to identify and assent to clear and intelligible propositions about God.[17]

Vickers picks up the concern about the disconnection between the Holy Spirit and worship: "Whereas knowing, trusting and loving God had long been regarded as dependent on the presence and work of the Holy Spirit human beings could now obtain saving knowledge simply by doing their epistemic best."[18] His argument continues at a later point:

> Among the many things lost in this shift in the conception of salvation, none was more crucial than the presence and work of the Holy Spirit. The appeal to reason meant that the presence and work of the Holy Spirit was no longer needed in the discernment of divine revelation and in the interpretation of scripture. To the degree that assent to clear and intelligible propositions in

14. Davies, *Worship of the English Puritans*; *Worship and Theology*.

15. Lim, *Mystery Unveiled*; Vickers, *Invocation and Assen*; Dixon, *Nice and Hot Disputes*.

16. Vickers, *Invocation and Assent*, 1.

17. Vickers, *Invocation and Assent*, xviii.

18. Vickers, *Invocation and Assent*, xv.

scripture was all that was needed for salvation, even the work of
the Holy Spirit in ecclesial practices such as baptism, worship
and the Eucharist was not sufficiently emphasized.[19]

Owen's drawing attention to the connection between the Holy Spirit and
worship was a strong counter to some of the prevailing trends of his day.
Interestingly enough, despite Owen's criticism of those who were overly "enthusiastical," he himself was criticized by Sherlock and Clagett for being too
enthusiastical himself, as Lim points out in *Mystery Unveiled*. "The mystical,
Trinitarian and Calvinistic spirituality of Owen, for instance, was excori-
ated for verging on Enthusiasm by William Sherlock and William Clagett
during the Restoration period."[20] Lim goes on to detail the arguments between Owen and Sherlock and Clagett. Both Vickers and Lim point to the
seventeenth-century rise of rationalism as part of their argument about the
demise of the doctrine of the Trinity during that century and the loss of the
connection between Trinitarian understanding and worship. While Vickers
addresses issues to do with rationality and scripture, Lim examines the demise of mystery, pointing to Owen's emphasis on a more mystical, apophatic
approach to theological understanding arising out of his particular views
about the Holy Spirit and worship.

Owen's Approach to Worship

Owen wrote against the backdrop of considerable controversy with regard
to worship in the church in England. This controversy was reflected in the
1662 Act of Uniformity, with its wider reference to authority and the need
for bishops in an established church, seeking to bring stability after a period
of political and religious turmoil in England.[21] His writings about worship

19. Vickers, *Invocation and Assent*, 57.

20. Lim, *Mystery Unveiled*, 14. "Enthusiasts" is a term used in a variety of ways, of a
range of groups. In the journal *Religion* Michael Heyd outlined some of the diversity of
views that the term "enthusiasts" covered: "My own research, however, led me to the conclusion that 'enthusiasm' was primarily a derogatory label, not a neutral designation of
any homogeneous group in the sixteenth, seventeenth, and eighteenth centuries. It was
applied to a broad and diversified spectrum of movements and individuals: to radical
sects such as the German Anabaptists, the English Quakers or the Dutch Collegiants, to
Millenarian movements like the Fifth Monarchy Men in England or the French Hugue-
not Prophets who spread in Europe from Southern France after 1700, but also to more
loosely defined movements like the Puritans in England or the Pietists in Germany.
Moreover, in Restoration England, Catholics themselves were accused of 'enthusiasm'"
(Heyd, "Reaction to Enthusiasm").

21. Amongst the various stipulations of the 1662 Act of Uniformity, with regard to

reflect both his pneumatological understanding and his non-conformist position. Owen argues that Jesus came to set people free, and that, for example, having liturgies imposed on the regular Sunday worship cuts against freedom. Arising out of the debate on the use of set liturgies, he makes the argument for the shape of worship being determined only by Christ from within a scriptural setting. This becomes clear in his "Brief instruction in worship of God" in Question 12 and his answer:

> *Question 12:* What is principally to be attended unto by us in the manner of the celebration of the worship of God and observation of the institutions and ordinances of the Gospel?
> *Answer:* that we observe and do all whatever the Lord Christ hath commanded us to observe, in the way that he hath prescribed, and that we add nothing unto or in the observation of them that is of man's invention or appointment. (Deut 4:2; 12:32; Jer 7:27; Matt 15:9, 13; 17:5; 28:20; Col 2:3; Heb 3:3–6)[22]

For Owen, worship plays an integral role in his understanding of God and of the Christian life, as indicated in his "Five Principles," moving from worship to the Trinity. McGraw, in his book on Owen, *A Heavenly Directory: Trinitarian Piety, Public Worship and a Reassessment of John Owen's Theology,* draws attention to the way in which the theme of worship, and in particular, public worship, runs through Owen's writings. "Owen tended to include treatments of public worship wherever they fit logically into his writings. This highlights his continued preoccupation with this subject along with his stress on communion with God as triune."[23] The concern with public worship reflected a range of areas of interest, from the theological to the pastoral and from the practical to the critical, as is seen in the titles of some of the most central of Owen's work in regard to theology and worship outlined below in these four different categories.

------

authority in the church, this Act laid down the use of the *Book of Common Prayer* in Sunday services, and required the assent of the priest to this use. Those who refused to assent to the range of requirements laid down were ejected from the Church of England. See full text in "Charles II."

22. Owen, *Works*, 15:462. From "A Brief Instruction in the Worship of God and Discipline of the Churches of the NT by Way of Question and Answer" (446–530).

23. McGraw, *Heavenly Directory*, 118. One note of caution with regard to McGraw's book is the weight he gives throughout his book to a particular sermon of Owen's, published sixty years after his death, based on the notes taken at the time of preaching.

Owen's Theological Approach to Worship

Owen's theological concern with regard to worship focuses on the Trinity, with particular attention to the work of the Holy Spirit. As referred to previously, his approach to the Trinity is seen in *Of Communion with God the Father, Son, and Holy Ghost* and his understanding of the Holy Spirit is developed in *Pneumatologia or, a Discourse Concerning the Holy Spirit*.[24] Owen writes on the particular key role of the Holy Spirit in worship:

> Hereby, then, the apostle informs them wherein the foundation of all church relation, order, and worship, did consist: for whereas they had all respect unto the Lordship of Christ and their acknowledgment thereof, this was not from themselves, but was a pure effect of the operation of the Holy Ghost in them and towards them. And any thing of the like kind which doth not proceed from the same cause and fountain is of no use to the glory of God, nor of any advantage unto the souls of men.[25]

Owen gives weight to the significance of the Holy Spirit at the heart of worship, seeing the Holy Spirit as the person of the Trinity who draws worship out from the human heart. He is continually at pains to insist that worship is not only a matter of human devising but is in response to the three-fold nature of the Trinity. Owen's thinking on the theme of public worship which is touched on in these two works is further drawn out in many of his sermons, and in particular in *Sermons: III and IV: The Nature and Beauty of Gospel Worship*.[26]

Owen's Pastoral Approach to Worship

Owen saw worship as at the heart of receiving the Holy Spirit. In the gathered community of believers attentive to the Word of God, the Holy Spirit would be present and the work of regeneration, followed by sanctification, would happen. For Owen, worship both prepares people for the work of the Holy Spirit and is the place of encounter with the Holy Spirit.[27]

24. Owen, *Works*, vols. 2–3.

25. Owen, *Works*, 3:19.

26. See Owen, *Works*, vol. 9. Many were published posthumously and based on notes taken by some of his hearers.

27. His references to worship are found in various parts of *Pneumatologia* (including book 7, "A Discourse of the Work of the Holy Spirit in Prayer" [Owen, *Works*, 4:236–352]). He also wrote on worship in "A Brief Instruction in the Worship of God and Discipline of the Church of the New Testament," and "A Discourse Concerning

The pastoral aspects of Owen's theological thinking about public worship come out in his further writing on the Holy Spirit: *A discourse of the work of Holy Spirit in prayer, A discourse on the Holy Spirit as a Comforter, A discourse of spiritual gifts,* and in his sermons in *Works,* Volume 9, "Sermons."[28] Owen had a strong concern to support the lives of individual Christians in their growth in the faith. His writings describe the connection he makes between the Holy Spirit and the Christian's life. They are not a series of spiritual "self-help" exercises but point to the priority of the Holy Spirit in the person's life and the possibility of growing in trust and dependence on the Triune God through the sanctifying work of the Spirit. Chapter 8 on transformation looks in more detail at the nature of this sanctification.

Owen's Practical Approach to Worship

While the primary purpose of this book is neither historical nor a focus on the practical aspects of worship, it is worth noting the practical principles of Owen's work as well as his historical setting. This gives a further indication of Owen's desire to hold together theology and the practice of worship as seen in particular in the regular offering of Sunday services. *A brief instruction in the worship of God and discipline of the church of the New Testament* illustrates the way in which Owen translated his theological thinking into practical principles for the conduct of worship based on his understanding of the scriptural priority of Jesus's teaching about worship.[29] The question arises as to what exactly it is that the *"Lord Christ hath commanded us to observe."* Jesus came out of the Jewish synagogue and Temple traditions and added to this in his gift to his followers of Baptism and the Lord's Supper. His own practice of prayer gives a model for praying, as does his teaching on prayer in the Lord's Prayer. Owen's further formal references to worship and what constitutes worship are found more in the Epistles than the Gospels. Owen himself makes this clear in the biblical references he quotes in response to Question 17, "Which are the principal institutions of the Gospel to be observed in the worship of God?" when he outlines the answer to his question:

Liturgies and Their Imposition" (see Owen, *Works,* vol. 15); "Twelve Arguments against Conformity to Worship Not of Divine Institution" (*Works,* 16:240); "Three Discourses Suitable to the Lord's Supper" (*Works,* 17:595–99); "Two Short Catechisms" (*Works,* 1:418–64); "Of the Sacraments of the New Covenant," and "Of the Lord's Supper"; and in various sermons on the sacraments (see *Works,* vol. 9).

28. Owen, *Works,* vols. 3–4 (many sermons published posthumously). For a comprehensive Owen bibliography, see Burden, "John Owen." This is the first bibliography to list Owen's manuscript writings as well as his printed works.

29. Owen, *Works,* 15:446–530.

> Answer: the calling, gathering and settling of churches with
> their officers as the seat and subject of all other solemn institut-
> ed worship; . . . prayer with thanksgiving; . . . singing of Psalms;
> . . . preaching the Word; . . . Administration of the sacraments
> of Baptism and the Supper of the Lord . . . Discipline and rule of
> the church collected and settled; most of which have also Sun-
> day particular duties relating unto them and subservient unto
> their due observation.[30]

This brief outline of Owen's practical principles with regard to the nature
of worship reflects the simplicity of his approach to the content of services.
This serves as an illustration of his seventeenth-century concerns about the
imposition of formal liturgies and leads us into an examination of his critical approach to the nature of the offering of worship.

Owen's Critical Approach to Worship

Owen's critical approach to worship arises out of his historical context.
His critique focuses on his seventeenth-century Reformed concerns with
what were seen as "Romish" practices, against which he writes strongly. Not
surprisingly in terms of the controversies of the later seventeenth century
over worship, reflected in part in the references to worship in the Act of
Uniformity in 1662, Owen also wrote in no uncertain terms about any worship which he perceived to be imposed by human authorities rather than
coming from the Holy Spirit, as in *A Discourse concerning Liturgies and
Their Imposition* (London, 1662) and *An Answer unto Two Questions: With
Twelve Arguments against Any Conformity to Worship Not of Divine Institution* and *Three Discourses Suitable to the Lord's Supper*.[31] While Owen was
sympathetic to the use of the Prayer Book, he rebelled against the idea that
it should of necessity be used each Sunday. In this debate we also see his
thinking about the separation of Church and State, with the Church having
the freedom and responsibility for the conduct of worship under the guidance of the Holy Spirit.[32]

30. Owen, *Works*, 15:478. Owen offers extensive biblical references for each point
raised in his Answer.

31. See Owen, *Works*, vol. 15; "An Answer to Two Questions: With Twelve Arguments against Any Conformity to Worship Not of Divine Institution" (Owen, *Works*,
21:595–99).

32. Horton Davies indicates the strength and polemical nature of some of Owen's
writings in this area when he refers to the representative nature of Owen's thinking
and the strength of Owen's views: "Owen spoke for all the ejected Nonconformists
ministers of 1662 when he accused the imposers of liturgies of bringing 'fire and faggot

Contribution and Critique

Contribution

Owen's focus on the Holy Spirit has three consequences. The first of these is to re-focus worship away from the detailed wording of set prayers and orders of service to the wider presence of God in worship. Keeping this focus on the Spirit (for which, as we have seen, Owen has been criticized as being both too enthusiastical and too mystical) is drawing attention to the way in which worship has its origins in the divine rather than the human. The second consequence is the drawing together of worship and theology. Owen's pointing to the nature and activity of the Holy Spirit, within the setting of the Trinity, draws together the trinitarian nature of worship with the theological understanding of the Trinity. The third consequence is the holding together of the activity of the Holy Spirit within human experience thus keeping the doctrinal understanding of God closely linked to the human experience of God in body, mind, and spirit.

Critique

As well as the advantages of looking at the seventeenth-century context of Owen's thought, there are limitations in transferring Owen's arguments directly to the twenty-first century. His strong anti-Roman Catholic views are colored by the relatively recent period (in his day) of the Reformation. The twentieth century has seen a greater ecumenical development and understanding between Reformed and Catholic traditions.[33] The lack of specificity in outlining the nature and content of services can lead to a weakness in the content and framework of worship. The argument against the regularity of a set liturgy can take away from the value of a regularly repeated framework in deepening the faith. Owen's critique of "man-made" liturgies, while serving to point to human dependence on God, can neglect the role of human activity in shaping spoken or written words. The final critique at this point refers to Owen holding together, in an apparently contradictory way, the view that that some aspects of the work of the Holy Spirit ceased after the period of the Old and New Testaments while other areas of the Holy Spirit's work continue. The third quadrilateral point, on truth, will look at the idea of origins and originality in order to respond to this particular view.

---

into the Christian religion'" (*Worship and Theology*, 193).

33. This will be looked at further in the final chapter.

ZIZIOULAS'S CONTEXT AND APPROACH TO WORSHIP

The strength of the Orthodox position with regard to the role of worship is clearly outlined in Schmemann's *Introduction to Liturgical Theology*.[34] He begins with a critique of what he argues is the Western separation of worship from doctrine. "At this point it is only necessary to emphasize that in appropriating the structure and method of the West our theology has for a long time been cut off from one of its most vital, most natural roots—from the liturgical tradition."[35] He continues with a reference to the rise of the liturgical movement (in both East and West) following the First World War:

> What is important for us here is its substance. And its substance lies in the genuine discovery of worship as the life of the Church, the public act which eternally actualizes the nature of the Church as the Body of Christ. . . . It is a return from the pietistic and individualistic understanding of worship to worship once more conceived as the eternal self-revelation of the Church. Once more the catholic view of worship was discovered as the public service of the spirit-filled people of God.[36]

Jillions points to the wider Orthodox understanding of how theology, spirituality, and liturgy are to be held together and refers to Zizioulas's contribution to this understanding:

> The worship experience of generations has shaped liturgy as the theological source par excellence, *theologia prima*. Ancient scripture and patristic writings are filtered through and stamped with the corporate life of prayer which remains in every age "ever full of sap and green" [Psalm 91(92):14]. This accounts for the universal orthodox experience of the liturgy as "today" in spite of its ancient form. John Zizioulas has called this "liturgical dogmatics" Orthodoxy's particular gift to the twenty-first century. This point is an important counterbalance to the emphasis on theology as an intellectual discipline somewhat divorced from prayer and worship.[37]

The bringing together of theology and worship—so that both the understanding of God is shaped in the encounter through the Holy Spirit in

---

34. Schmemann, *Introduction to Liturgical Theology*.

35. Schmemann, *Introduction to Liturgical Theology*, 10.

36. Schmemann, *Introduction to Liturgical Theology*, 14.

37. Jillions, "Orthodox Christianity in the West," 279.

worship and also that worship informs the intellectual discipline of theology—is a key argument of this book.

An understanding of the priority of worship undergirds Zizioulas's
writing, beginning with the book of his doctoral thesis, *Eucharist, Bishop,
Church,* followed by *Being as Communion* and continued in the series of
books next published, mostly over twenty years after *Being as Communion.*[38]
In the Preface to *Eucharist, Bishop, Church,* Zizioulas outlines the setting
for his early thinking with regard to worship at the same time addressing a
critique that has been levelled at the Orthodox Church:

> The reproach levelled at our Church that she has remained
> through the centuries a "community of worship" today, proves
> to be the best guarantee of a sure route back to the conscious-
> ness of the ancient undivided church. For the liturgical life of
> our Church which is characterised by its conservatism and
> traditional character has not succumbed to overloading with
> non-essential later elements, but continues to reflect in a chang-
> ing contemporary world the one, holy, catholic and apostolic
> Church of every age, worshipping in one body.[39]

While this slightly defensive approach could be seen as pointing to difficult
issues in relation to an understanding of change, it clearly focuses on the
value that Zizioulas gives to the sustaining and continuing role of worship
in the life of the church. When I turn to look at the nature of truth and the
role of the Spirit in "leading into truth" I will examine Zizioulas's later writings in order to highlight the possibility of a more developmental role of the
Spirit than is outlined at this point.

In developing his understanding of worship, Zizioulas highlights
the relationship between the communion within the Trinity and the significance of that communion being embodied in the Eucharist through the
constitutive work of the Holy Spirit. Zizioulas maintains that Pneumatology
has saved the life of the Orthodox churches and asks the question whether
it is liturgy that still saves Orthodoxy?[40] In liturgy, he maintains that the
church is held together by the coming together of the "one" and the "many."
The church is fully present in each place as the Spirit constitutes the Body of
Christ in each place. The Eucharist holds together the local and the universal
in terms of the same Eucharist being celebrated in each different and particular place. The Eucharist also holds the bishop and the people together in a

---

38. Zizioulas, *Eucharist, Bishop, Church*; *Being as Communion*; *Communion and
Otherness*; *Lectures*; *One and the Many.*

39. Zizioulas, *Eucharist, Bishop, Church,* 1.

40. Zizioulas, *Being as Communion,* 141.

mutuality of community and ministry, with "no ministry that does not need the other ministries."[41] The Eucharist holds the church together. However, before he could be accused of just developing a kind of "congregationalism," Zizioulas goes on to maintain that there is a simultaneity between the local and the universal. There is both the local and the universal, but one is not prior to the other. He develops this further in terms of conciliarity and the role of the bishop.

While Zizioulas develops his thinking in response to twentieth-century philosophers such as Heidegger and relatively recent Orthodox theologians such as Lossky, Florovsky, and Afanasiev, his thinking is primarily rooted in the Early Fathers, and particularly in the Cappadocian Fathers, pointing to their understanding of the close relationship between theology and liturgy.[42] The particular arguments made will be examined further in terms both of the Trinity and personhood, and of the varying epistemological considerations between Zizioulas and these writers. Zizioulas's concern for the unity of the church leads him to look back to the days of the undivided church in the early centuries of Christianity in order to recover the fruits of a shared understanding of the faith before the gradual separation of the churches of East and West culminating in the events of 1054. He argues for the value of the unbroken yet diverse tradition of Orthodoxy with its constant Trinitarian focus and the embodiment of this focus in the worship offered by the church. While there is a diverse range of appreciation of Zizioulas from within the Orthodox community, the issues raised focus more on his particular interpretation of personhood and ontology as they arise out of the Cappadocian Fathers than on his understanding of worship and the role of the Eucharist.[43] There has been some discussion as to whether the disagreements with Zizioulas come more from Anglophone Orthodox writers.[44]

---

41. Zizioulas, *Being as Communion*, 139.

42. This latter influence, particularly that of Basil, has been referred to in chapter 2. It is developed in chapter 5 of Zizioulas, *Communion and Otherness* ("Pneumatology and the Importance of the Person: A Commentary on the Second Ecumenical Council"). Here Zizioulas highlights the significance of Basil's interpretation of the Holy Spirit, arising out of his doxology "Glory be to the Father with (*meta*) the Son, with (*syn*) the Holy Spirit."

43. Knight, *Theology of John Zizioulas*. In chapter 2, "On the Criticism of Being as Communion in Anglophone Orthodox Theology," Alan Brown does an interesting piece of research on these arguments, looking in particular at the critiques offered by Louth, Turcescu, and Behr and—in response—positively analysing Zizioulas's writings, based on the writings of the early Fathers.

44. These arguments will be looked at further in chapter 5.

I move to provide an overview of Zizioulas's thinking about worship by referring to the theological, pastoral, practical, and critical categories in order to lay the foundations for the argument with regard to the quadrilateral framework.

Zizioulas's Theological Approach to Worship

In Zizioulas's *Lectures in Christian Dogmatics*, he began by writing that "theology starts in the worship of God and in the Church's experience of communion with God."[45] This understanding of the interplay between theology and worship runs through and undergirds his writing. His thinking focuses directly on the Trinity, in terms of personhood and relationality, and the way in which these characteristics are embodied in the Eucharist. He wrote in terms of the particular relationship between humanity and God that is made possible in the Trinity: "God is 'the one who is' and he is that 'being' whom we can address in worship and the Eucharist."[46] The significance of worship as offered within the community of the church, not only by individuals on their own, is stressed. "The community of the Church and its worship is the context that gives doctrine its authority."[47]

Worship is further expanded in terms of the sacraments: "We have said that theology is first worship of God and that the fundamental logic of theology is given in the event of baptism and Eucharistic worship."[48] As referred to in chapter 3, Zizioulas emphasizes the particular role of the Eucharist in relation to the church and to the relationship of the church to God: "The Eucharist . . . is the heart of the church, where communion and otherness are realised par excellence. If the Eucharist is not celebrated properly, the Church ceases to be the Church."[49]

In his early writing, Zizioulas inextricably links the Eucharist with the Bishop and the Church, thus preserving the unity of the church. He argues against the greater priority given by Afanasiev to the local congregation as reflecting the fullness of the church, with a differently nuanced understanding of the role of the bishop in relation to the congregation.[50] However, an examination of the more structural elements of Zizioulas's thinking with

---

45. Zizioulas, *Lectures*, 1.

46. Zizioulas, *Lectures*, 55.

47. Zizioulas, *Lectures*, 6.

48. Zizioulas, *Lectures*, 6.

49. Zizioulas, *Communion and Otherness*, 7.

50. Afanasiev, *Church of the Holy Spirit*.

regard to the church are outside the purview of this book, which is focused on the Holy Spirit and worship. At this point what is being noted is the orientation of worship to theology which runs through Zizioulas's writing. Chapter 7 focuses on the epistemological factors undergirding an approach to understanding God that is rooted in the divine presence in the relationship and activity of worship.

Zizioulas's Pastoral Approach to Worship

Zizioulas's writings on worship are primarily theological. However, his pastoral approach grows out of his emphasis on the importance of the activity of God in the Eucharist for constituting the church in each place. In this act of worship, which is also the central point for the work of the Holy Spirit, the people approach God and encounter God. Zizioulas argues for an encounter with God which engages the whole of the person:

> Christians have a relationship of direct and personal familiarity with the Church and the saints. The relationship is personal and involves our entire being, not merely our minds or feelings. . . . The liturgy is simply the realisation of our relationship to God, the whole communion of his saints and the entire world.[51]

I move in the next chapter to look at the way in which in this encounter with the personal and relational God, human persons rise to their full humanity.

Zizioulas's Practical Approach to Worship

Zizioulas also considers practical aspects of the offering of worship, ranging from the words said in the Eucharistic prayer to a consideration of practices such as the lighting of candles and people signing themselves with the cross.[52] Zizioulas recently has added a new dimension to his thinking in his writing about the created world and its link with his theological understanding.[53] In an article originally published online in 2015 Zizioulas writes: "This Eucharistic ethos is the first thing that we need today at a time of severe ecological crisis. This is a spirituality that flourished in the desert Fathers but has been forgotten in the meantime. It has to be recovered

51. Zizioulas, *Lectures*, 125.

52. Zizioulas, *Lectures*, 150–51. Here, Zizioulas looks at phrases from the Eucharistic prayers of Basil and St John Chrysostom, and links these to the holiness of the church, as in the phrase in the Liturgy beginning "the holy things unto the holy . . . "

53. See Zizioulas, "Humanity and Nature."

urgently, now that we need to be redeemed from humanistic and human-centered attitudes to existence."[54] Drawing together the Eucharist and a practical concern for creation is an example of the way in which Zizioulas's thinking connects between his understanding of worship and its practical application, particularly in response to the contemporary setting in which he is writing.

Zizioulas's Critical Approach to Worship

Zizioulas argues that the churches of the West have become overly institutional because of what he sees as a more Christo-monist approach, unlike the churches of the East, with what Zizioulas sees as their more Pneumatological approach. This critical approach is taken forward in Zizioulas's focus on the nature of the Eucharist as the place of constitution of the church through the power of the Holy Spirit, and thus the centrality of worship in the life of the church. The nature of this focus on Pneumatology provides part of the argument of this book regarding the Holy Spirit and worship.

Contribution and Critique

Contribution

Zizioulas makes a major contribution to a deeper understanding of worship. At the heart of what he offers is the centrality of worship for the life of the church and the way in which worship is connected with both doctrine and the world. He argues that worship is the primary category in which God is both known and encountered. Zizioulas's particular focus on worship is on the Eucharist, which forms part of the argument in this book for the embodiment of the Holy Spirit. Zizioulas argues that worship is the place in which each person finds himself or herself as person, rather than individual, drawn into relational identity in response to the triune God who is three persons in one. Zizioulas holds together the church and the kingdom of God, with the church as the embodiment of Christ, realizing the kingdom in the world.[55]

54. Zizioulas, "Come, Holy Spirit."
55. This argument is taken further in chapter 8 on transformation.

Critique

Zizioulas has been critiqued from several angles, from both within and out-side the Orthodox world. His particular approach in seeing the centrality of the church to the kingdom could be argued to place too much emphasis on the church and not enough on the world. This aspect, which will be looked at further, could imply a neglect of other areas of worship such as preaching and to fall into the trap of becoming overly liturgically dependent rather than dependent on the Holy Spirit. His linking worship with the key Eucha-ristic presidential role of the bishop could be seen as limiting a wider role for ordained and lay people in the leading of worship, and giving a specific structure to the church that is unwarranted in either the tradition of the church or the contemporary ecumenical movement.

SIMILARITIES AND DIFFERENCES BETWEEN OWEN AND ZIZIOULAS

In terms of context, culture, and confessional identity, Owen and Ziziou-las inhabit two different worlds. In terms of the centrality of the Trinity to the Christian faith, the role of the Holy Spirit within the Trinity and the church, and the significance of worship as the point of encounter with the triune God, these worlds overlap. I argue in this book that what can be seen as the multi-vocal nature of their different writings is not a statement of fundamental and irreconcilable difference but a reflection of the nature of the diversity that is the gift of the Holy Spirit, which Spirit is a unifying factor between these two theologians. Their significance and orientation are shown in the resurgence of writing on Owen and the range of contemporary engagement with Zizioulas, indicating the wider interest that each one is currently undergoing.

Sources and Settings

Zizioulas's deep rootedness in the early Fathers, particularly the Cappado-cians, and his engagement with the twentieth-century philosophical and theological context in his desire for an undivided church stands in contrast to Owen's writing in a time of political and religious change, turmoil, and ecclesial separation that was in part the result of the European Reformation. However, there is a similarity in terms of the desire to go back to origins. For Owen, the scriptural basis of his thinking is critical, along with his ap-proach to the centrality of worship. It is significant to note, as referred to previously, the way that Owen balances tradition and scripture. As already noted, in *Pneumatologia* Owen refers widely to the writings of the early Fathers, however with a less specific focus on the Cappadocians than Zizioulas. While the consequences of the Reformation could be seen as a further dividing of the church after the long slow upheaval that led to the separation of the churches of the East from the churches of the West culminating in the events of 1054, Owen's concern for faithfulness to the origins of the faith, in the Trinity, in scripture, and in the early church, offers a parallel for Zizioulas's concern for a church rooted in tradition. While Zizioulas's approach to scripture is balanced by his rootedness in tradition and his engagement with contemporary philosophical approaches, he nonetheless offers distinctive references to scripture as a key part of his argument and discussion.

I move to look further at the range of their similarities, after which I will identify some of their differences.

Similarities

The Centrality of Worship

The weight given to worship, particularly the connection between worship and doctrine with specific reference to the Trinity, is a uniting theme in Owen and Zizioulas, as is the key role of the Holy Spirit in constituting the church through worship. Both Owen and Zizioulas see the importance of worship as being the locus for the knowledge of God and the point at which people are drawn into the communion of the Trinity. In so doing, they share a theological understanding of the significance of worship and worship offered in the setting of the church. Despite their confessional differences, there are unexpected congruities between the two theologians where the interplay of theology and worship and the role in this of the Holy Spirit is concerned.

Re-casting Epistemology

It can be argued that Owen and Zizioulas each seek, in their focus on the significance of worship in encountering and understanding the Trinity, to re-shape a more rationalist epistemological focus. This rationalist focus takes reason as the sole epistemological criterion in contrast to a more holistic understanding of human experience involving body, mind, and spirit. Owen and Zizioulas both, from different perspectives, argue that the Holy

Spirit in worship brings people to an encounter with the triune God that leads to knowledge of God by being brought into a full-bodied relationship with God.[56]

The "Embodiment" of the Holy Spirit in Worship

Owen and Zizioulas both hold that the inspiration of the Spirit is central to the worship offered by the gathered community. I am suggesting that this leads to an understanding of a Spirit that is embodied, both in the personal life of the individual and the community life of the church. This is not to say that the Spirit is bound by the worshipping community, or not active more widely than the worshipping community, but to argue that there is a dimension of the Spirit's nature and activity which can be described as embodied *in* worship.

The Effectual Impact of the Holy Spirit in Worship

Both Owen, in his emphasis on the Spirit leading people into sanctification, and Zizioulas, in his understanding of the Eucharist pointing to God's purpose for the whole created earth, offer diverse understandings of the Holy Spirit's role in transformation, which can be seen to complement each other, as will be seen in chapter 8. Owen and Zizioulas keep the focus on the overarching priorities with regard to worship, and the rootedness of worship in the divine life, rather than looking in detail at the structure and content of worship.

Simplicity

This book argues that there is a similarity between Owen and Zizioulas in their attitudes to essentials and non-essentials in the worshipping life of the church. Owen, by casting aside what he saw as some of the unhelpful accretions of the Roman Catholic Church, and Zizioulas, by seeking to return to what he sees as the essentials of the early church, have the effect of arguing for a greater simplicity in the nature and content of worship and in the life of the church. The issue of essential and non-essential items of worship is one that is raised by Owen and Zizioulas.

---

56. This argument will be explored further in chapter 7 on epistemology and truth.

Suspicion of the "Structural Institution"

Following on from this point about simplicity, there is a further similarity in Owen's and Zizioulas's ideas about the church as an institution. While Owen has a strong emphasis on the need for discipline within the local church, and Zizioulas has a strong emphasis on the role of the bishop as the focal point for the church and worship, the centrality they both give to the living encounter with God in the worship of the church puts into a different perspective a more institutional focus on the church with an emphasis on structure as the starting point. The encounter with the triune God becomes the first order issue, and the structure becomes a second order issue.

Subjectivity and Objectivity

Both Zizioulas and Owen, in their balancing the subjectivity of human experience in worship with what might be argued is the objectivity of the encounter with God through the power of the Holy Spirit, support a pneumatological theology of worship which holds together human experience and divine encounter.

Differences

Scripture and Tradition

While both Owen and Zizioulas base their theological interpretations in scripture, Owen takes a closer approach to scripture, using Biblical quotations to support each part of his argument, while Zizioulas has less frequent quotations from scripture. Owen lived in a pre-critical era in terms of scriptural interpretation. However, it is interesting to note his criticism of the Socinians as overly biblically literalist and giving insufficient weight to tradition. Owen sought to reclaim the role of tradition, as evidenced in his use of the early Fathers, while holding on to the priority of a scriptural justification for his arguments. For Zizioulas, tradition plays a larger role in terms of his particular focus on the Cappadocian Fathers on whom he reflects in considerable depth. Owen's use of tradition includes a less in-depth approach to particular theologians from the early church, with a broader range of theologians quoted, balanced by his references to those in the Reformed tradition.

The Nature and Content of Worship

While both Owen and Zizioulas are clear about the Trinitarian nature of worship and the way in which a development of a theological understanding in the church arises out of worship, their particular interpretations of worship vary widely. Zizioulas focuses on the Eucharist and Owen on a more informal pattern of worship where the general aspects of worship are outlined, with an emphasis on opening the Word of God but without a specific order of service.[57] While they share a similar theological orientation, their outworking of this orientation differs. For Owen, worship arises out of the Word, preached and discerned by the community of believers, as inspired by the Holy Spirit. For Zizioulas, worship is centered on the Eucharist in which the triune God is encountered through the power of the Holy Spirit. While Owen's practical concerns are focused in the particular practices of worship, Zizioulas adds an understanding of the created world.[58]

The Particular Significance Given to the Role of the Holy Spirit in Worship

The similarities and differences of Owen's and Zizioulas's approaches will be looked at in the details of the quadrilateral framework for which I am arguing, looking at personal relationality, immediacy, truth, and transformation. Their diversity of views in each of these areas will be examined, with the concluding chapter returning to the ecumenical implications of such a multi-vocal approach to the Spirit.

The Holy Spirit in their Understanding of the Church

The two different confessional backgrounds of Owen and Zizioulas mean that it is unsurprising to discover that they offer two different interpretations of the Holy Spirit in the life of the church. Owen places weight on the Spirit giving life to the congregation in each place. While Zizioulas sees the Spirit in the life of each act of worship, he has an additional emphasis on the bishop as the person who offers a focus of unity, yet within the sharing of ministry among the worshipping people of God.

---

57. It would be possible in another book to enter into a detailed comparison between the two, but that is not the aim here.

58. Zizioulas, "Humanity and Nature."

Different Contexts: Insider/Outsider Approaches

Zizioulas's context is very different to that of Owen, whose critical analysis was directed towards his seventeenth-century situation when there was turmoil in the country and in the church. Zizioulas's critical analysis is not directed in the same way to the situation of the Orthodox churches in their context but focuses rather on matters of contention between Eastern and Western churches. Owen began as an "insider" with the ascendancy of Cromwell, but then, after the 1662 Act of Uniformity, became an "outsider" to the church and mainstream theological discussion. Zizioulas's critical analysis is concerned with what he sees as the orientation and influence of Western churches as well as with what he sees as some of the theological areas needing development from within the Orthodox tradition.

The Difference in Philosophical and Theological Frameworks

I have already pointed out the difference in Owen's and Zizioulas's theological and philosophical outlooks and frameworks, as well as in their sociological and historical settings, a theme which continues to run throughout this book, with the aim of seeing where such diversity reflects the multi-vocal understanding of the nature of the Holy Spirit.

TAKING THE ARGUMENT FORWARD

I proceed now to the way in which the Holy Spirit can be seen as "embodied" in the church through worship before moving on to look at a series of theses which describe worship in response to the Holy Spirit.

The "Embodiment" of the Holy Spirit—Embodied in the Church Through Worship

The manifestation of the Holy Spirit in both the relationships and the activity of worship points to the embodiment of the Holy Spirit, an embodiment particularly manifest in the constitution of the church by the Spirit's presence. Eugene Rogers, in *After the Spirit*, has pointed to the immanence and embodiment of the Holy Spirit, going so far as to say, in introducing his book, "that the Spirit had grown dull because unembodied, and bodily experience unpersuasive because un-Spirited, was one of the initial insights for this book."[59] This volume touches on one particular aspect of embodiment, which is the way in which the Holy Spirit is embodied in the worship offered by the church. This is not to say that the Spirit becomes the church or the church becomes the Spirit. It is to argue rather for synchronicity—that the Spirit is present in the Christian community in a relationship of mutuality between persons and the Spirit.

The argument about the embodiment of the Spirit has been a contentious one, as LeRon Shults and Andrea Hollingsworth point out with reference to the writing of Origen: "Origen sometimes seems to share the Gnostic aversion to embodiment and materiality. God is incorporeal, 'without any material substance, and without partaking in any degree of a bodily adjunct.'"[60] The argument of this book is that the offering of worship in the church requires a particular location, visibility, and group of people. Yet this worship is not of human origin and determination but a response to the work of the Holy Spirit in that particular location and amongst those particular people. The theological and philosophical arguments in the seventeenth century that led to a sense of disconnection between the Trinity and worship point to the way in which the doctrine of the Trinity became disembodied, located within a realm of ideas to be argued over rather than connected with a full-bodied approach to the human condition, in which body, mind, spirit, and emotions are held together. The argument about the synchronicity between the person and the Spirit will be taken forward in looking at the nature and understanding of immediacy.

In his seminal book *Worship, its Theology and Practice*, the Reformed theologian J. J. von Allmen describes the centrality of worship for constituting the church, a point which is echoed by John Zizioulas in his argument about the Spirit constituting the church. Von Allmen writes: "By its worship the Church becomes itself, becomes conscious of itself and confesses itself as a distinctive entity. Worship thus allows the Church to emerge in its true nature."[61] He echoes this point further on in chapter 2 when he writes:

> It is in the sphere of worship, the sphere *par excellence* where the life of the Church comes into being, that the fact of the Church first emerges. It is there that it gives proof of itself, there where it is focused, and where we are led when we truly seek it, and it

---

59. Rogers, *After the Spirit*, 3.

60. Schuts and Hollingsworth, *Holy Spirit*, 23, quoting Origen, *On First Principles* 6.4.

61. Allmen, *Worship*, 42.

is from that point that it goes out into the world to exercise its mission.[62]

Colin Gunton, in his chapter comparing Owen and Zizioulas on the church in *Theology Through the Theologians*, places von Allmen's thinking in a pneumatological perspective when he writes: "The heart of the constitution of the Church by the Spirit is to be found in worship. Every act of worship that is in the Spirit is a constituting of the Church."[63] This book seeks to highlight the way in which the Spirit brings about the relationship with God by drawing people into acts of worship. While it could be considered that the Spirit is always present in worship, consciousness of the Spirit's presence and awareness of the way in which the Spirit is present can vary.

The argument in this volume arises out of an understanding of the Holy Spirit as constituting the church through the worship offered by the church, worship that is a sign of the relationship between people and God. In order to unpack this theme, I draw out from Owen and Zizioulas four characteristics of the Holy Spirit that reflect the nature of the relationship of worship and come to be signs of embodiment of the Holy Spirit in the particular moments of worship offered by the church. I look at particular characteristics of the Holy Spirit that are embodied in worship, the way the Holy Spirit draws people into a relationship with God that can be characterized as that of worship, and the way in which embodiment describes the nature and activity of the Holy Spirit. This book is developed in response to the consideration of the Pentecostal revival over the last century with its strong focus on a Spirit-led, Spirit-filled embodiment in worship, in order to re-affirm the presence of the Holy Spirit across the worship offered by the church as a whole and to offer new insights for the way in which the Spirit may be said to be present in worship.

Ten Theses on the Holy Spirit and Worship

In concluding this chapter, I move to offer ten theses that look at the nature of worship. These are developed from reflection on Owen's and Zizioulas's writing in relation to the activity of the Holy Spirit in drawing people into a relationship of worship with the triune God. They are drawn out to supplement the quadrilateral framework, with the quadrilateral framework referring primarily to the nature and activity of the Holy Spirit in worship, while the ten theses look at the nature of worship in and of itself. This distinction

---

62. Allmen, *Worship*, 44.

63. Gunton, *Theology through the Theologians*, 202.

between quadrilateral and theses is about looking from different perspectives on the Holy Spirit and worship: the first of the offering of worship and the second of the nature and activity of the Holy Spirit. The nature and work of the Holy Spirit take priority and lead into looking at worship, thus the quadrilateral framework focuses on the Holy Spirit and the ten theses develop an understanding of worship in order to indicate both the distinction between the two and yet the interrelatedness of the Holy Spirit and worship. These ten theses arise out of the reflection on the Holy Spirit and worship in the first half of this volume and point to areas to be developed in the second half of this work.

1. Worship is evoked in response to the one triune God, who is fully one and fully three, Father, Son and Holy Spirit, who draws all created things into being, offers redemption in response to the fallenness of the human condition, and brings creation into new life. (Chapter 2 looks at the personal and relational Trinitarian understanding of Owen and Zizioulas.)

2. Within the life of the Trinity, the particular activity of the Holy Spirit involves drawing people to the fullness of God. (Chapter 3 looks at a personal understanding of the Holy Spirit within the Trinity.)

3. The encounter with God, taking place in the setting of the offering of worship, defines the nature of the relationship between the created and the creator. (Chapter 4 looks at worship.)

4. The encounter taking place in worship involves the whole person: body, mind, and spirit. (Chapter 4.)

5. This encounter opens up a personal relationship with God, not in terms of a relationship between equal partners, but in terms of a relationship in which the "other" is glimpsed, while not being fully known. (Chapter 5 looks at personal relationality as the first aspect of the quadrilateral framework.)

6. The Holy Spirit opens up the immediate encounter with God, mediated within the personal and communal framework of worship. (Chapter 6 looks at the immediacy of the Holy Spirit as the second aspect of the quadrilateral framework.)

7. The immediacy of the knowledge of God is connected with particular times and places, but not restricted to these times and places. (Chapter 7 examines epistemological issues in terms of a relational understanding of truth, as the third aspect of the quadrilateral framework.)

8. The immediacy of the encounter is not such that it limits God to being a known object but is such that the person is faced by the unknowability and otherness of God. (Chapter 7.)

9. The immediacy of the encounter leads to personal transformation and to a renewal of vocation. (Chapter 8 explicates the role of the Holy Spirit as transformational as the fourth aspect of the quadrilateral framework.)

10. Seeing the Holy Spirit in worship as the one who draws us into the encounter with the Trinity opens up the possibility of a renewed ecumenical appreciation of the varieties of possibility of ways of worship, offered to the one divine source. (Chapter 9 concludes with a brief look at ecumenical implications of this approach to the Holy Spirit and worship.)

5

The Quadrilateral, Part One

The Holy Spirit and the Trinity—
Personal and Relational Understanding

INTRODUCTION

This chapter develops the first part of the four-fold argument that I am making in this book about the nature of the relationship between the Holy Spirit and worship, developing the argument in the setting of a quadrilateral framework. The four sides, held together, provide an interpretative framework for understanding the nature and activity of the Holy Spirit in relation to worship. While each side of the quadrilateral can be seen as standing on its own, there are greater theological benefits in holding all four sides together.

This chapter takes forward the argument for the first side of the quadrilateral by looking at the significance of Owen's and Zizioulas's views of the Trinity as personal and relational, providing the context for understanding the role of the Holy Spirit in worship. My focus is on the understanding of "person" initially in relation to the Trinity and consequentially in relation to the human person. The emphasis is on seeing the Holy Spirit as a personal rather than impersonal power (or an amorphous and generalized "spirit"). This first side of the quadrilateral argument is developed through an examination of Owen's and Zizioulas's explication of the Holy Spirit as personal and relational and the way in which this understanding is seen as being embodied in worship. Their differences of approach and yet the similarities of their conclusions are identified.

An understanding of "person" in relation to the Trinity has long been a contested matter in terms of whether it is possible to conceptualize what is seen to be the revelation of God in scripture in personal terms in relation to God, particularly when three "persons" are caught up in one shared identity. The question of the definition of "person" in and of itself, as well as the definition of person as applied to the different persons of the Trinity, is one that has been wrestled with over many centuries.[1] Angel Cordovilla Perez outlines the historical debate with regard to the original derivations of *persona, prosopon,* and *hypostasis,* looking at "fundamental milestones" of the history of the concept of person, from the early Fathers, through to the medieval period, moving on to the psychological turn of modern philosophy and then to the contemporary debate between "mono-subjectivity and inter-personality."

Grenz makes a transition between Trinitarian thinking about the nature of person and the range of contemporary ways of thinking about the human person, referring to the "widely accepted philosophical conclusion that 'person' has more to do with relationality than substantiality and that the idea stands closer to the idea of communion or community than to the individual in isolation or abstracted from communal embeddedness."[2]

From a sociological perspective, Christian Smith offers a helpful analysis of the emergence of personhood and the range of contemporary understandings of person. Charles Taylor in *Sources of the Self: The Making of the Modern Identity* comes from a different angle. Looking at the development of the "self" in terms of human identity, he makes an argument for going back beyond the Enlightenment to writers as early as Augustine for the origins of the modern self and looks both positively and critically at what he identifies as the decline of the view of the self as relational.[3]

The recent wealth of material on the Trinity includes a number of writings on the personal and relational aspects of the Trinity. These provide a renewed opportunity to look at this particular interpretation of the Trinity in a way which can be helpful and fruitful to the church in what has been described in the West as postmodern times.[4] Najib Awad builds on his

1. See Perez, "Trinitarian Concept of Person."

2. Grenz, *Social God,* 4.

3. Smith, *What is a Person?*; Taylor, *Sources of the Self.*

4. McCall's *Which Trinity?* offers a summary of those who critique (19–23) and

doctoral thesis on the personal individuation of the Holy Spirit by looking at modernist and postmodernist perspectives on a Trinitarian understanding of personhood and relationship.[5] Torrance delves into the understanding of "One Being and Three Persons," pointing to the Council of Alexandria in AD 362 and the way in which Athanasian and Cappadocian approaches were brought together under the theme *One Being, Three Persons*. Torrance points to the way in which "The 'whole' with which we are concerned is that of the divine Triunity in which 'the One and the Three' and 'the Three and the One' are the obverse of one another."[6] Fox draws out a comparison and mutual critique between Elizabeth Johnson and John Zizioulas, showing the mutual learning on the basis of an understanding of personal relationality that can take place between what might, once again, seem like two widely diverging theologians.[7]

The contributions of Owen and Zizioulas from what at first sight appear to be separated and therefore divergent Western and Eastern perspectives helps to build a bridge between two different angles of interpretation while offering a helpful dynamic for re-interpreting the personal and relational nature of the Trinity. Owen's and Zizioulas's respective emphases on the Holy Spirit as personal arise out of their approach to the Trinity as personal, not in terms of a social Trinitarianism or an individualistic "center of self-consciousness" model, but in terms of their understanding of the relational nature of the triune God. Out of this understanding comes a reshaping of the relational nature of the human person.

Owen and Zizioulas approach the personhood of the Holy Spirit in distinctively different ways. Owen's argument arises from his close examination of the references to the Holy Spirit in scripture, while Zizioulas bases his explication on the philosophical and theological understanding of the Cappadocian Fathers and on more recent philosophical and theological thinking. While Owen and Zizioulas come from two different starting

those who defend social Trinitarianism (23–39). Karageorgi, "Examination of the Contribution of John Owen," looks further at Owen's relationship to Eastern and Western thinking. Horrell, "Toward a Biblical Model," emphasizes relationality, but with greater weight given to the self-consciousness of each person within the Trinity than this chapter would allow. Metzler, "Trinity in Contemporary Theology," critiques social Trinitarianism but then raises up the "dynamically personal" nature of the Trinity that gives the appearance of avoiding the question of the way in which the persons of the Trinity might relate to each other.

5. Awad, *Persons in Relation*.

6. T. F. Torrance helpfully explores similar themes to Zizioulas with reference to the Cappadocian Fathers. See Torrance, *Christian Doctrine of God*, 112–35, 136–67.

7. Fox, *God as Communion*.

points and two different ways of analyzing the nature of the Holy Spirit, they both give weight to the personal nature of the triune God. I look at the way in which they each from their different perspectives point to the concept of person being shaped by the personal relationality within the Trinity, rather than an individualistic conception of the human person based around its self-conscious subjectivity.

Four aspects of this argument will be drawn out:

a. the personal and relational nature of the Holy Trinity;

b. the Holy Spirit drawing people into relationship with God;

c. this relationship focused in worship, embodying communion with the triune God; and

d. the development of people into full personhood in this worshipping relationship.

Worship offered corporately by the Christian church carries a dual significance. Firstly, it embodies the relationality into which people are drawn by God, and through this embodiment of relationality becomes the place where humans become fully persons. Secondly, in worship there is an emphasis on mystery, complementing the doctrinal understanding of the three persons of the Trinity. Worship points to the way in which the persons of the Trinity are encountered both in the visibility of the Word and the Sacrament and in the mystery of the presence of God beyond all human knowing. The offering of worship points to the way in which human persons can share in the sense of encounter and mystery.

I turn to look in more detail at Owen's and Zizioulas's rationale for emphasizing the personal nature of the Holy Spirit, before moving to refer to the similarities and differences between Owen's and Zizioulas's interpretations, and then offering a critique of their arguments and some conclusions.

OWEN AND THE PERSONAL NATURE OF THE HOLY SPIRIT

In *Pneumatologia* Owen has a thoroughgoing emphasis on the Holy Spirit as personal. I begin by looking at the historical setting of Owen's thinking about the Holy Spirit as personal and the particular framework of scripture and the early Fathers that shapes his thinking. This leads into a detailed analysis of his approach based on his drawing out from scripture of three characteristics of the nature of the Spirit and two activities of the Spirit.

It is interesting to note that the late twentieth century has seen echoes of Owen's scriptural arguments, for example, in Gordon F. Fee's extensive work *God's Empowering Presence* that helpfully outlines the range of the scriptural discussion about the nature and activity of the Holy Spirit.[8]

The Historical Context For Owen's Understanding of the Holy Spirit as Person

In Owen's emphasis on the nature of the Holy Spirit as person, he is countering the views of those in his day (such as the Socinians, Unitarians, and Quakers referred to previously) who developed a range of ideas about the Spirit as less than or other than personal and, Owen thought, diminished the Trinitarian nature of God and the personal nature of the Spirit.[9] Owen wrote countering views that regarded the Spirit as an abstract principle in nature as a whole, a description of the way in which God generally manifests himself in creation, an impersonal power, or a particular aspect of human nature such as "the light within." Owen wrote, at times polemically, against these views which he saw as representing a limited and (in terms of personhood) non-specific view of the Holy Spirit. Out of this wrestling with views he felt were insufficient, Owen developed his thinking about the personal nature of the Spirit and the way in which the Spirit fully shares in the divinity of the persons of the Trinity. Owen sums his thinking up as follows: "The sum is that the Holy Ghost is a divine, distinct person, and neither merely the power or virtue of God, nor any created spirit whatever."[10] Owen continues at this point with five arguments demonstrating the equality of divinity of the Holy Spirit with the Father and the Son, the personal nature of Father, Son, and Spirit, and that the same obligation of worship as is due to the Spirit as to the Father and the Son. By focusing in this way on the Spirit, Owen developed his own understanding of the Spirit as personal. Nuttall comments approvingly: "A theology based on the doctrine of the Holy Spirit would start from faith in God as at least not less than personal, as not abstract, ideal or a principle of coherence or perfection."[11]

8. Fee, *God's Empowering Presence.*

9. See "A Brief Declaration and Vindication of the Trinity," in Owen, *Works,* 2:366. Owen outlines the range of the arguments he seeks to counter, such as that of a created spirit rather than the uncreated Spirit or a spirit without "personality" or that the Spirit was only "the Spirit of Christ" without a separate distinctive identity.

10. See Owen, *Works,* 2:401. Here, Owen responds to the views of the Socinians, and others, with an extensive counter argument followed by his five points about the Holy Spirit and the Trinity and the worship due equally to each person of the Trinity.

11. Nuttall, *Holy Spirit in Puritan Faith,* 172.

In taking the view of the Holy Spirit as "person," Owen is following in the tradition arising out of the much earlier thinking of the Cappadocian Fathers. In taking the argument to those in the seventeenth century who wanted to move away from the thought of the Spirit as "person," Owen holds together both his strong Trinitarian understanding of God and his belief in the particular and specific role of the Holy Spirit within the Trinity. Owen keeps his definition of the Spirit within the mainstream of the Christian tradition while drawing out his distinctive approach to the personhood and efficacy of the work of the Spirit.

Owen's Basis For His Interpretation: The Balance Between Scripture and Tradition

While Owen was deeply rooted within the Reformed tradition's strong emphasis on scripture as the source for knowing God's revelation, he also had a concern to hold this emphasis and its interpretation within the wider setting of the church as a whole. Throughout *Pneumatologia* his concern to give weight to the voice of tradition, as expressed by the early Fathers, alongside scripture, can be seen.

Owen's thinking about the personal nature of the Spirit drew together the early Fathers and scripture. Letham comments: "Like the Cappadocians and Calvin before him, Owen stresses that the Fathers' terms convey the sense of Scripture. 'They are expository of what is contained.' To deny this on the pretext of reverence for Scripture is to render Scripture useless."[12] Owen's awareness of the Cappadocian tradition within the wider thinking of the early church is seen at an early point when he quotes Basil and Gregory of Nyssa in support of his argument:

> Whereas the order of operation among the distinct persons depends on the order of their subsistence in the blessed Trinity, in every great work of God, the concluding, completing, perfecting acts are ascribed unto the Holy Ghost.[13]

In Owen's taking up of the phrase "concluding, completing, perfecting acts" he not only points to the particular role of the Holy Spirit within the Trinity, bringing God's work to fruition, but also gives a hint of the argument

---

12. See Letham, "John Owen's Doctrine of the Trinity," 190, referring to Owen, *Works*, 2:379, where Owen quotes Gregory Nazianzus, *Oration* 31.3.21–23; Calvin, *Institutes* 1.13.7–29.

13. Owen, *Works*, 3:94. Owen quotes both Gregory of Nyssa (ad Ablabium) and Basil (de Spir. Sanc. cap. Xvi) in support of his thinking at this point.

that Zizioulas makes about the eschatological nature of the role of the Holy Spirit in drawing people from the present to the future.

Owen's emphasis on the personhood of the Spirit relates both to his reflection on the personal qualities of the nature of God and to the way in which he sees the significance of the personal in human identity. Owen held to the Cappadocian view that the Spirit is a distinct "person" within the Trinity.[14] He based his argument about the Spirit as a person not so much on a philosophical understanding of "spirit" or "person" but on the basis of what he perceives to be the revelation of God in scripture, with scripture itself being inspired by the Holy Spirit. Owen's "personal" understanding of the Holy Spirit was argued from the grounds that the descriptions of the Spirit in scripture portray the Spirit as personal.[15]

Trueman points to Owen's framework of scriptural interpretation which undergirds his thinking with regard to the Holy Spirit, referring to the way in which Owen argues that biblical interpretation is to be conducted with reference to the Trinity.

> If the Trinity is rejected, it will quickly become apparent that nothing of value can be derived from the Scriptures. The Trinitarian economy of salvation thus provides the hermeneutical key for unlocking the meaning of the Scriptures, a key which gives due weight to both the eternal and historical dimensions of scriptural teaching.[16]

Trueman continues by pointing to the way in which in his Trinitarian thinking, Owen is concerned to hold doctrine not only as the basis for a rational argument pursued with the mind, but in the setting of a personal relationship with God. "This Trinitarian interpretative device is not abstract doctrine but helps to maintain the link which Owen has argued exists between doctrine and piety."[17] This link between doctrine and piety is being taken forward in this book in terms of an interpretation of piety in the setting of

---

14. A small sign of the weight that Owen gives to the Cappadocian Fathers is the way in which he quotes Basil twice as much as Calvin (in *Pneumatologia*: Basil six times, Gregory of Nyssa three times, and Calvin three times).

15. The argument with regard to the authority of scripture and the nature of revelation will be taken further in chapter 7.

16. Trueman, *Claims of Truth*, 97. At this point, Trueman references Owen, *Works*, 16:340: "Here reason is entangled; yet, after a while, finds evidently, that unless this be embraced, all other things wherein it hath to do with God will not be of value to the soul."

17. Trueman, *Claims of Truth*, 98.

the shared worship offered in the church, rather than focusing on an individual interpretation of piety as a matter for a person on his or her own.

Kapic in *Communion* emphasizes Owen's starting point in scripture and the way in which the Holy Spirit is seen amongst the people of God by looking to the way in which Owen's logic can be seen as moving "backward," from the external works of God to the internal, establishing the Spirit's ontological relationship to the Father and Son.[18] This holding together of a scriptural framework alongside a Trinitarian interpretation arising from the early church serves to demonstrate the epistemological framework within which Owen thought.[19]

Personal Characteristics and Activities of the Holy Spirit

Owen begins his argument about the personal nature of the Holy Spirit by identifying three personal characteristics: wisdom or understanding, will, and power.[20]

Firstly, Owen turns to wisdom, a key word for him throughout *Pneumatologia*, starting by quoting phrases from 1 Corinthians 2:10–12:

> These things God has revealed to us through the Spirit; for the Spirit searches everything, even the depths of God. . . . We speak of these things in words not taught by human wisdom, but taught by the Spirit, interpreting spiritual things to those who are spiritual.[21]

In this passage from Corinthians, Owen sees Paul pointing to the wisdom of the Spirit revealing God's wisdom. Insofar as wisdom is a personal characteristic, rather than a characteristic of an inanimate object, Owen maintained that the Spirit, in showing wisdom, was also revealing the personal nature of the Spirit. The Spirit is both the embodiment of wisdom and imparts wisdom. Fee comments on this passage from Corinthians:

> Paul transformed wisdom from a philosophical, rhetorical term, into a historical, soteriological one. . . . The Gospel can never be perceived as divine wisdom by those who are pursuing *sophia*; it

---

18. Kapic, *Communion with God*, 197. There is an interesting debate to be had as to whether God's movements can be seen as either "forward" or "backward" in the way in which Kapic implies, or whether this refers more to the different approaches that arise out of the varying perspectives of human understanding.

19. This area will be looked at further in chapter 7.

20. Owen, *Works*, 3:78, 80, 81.

21. Owen, *Works*, 3:78, 79.

is recognised as such only by those who have the Spirit, since it comes only by the Spirit's revelation.[22]

Fee's pointing to the movement from philosophy to soteriology reflects the changing nature for Paul of the concept of wisdom as imparted by the Holy Spirit, from a more abstract concept, which people could pursue independently from a faith in God, to a personal and relational understanding that flows out of the nature and work of the Spirit.

Owen continues:

> Add hereunto that this Spirit is the author of wisdom and understanding in and unto others, and therefore he must have them in himself; and that not virtually or casually only, but formally also 1 Cor 12:8, wisdom and knowledge are reckoned among the gifts bestowed by him. For those of faith and tongues, it is enough that they are in him virtually; but wisdom and understanding, they cannot be given by any but he that is wise and understandeth what he doth; and hence is he called expressly a "Spirit of wisdom and understanding, of counsel and knowledge" (Isa 11:2).[23]

For Owen, wisdom has a spiritual quality, drawing people into search for the "deep things of God." Wisdom is a gift which is deepened when received from the Holy Spirit, whose nature is wisdom. The contrast between human wisdom and the Spirit's wisdom is threefold: the Spirit's wisdom is boundless whereas human wisdom is constrained by the boundaries of human understanding; the Spirit's wisdom is a gift to be received and shared rather than a possession to be exploited for personal gain; and the Spirit's wisdom leads into a knowledge of God, rather than being restricted by the limitations of human knowing.

Secondly, Owen identifies the Spirit as personal because the Spirit can be said to share the characteristic of will. Owen describes will as "the most eminently distinguishing character and property of a person."[24] Owen quotes 1 Corinthians 12:11 with regard to the way in which the Holy Spirit wills to distribute gifts: "all these worketh that one and the self-same Spirit, dividing to every man severally as he will."[25] Owen maintains that the Spirit is acting "by his own will, his own choice and pleasure."[26] Owen argues that the fact

---

22. Fee, *Empowering Presence*, 96.

23. Owen, *Works*, 3:81.

24. Fee, *Empowering Presence*, 80.

25. Owen, *Works*, 3:81.

26. Owen, *Works*, 3:81.

that the Spirit wills things to happen, demonstrates the personhood of the Spirit. "What can be spoken more fully and plainly to describe an intelligent person, acting voluntarily with freedom and by choice, I know not."[27]

Fee comments on this verse with regard to the sovereignty of the Spirit in the distribution of gifts arguing that "the gifts . . . ultimately express the Spirit's sovereign action in the life of the believer and the community as a whole." He concludes by expressing the ongoing hope that the Spirit provides "that the one and the same Spirit will do as he pleases, despite the boxes provided for him by those on both sides of this issue" (the issues being settling for the ordinary or justifying settling for the ordinary).[28]

These expressions about the Spirit's will raise the issue of "will" within God, as to whether there can be three wills within the Godhead if there is only one God. In response to the question of whether Owen could be accused of tritheism, each person of the Trinity having a separate will, Kapic comments and quotes Owen in rebuttal:

> Owen does not hesitate to speak of the Spirit's will. . . . Does such a claim move Owen toward tritheism? He would certainly deny the charge. Although he mentions three wills, he grounds such language in the following presupposition: "the will of the Father, Son and Holy Ghost is essentially the same; so that in the acting of one there is the counsel of all and each freely therein."[29]

Also, in laying the foundations in *Pneumatologia* for his understanding of the unity of the Trinity, Owen writes, "The several persons are undivided in their operations, acting all by the same will, the same wisdom, the same power."[30] Owen illustrates a further paradox of faith with regard

27. Owen, *Works*, 3: 81.

28. Fee, *Empowering Presence*, 174, 75.

29. Kapic, *Communion with God*, 197, quoting Owen, *Works*, 2:235.

30. Owen, *Works*, 3:93. "Intending to treat of the operations of the Holy Ghost, or those which are peculiar unto him, some things must be premised concerning the operation of the Godhead in general, and the manner thereof; and they are such as are needful to guide us in many passages of the Scripture, and to direct us aright in the things in particular which now lie before us. I say, then—

1. That all *divine operations* are usually ascribed unto *God absolutely*. So it is said God made all things; and so of all other works, whether in nature or in grace. And the reason hereof is, because the several persons are undivided in their operations, acting all by the same will, the same wisdom, the same power. Every person, therefore, is the author of every work of God, because each person is God, and the divine nature is the same undivided principle of all divine operations and this ariseth from the unity of the persons in the same essence. But as to the manner of subsistence therein, there is distinction, relation, and order between and among them; and hence there is no divine

to the Trinity in supporting the view that there might be three persons but with a single will.

Thirdly, Owen identifies the characteristic of power as a characteristic attributable to the Holy Spirit, and, in being so attributable, demonstrating the personal nature of the Spirit. "A Power whereby any one is able to act according to the guidance of his understanding and the determinations of his will, declares him to be a person."[31] Owen cites a range of the effects of the Spirit in order to demonstrate the impact of the power of the Spirit in both redemption and creation.[32] Owen refers also to Isaiah 11:2: "As he is called a 'Spirit of wisdom and understanding,' so is he also of 'might' or power." He goes on to counter the argument that the effects of the Spirit might not be integral to the nature of the Spirit on the basis that "although it may be granted that the things there mentioned are rather effects of his operations than adjuncts of his nature, yet he who effecteth wisdom and power in others must first have them himself."[33] While comparisons could be drawn with the Spirit and Sophia, or wisdom, the personal nature of the Spirit for which Owen argues indicates that the Spirit is not impersonal wisdom but is the

---

work but is distinctly assigned unto each person, and eminently unto one. So is it in the works of the old creation, and so in the new, and in all particulars of them. Thus, the creation of the world is distinctly ascribed to the Father as his work, Acts 4:24; and to the Son as his, John 1:3; and also to the Holy Spirit, Job 33:4; but by the way of eminence to the Father, and absolutely to God, who is Father, Son, and Holy Spirit.

The reason, therefore, why the works of God are thus distinctly ascribed unto each person is because, in the undivided operation of the divine nature, each person doth the same work in the order of their subsistence; not one as the instrument of the other, or merely employed by the other, but as one common principle of authority, wisdom, love, and power."

31. Owen, *Works*, 3:81. Owen continues, "It is not the mere ascription of power absolutely, or ability unto anything, that I intend; for they may signify no more but the efficacy wherewith such things are attended in their proper places, as instruments of the effects whereunto they are applied. . . . But where power, divine power, is absolutely ascribed unto anyone, and that declared to be put forth and exercised by the understanding and according to the will of him to whom it is so ascribed, it doth undeniably prove him to be a divine person; for when we say the Holy Ghost is so, we intend no more but that he is one who by his own divine understanding puts forth his own divine power. So is it in this case: Job 33:4, "The Spirit of God hath made me, and the breath of the Almighty hath given me life." Creation is an act of divine power, the highest we are capable to receive any notion of; and it is also an effect of the wisdom and will of him that createth, as being a voluntary act, and designed unto a certain end. All these, therefore, are here ascribed to the Spirit of God."

32. Owen, *Works*, 3:81. Owen refers to James 1:21 "able to save our souls"; Acts 22:32 "the word of God's grace, building us up"; Job 33:4 "the Spirit of God hath made me and the breath of the Almighty hath given me life" (Owen, *Works*, 3:82).

33. Owen, *Works*, 3:82.

one who offers wisdom and draws people into wisdom. The power of the Spirit is not about force or coercion but about the drawing of people into the fullness of wisdom and the manifestation of God's saving love. The notion of power and its nature will be looked at further in the fourth part of the quadrilateral argument, on transformation.

I turn now from Owen's explication of the characteristics of the Holy Spirit to his references to the activities of the Spirit. Owen complements the personal characteristics of the Holy Spirit with what he sees as the activity of the Holy Spirit as described in scripture, and in this description, reinforces his understanding of the personal nature of the Holy Spirit. He describes this activity in terms of "works and operations" and makes the argument about the personal nature of the Holy Spirit:

> To complete this argument, I shall add the consideration of those *works* and *operations* of all sorts which are ascribed to the Spirit of God; which we shall find to be such as are not capable of an assignation unto him with the least congruity of speech or design of speaking intelligibly, unless he be a distinct, singular subsistent or person, endued with divine power and understanding.[34]

Owen continues by saying that these works and operations are to be taken not separately, but as a whole, and as a whole they point to the way in which the Spirit acts personally. He identifies two areas of activity in particular, that of teaching and of calling, in support of his argument.

Owen saw the work of the Holy Spirit as teacher as evidence of the personal nature of the Holy Spirit. Owen pointed to such texts as Luke 12:12 and John 14:26 in support of his argument. Luke 12:12 is set in the context of the persecution of the early Christians and the anxiety about people knowing what they need to say to defend themselves. "Do not worry about how you are to defend yourselves or what you are to say, for 'The Holy Ghost shall teach you what ye ought to say.'"[35] John 14:26 is set in the middle of the "Last Supper discourse" of Jesus, when Jesus reassures his disciples about the future. "The Comforter, which is the Holy Ghost, whom the Father will send in my name, he shall teach you all things, and bring all things to your remembrance."[36] A teacher is not an abstract proposition or an immaterial substance. Whereas learning can happen in a range of ways, as in reading a book or studying the law, a teacher engages with individuals to support

34. Owen, *Works*, 3:83.
35. Owen, *Works*, 3:83.
36. Owen, *Works*, 3:83.

and encourage them. Owen is emphasizing this personal engagement of the Spirit, leading people to a fuller knowledge of God, encouraging them in the fullness of life, giving them words to say in times of trial. The Spirit, in engaging in these roles, could not be less than personal.

Owen also sees the Spirit as personal in terms of giving a call to people to particular ministries. He cites Saul and Barnabas and those who are called to be overseers. There is a specificity about the work of the Spirit which carries a greater personal weight than those conceptions of the Spirit which emphasize the Spirit's impersonal nature. Owen argues that the Spirit calls people to certain roles within the community of believers and maintains that this personal action is a further illustration of the personal nature of the Spirit.

The combination of the scriptural descriptions of the Spirit having the characteristics that would be seen in a person rather than in what Owen describes as a substance or an emanation, as well as the activities of the Spirit which would flow out of a person, lead Owen to conclude that the Spirit has a personal identity. It is out of both the characteristics and the activity of the Spirit, that the Spirit is transformative in human life.

Critique and Conclusions

The emphasis that Owen places on the Spirit as personal raises a number of issues. It could be argued that in Owen's emphasis on the personal identity of the Spirit, he both diminishes the role of the Spirit as divine and unduly separates out the Spirit from the fullness of the life of the Trinity. It could also be argued that Owen, in the very way he takes up examples of personal characteristics and activity that are specific to the human being, is creating the Spirit in the image of a human being rather than honoring the Spirit's Trinitarian identity and divine otherness.

However, Owen argues that these personal characteristics do not make the Spirit less than God or separate from the Trinity. Owen maintains that "the Holy Spirit is a divine, self-subsisting, self-sufficient person . . . expressly called God—therefore he must have the nature of God."[37] In so far as the Spirit has the nature of God, divine properties are assigned to him, which Owen makes clear through a further set of scriptural citations.[38]

---

37. Owen, *Works*, 3:89.

38. Owen, *Works*, 3:91. "Add hereunto, in the last place, that divine properties are assigned unto him, as eternity, Heb 9:14, he is the 'eternal Spirit';—immensity, Ps 139:7, 'Whither shall I go from thy Spirit?'—omnipotency, Mic 2:7, 'The Spirit of the Lord is not straitened,' compared with Isa 40:28; 'The power of the Spirit of God,' Rom

Owen's understanding of the personal nature of the Spirit is not without its critics. Kapic points to some of the tensions within Owen's argument about the nature of personhood while also emphasizing the way in which, for Owen, the personal and relational knowledge of the Trinity is encountered in worship:

> Owen still has difficulties with the persons, betraying his Western roots. At the same time, this is as much due to the impossibility of defining persons. The human person is made in the image of God, who is incomprehensible, and so shares an element of incomprehensibility on a creaturely level. However, the Eastern approach has greater merit here, dealing with the revelation of the three in the Bible as given, following the way we come to know them in salvation. After all, while we relate to an object by definition, to a person it is more appropriately through recognition and communion. Hence knowledge of God the Trinity is grounded in worship. To that great goal Owen was pointing.[39]

The language of mystery points to the unknowability of God, who is yet revealed in three-fold identity. This mystery, reflected in the "persons" of the Trinity, points to the limitation of the language of personhood about God, and thus raises the possibility of a level of mystery about the identity of the human person.[40]

The significant feature that Owen draws out is the issue of Trinitarian relationality, which can be seen from a range of perspectives. The twentieth and twenty-first centuries have seen a broader exploration of the nature of relationality, from a scientific as well as a theological perspective. Wildman, in his "An Introduction to Relational Ontology," indicates the broad sweep of understandings that relationality offers in the twenty-first century, embracing scientific, philosophical, and theological understandings.[41] Owen, from within a different scientific era, offers insights about the significance of the nature of relationality that feed in to a more contemporary twenty-first-century approach to relationality.

15:19;—prescience, Acts 1:16, This scripture must be fulfilled, 'which the Holy Ghost by the mouth of David spake before concerning Judas';—omniscience, 1 Cor 2:10, 11, 'The Spirit searcheth all things, yea, the deep things of God;'—sovereign authority over the church, Acts 13:2, 4; 20:28."

39. Kapic and Jones, *Ashgate Research Companion*, 197.

40. Chapter 7 includes looking at the relationship between the comprehensibility and incomprehensibility of the knowledge of God and the way in which these two aspects are held together by the Holy Spirit drawing people into worship.

41. See Wildman, "Introduction to Relational Ontology."

Trueman points to a further perspective on relationality offered by covenant theology and affirms Owen's fundamental belief that theology is relational.[42] Kapic quotes Trueman's research as further contributing to this area of study as he lays out the structure of Owen's most systematic work *Theologoumena Pantodapa*, which has a historical framework organized around the covenants:

> Underlying this choice of organization is Owen's fundamental belief that theology is relational; that is, it depends upon the nature of the relationship that exists between God the revealer and the one revealed, and humans, the recipients of that revelation. In this context, the progressive nature of the covenant scheme serves to take account of the fact that theology requires a divine-human relationship, and that the biblical record shows that relationship has itself not been static but subject to historical movement, a movement which can be articulated by setting forth in order the key points at which God has explicitly defined his relationship with humanity: the various covenants which are found within the Bible.[43]

Whereas Wildman's thinking about relational ontology could be seen as referring to the immanent Trinity in terms of the inner relations between the three persons of the Trinity, covenant theology focuses more on the economic Trinity in terms of the external relations between God and humanity. Owen's later writing embraces both the immanent and the economic Trinity in its dual focus on the Holy Spirit as personal within the life of the Trinity and its emphasis on the role of the Spirit as drawing people into relation with God.

ZIZIOULAS'S EMPHASIS ON THE PERSONAL NATURE OF THE HOLY SPIRIT, ARISING OUT OF HIS TRINITARIAN FRAMEWORK

Introduction

Zizioulas's understanding of person arises out of the long historical context of the influences on him of the Cappadocian fathers. His argument is made in response to what he understands as an overly-strong Enlightenment

---

42. Trueman, *Claims of Truth*, 80.

43. Trueman, *Claims of Truth*, 49.

approach to the person as an individual rather than as being in relation.[44] He focuses on the definition of person arising out of a relational understanding of personal identity within the Trinity rather than an understanding that begins from individual self-consciousness.[45]

He thus holds that the personal nature of the Holy Spirit, embodied in worship, draws the individual into participation in the triune life and thus into full personhood. In order to develop the personal and relational understanding of the Trinity and the way this is evoked in the Holy Spirit, this section examines in more depth Zizioulas's understanding of "person" in terms of the way in which the personal and relational nature of the Trinity is manifest in the Holy Spirit. Zizioulas's understanding of communion leads him to look more closely at the nature of relationality within the personhood of the Trinity and, as a consequence of this thinking, about the nature of relationality in terms of the human person.

Zizioulas's thinking about the personal aspects of the Trinity, giving relationality as a key identifier of "person," offers the possibility for a broader understanding of person than that which focuses on the self as autonomous. A prior emphasis on relationality means that the self is primarily known in relationship and only secondarily in terms of individuality.

Zizioulas's Rootedness in the Cappadocian Fathers

Zizioulas builds positively on the thinking of the Cappadocian Fathers in order to counter what he sees as the development of the concept of person in the period from the Enlightenment onwards: "[The concept of person] should not be understood as an 'individual' in the sense of an identity conceivable in itself, an 'axis of consciousness' and a concurrence of natural or moral qualities, or a number that can be subject to addition or combination."[46] Zizioulas sets his argument in the context of a critique of Boethius and Augustine:

> With the help of a cross-fertilization between the Boethian and the Augustinian approaches to man, our Western philosophy and culture have formed a concept of man out of a combination

44. Compare with Charles Taylor's argument in *Sources of the Self.*

45. There is a range of recent PhD dissertations that have found Zizioulas's personal understanding of the Trinity and its implications a focus for further development, for example, Robinson, "Towards a Definition"; Tibbs "East Meets West"; Folsom, "Comparative Assessment"; and Awad's comparison of Zizioulas and Gunton, "Pneumatology and the Defence."

46. Zizioulas, *Communion and Otherness,* 171.

of two basic components: rational individuality on the one hand and psychological experience and consciousness on the other. It was on the basis of this combination that Western thought arrived at the conception of a person as an individual and/or a personality, that is, a unit endowed with intellectual, psychological and moral qualities centered on the axis of consciousness.[47]

Zizioulas goes back beyond Boethius and Augustine, identifying his most significant influences as being those of the Cappadocian Fathers.[48] He places particular weight on their theological re-interpretation of the nature of God as person:

> The Cappadocian Fathers made some fundamental contributions to the doctrine of God. . . . They shifted the sense of "hypostasis" from its original sense of "essence," and transferred it to the person, making "person" a fundamental category.[49]

He offers a more detailed argument from Gregory of Nyssa about the priority of an understanding of personhood arising out of the Trinity rather than from reflection on the nature of human personhood, "Therefore . . . we must avoid applying to the Trinity things 'which are not to be seen in the Holy Trinity.'"[50] This argument about the nature of personhood deriving from the nature of the Trinity is key to this book, particularly in relation to the way in which the Holy Spirit, in worship, brings persons to personhood. Zizioulas also points to the influence of Basil:

47. Zizioulas, *Communion and Otherness*, 210–11. In the footnotes, Zizioulas comments on rational individuality, "On the basis of Boethius's definition as *naturae rationabilis individua substantia*" (210n6), and on psychological experience and consciousness, "Augustine's *Confessions* stand out as a decisive contribution to this psychological approach to person" (210n7).

48. While this influence is evident in *Being as Communion* and *Lectures*, it is particularly seen in the way he develops his argument with regard to personhood in *Communion and Otherness* in chapter 4, "The Trinity and Personhood: Appreciating the Cappadocian Contribution," and in chapter 5, "Pneumatology and the Importance of the Person: A Commentary on the Second Ecumenical Council." At the end of chapter 4, Zizioulas addresses, in an appendix, those such as Lucian Turcescu, who critique his understanding as a misreading of the Cappadocian Fathers.

49. Zizioulas, *Lectures*, 61.

50. Zizioulas, *Communion and Otherness*, 172. Zizioulas quotes four "deficiencies" mentioned by Gregory of Nyssa with regard to human personhood: (1) human mortality involving separation between human beings; (2) the possibility of addition or subtraction of human beings; (3) the transience and change of human persons; and (4) the derivation of human persons from different personal causes (PG 45:177–80) in order to develop the distinction between divine and human personhood.

> Basil . . . seems to be rather unhappy with the notion of sub-
> stance as an ontological category and tends to replace it . . .
> with that of *koinonia*. Instead of speaking of the unity of God
> in terms of His one nature, he prefers to speak of it in terms of
> the *communion of persons*; communion is for Basil an ontologi-
> cal category. The *nature* of God is communion. This does not
> mean that the persons have an ontological priority over the one
> substance of God, but that the one substance of God coincides
> with the communion of the three persons.[51]

At this point Zizioulas draws out a significant underlying aspect of his
argument, which is the importance of the persons of the Trinity being in
relationship rather than having separated and distinct identities. He summarizes his at times paradoxical argument about unity and multiplicity in
the Trinity in the matter of personhood as follows:

> With the help of the Trinitarian theology of the Greek Fathers,
> particularly the Cappadocians, and their understanding of what
> it means to be a person, first in God and then in the human
> being, communion and otherness are shown to be fundamental
> parts of the doctrine of the holy Trinity. God is not, logically
> or ontologically speaking, first one and then many, he is one in
> being many.[52]

Zizioulas treads with care the line between "God as One" and "God as
Three" in highlighting the way in which *koinonia* defines the substance of
God. Building on the Cappadocian Fathers' understanding of God, Zizioulas also emphasizes that knowledge of God comes through the worshipping
relationship found in the liturgy rather than as an abstract principle which
can be rationally proved outside a relationship with God. Weinandy points
to the way in which Zizioulas draws on the relational concept of person
within the dynamic of the Trinity, most fully expressed in worship:

> Secondly, . . . a proper understanding of "person" demands not
> simply one personal being existing in isolation, but rather nec-
> essarily implies relationships with other persons. "Person" by its
> very nature is a relational concept. Thirdly, by illuminating the
> significance of the notion of "person" within the Trinity Ziziou-
> las has brought to trinitarian theology a renewed and intensified
> dynamism, that is, the persons of the Trinity are not statically

---

51. Zizioulas, *Being as Communion*, 134. At this point Zizioulas footnotes a list of references from Basil's writings, including several references from *de Spiritu Sancto* and *Contra Eunomius*.

52. Zizioulas, *Communion and Otherness*, 11.

embedded within a singular substance, but actively relate to one another in a communion of love. Fourthly, this dynamism spills over in the Trinity's relationships to creation and with human persons. This eternal communion of love allows the persons of Trinity actively to reach out and embrace other persons, and this is most fully expressed and accomplished within the Eucharist.[53]

The emphasis on worship further points to a focus on mystery and the limitation of human words to describe the divine. Khaled Anatolios helpfully draws attention to this after his analysis of the debate between Gregory of Nyssa and Eunomius when he writes: "The nature of the relation between the infinite God and finite humanity is such that knowledge of God can only take place in the modality of receptivity, awe and worship."[54] This sense of mystery has a consequence with regard to human personhood, in drawing attention to the element of mystery in human identity.

Zizioulas draws together the Cappadocian basis of his thinking with his understanding of person as reflecting the image of God:

> It would seem, therefore, that the identification of *hypostasis* with person—this historic cross-fertilization between Greek and biblical thought that took place in the fourth century—has ultimately served to show that the notion of person is to be found only in God and that human personhood is never satisfied with itself until it becomes in this respect an *imago Dei*.[55]

I argue that the work of the Holy Spirit, sharing in the personal Trinitarian identity, is to draw people, through worship, into the full personhood that is the *imago Dei*. The Holy Spirit in worship draws people into the otherness of communion with God, an otherness which opens up both relatedness and freedom, constituent parts of the nature of the person.

Zizioulas's Understanding of the Holy Spirit as Personal

Zizioulas's significant contribution to thought about the nature of personhood arises out of the priority he gives to the way in which the nature of personhood is defined by an understanding of the way the triune God is revealed rather than being a human construct transferred to an understanding of God. The language of person and relationship is defined out of reflection on the nature of the Trinity rather than beginning with an anthropological

53. Weinandy, "Zizioulas, the Trinity, and Ecumenism," 410.
54. Anatolios, *Retrieving Nicaea*, 182.
55. Zizioulas, *Communion and Otherness*, 215.

approach which leads to a pre-existing definition of person being projected on to the Trinity. Zizioulas seeks to clarify the issue in relation to the significance he is placing on the writings of the Greek Fathers: "For the persons of the Trinity, according to the above Fathers, are not 'individuals,' either in the psychological sense of a center of consciousness or in that of a combination and concurrence of natural or moral qualities, or in the sense of a number that can be added or combined."[56] It is hardly surprising that placing an already existing definition of person onto the nature of God encounters difficulties in terms of trying to fit the ineffable mystery of God, who is yet revealed in the world, into a purely human pattern of personal understanding. The important insight that Zizioulas highlights, arising out of the arguments made by the Cappadocian Fathers, is that, when reflecting on the divine mystery, "person" is defined in terms of relationality. This emphasis on relationality stands in contrast to emphases on individuality or autonomy. It also marks the difference between an understanding of the social Trinity, which can seem to focus on three separate individuals within the Trinity, and a relational understanding of the Trinity, in which persons are primarily defined by relationship rather than self-consciousness.

In his introduction to *Communion and Otherness*, Zizioulas identifies three parts to his definition of person, arising out of his relational trinitarian perspective, parts which he develops throughout this book:

    a. The Person is otherness in communion and communion in otherness.

    b. Personhood is freedom.

    c. Personhood is creativity.[57]

The first part of his definition unpacks the theme of relationality and the way in which relationality in the Trinity points neither to God only as "One" nor to God only as "Three," but is a holding together of the one and the many. Zizioulas's paradoxical interpretation points to the way in which, in the Trinity, "otherness" is an intrinsic part of "communion."

The second part of his definition points to the way in which this "otherness" enables freedom. Zizioulas uses the language of *ekstasis* and *hypostasis* in order to lead into his understanding of freedom:[58]

> Thus, personhood implies the "openness of being" and even more than that, the *ek-stasis* of being, that is a movement towards

---

56. Zizioulas, *Communion and Otherness*, 171.

57. Zizioulas, *Communion and Otherness*, 9, 11.

58. Zizioulas, *Communion and Otherness*, 212–37. "Personhood as Ekstasis and Hypostasis of Being," in chapter 6, "Human Capacity and Human Incapacity."

> communion which leads to a transcendence of the boundaries
> of the "self" and thus to *freedom*.[59]

Freedom is therefore not to do with an understanding of the self in isolation, with the individual able to make decisions on his or her own, but relates to the going beyond the boundaries of the self in communion with the "other."

The third point that Zizioulas makes is about creativity. In drawing out what he means by creativity, Zizioulas offers the comparison between manufacturing and art, arguing that manufacturing is about turning humans into "things" and instruments towards ends.[60] On the other hand, art is the "'beginning of a world,' a 'presence' in which 'things' and substances (cloth, oil etc) or qualities (shape, colour etc.) or sounds become part of a personal presence. And this is entirely the achievement of personhood, a distinctly unique capacity of man."[61]

Zizioulas continues by developing his understanding about relationality in defining human personhood and the way that this is rooted in Christ, by the power of the Holy Spirit. He makes an argument for holding together "presence" and "absence" in human personhood rooted in an understanding of God the creator alongside the new creation offered in Christ in which human nature "overcomes its individualization."[62] At this point Zizioulas focuses on the Spirit. "A 'de-individualization' of Christ requires a conditioning of Christology by pneumatology, for it was in the Spirit that the de-individualization of Christ's humanity became possible."[63] Zizioulas continues: "At the same time man in relating to Christ in and through personhood affirms his existence only in communion, in the *koinonia* of the Spirit."[64]

It is the Spirit who draws the person into communion, a communion embodied in worship (for Zizioulas in the Eucharist) and shapes the person as person.

---

59. Zizioulas, *Communion and Otherness*, 213. Zizioulas puts in an interesting footnote commenting on the way in which, while *ek-stasis* is primarily known through the writings of Heidegger, the origins of this terms appear in the mystical writings of the Greek Fathers (Pseudo-Dionysius, Maximus, etc.). Zizioulas also quotes C. Yannaras's *The Ontological Content of the Theological Notion of Person* (1970) as a resource for the use of Heidegger in the re-interpretation of Eastern Orthodox theology.

60. Zizioulas, *Communion and Otherness*, 216.

61. Zizioulas, *Communion and Otherness*, 216.

62. Zizioulas, *Communion and Otherness*, 238.

63. Zizioulas, *Communion and Otherness*, 244.

64. Zizioulas, *Communion and Otherness*, 245.

The Role of the Holy Spirit as Embodying Communion

Zizioulas points to four characteristics of the Holy Spirit that are foundational for his thinking. Two of these that are significant but less foundational than the others are inspiration and sanctification. Zizioulas writes: "The Orthodox tradition has attached particular significance to the latter, namely the idea of sanctification."[65] However, he continues by identifying sanctification with the tradition of monasticism (in contrast to Owen who identifies sanctification with the renewed life of the individual Christian in each place) and so goes on to comment, "but monasticism—and the notions of 'sanctification' and 'spirituality' that lie behind it—has never become a decisive aspect of ecclesiology in the East."[66]

The reference to ecclesiology points to a central point of Zizioulas's thinking about the Holy Spirit, that it is the Holy Spirit who constitutes the church by embodying the *koinonia* of the Trinity as the people of God gather in the liturgy. Zizioulas outlines his argument in a sequence that emphasizes the relationship of the liturgy to the church and the way in which two foundational aspects of Pneumatology, that is, communion and eschatology, indicate the Spirit's presence and activity: "The Church is constituted in and through eschatology and communion."[67]

One aspect of this constitution is the way in which the Spirit, in embodying communion, draws people into a relationship with God such that full personhood is realized. Zizioulas takes the argument further in *Communion and Otherness* as he identifies the significance of the eschatological work of the Holy Spirit in shaping personal identity:

> The eschatological dimension of the presence and activity of the Spirit deeply affects the identity of the other: it is on the basis not of someone's past or present that we should identify and accept him or her, but on the basis of their *future*. And since the future lies only in the hands of God, our approach to the other must be free from passing judgement on him or her.[68]

Zizioulas further emphasizes the connection between the relational aspects of the Trinity and the embodiment of these in the church:

> All the observations we have made so far concerning faith in the Trinity, in Christ and in the Spirit take their concrete form

65. Zizioulas, *Being as Communion*, 131.

66. Zizioulas, *Being as Communion*, 131.

67. Zizioulas, *Being as Communion*, 131, 132.

68. Zizioulas, *Communion and Otherness*, 6.

in the Church. It is there that communion with the other fully
reflects the relation between communion and otherness in the
holy Trinity, in Christ and in the Spirit.[69]

This embodiment takes place most fully in the worshipping life of the
church. The central aspect of worship for Zizioulas is in the Eucharistic liturgy. (This is unlike Owen, for whom the Word in scripture and preaching
play a more central role.)

The Personhood of the Spirit and Worship

Zizioulas summarizes his thinking about the relationship between the Spirit
and worship as follows:

> The Eucharist is the inaugural event of freedom and the moment
> in which eschatological reality becomes the actual presence of
> this assembly brought together by the Holy Spirit. This is the
> work of the Holy Spirit, which is why the invocation (*epiclesis*)
> of the Holy Spirit is fundamental. The gifts that bear the body
> and blood of Christ bring us into increasing participation in that
> body. This event of person-to-person relationship takes place in
> the Spirit, between each of us and Christ. These eschatological
> events are seen, felt and tasted in the gathering of the Church.
> This gathering is the event in which the Holy Spirit opens us to
> life together in freedom.[70]

Worship involves being drawn by the Holy Spirit into a relationship with
the One who holds all relationships in being. The relationship with God
through the Holy Spirit which is embodied in worship is a relationship firstly
with the triune God. Flowing out of this relationship is the relationship into
which people are led with one another. Both relationships are characterized
by otherness, but this otherness is of a different order. The relationship with
God is characterized by the otherness between the created and the creator.
The relationship between people is characterized by that which is experienced by those who find their shared common origin in the creator. Within
this personalizing relationality, the Holy Spirit is both the one who (together

---

69. *Communion and Otherness*, 6. Zizioulas continues by reflecting on the role of
baptism, Eucharist, and ministry in the realization of communion. Here, one of his
differences from Owen is made clear in terms of Zizioulas's emphasis on the constitution of the church around the bishop, while Owen focused on the local church as fully
constituting the people of God in each place, without the addition of a bishop.

70. Zizioulas, *Christian Dogmatics*, 161.

with the Father and the Son) is worshipped and the one who has a particular role in engendering worship.[71]

Critique and Conclusions

Zizioulas draws out the significance of "person" in relation to the Trinity in a way which supports the first quadrilateral point with regard to the Holy Spirit and worship. His argument has not been without its challengers. For example, Loudovikos goes back to the origins of Zizioulas's understanding in the Cappadocian Fathers.[72] He argues that Zizioulas is not accurately reflecting the Cappadocian understanding of "person." However, there is a counter argument that Loudovikos himself is too heavily reliant on an Augustinian and sixteenth- and seventeenth-century Western development of the primary understanding of the person as the center of self-consciousness rather than as a being in relation.[73]

SIMILARITIES AND DIFFERENCES BETWEEN OWEN AND ZIZIOULAS

Affirming the Divinity of the Holy Spirit

There are interesting comparisons between Owen and Zizioulas in terms of the influences that lead them to see the significance of persons in relation to the nature and understanding of the Trinity. While they are shaped by their different backgrounds, it is noteworthy that similar threads run through their writings. The arguments they make are influenced by a desire to counter those who variously see the Holy Spirit as less then divine or as impersonal. For Owen, the Socinians, Unitarians, and Quakers provide

71. See Knight, *Theology of John Zizioulas*, 183–96. Knight helpfully analyzes Zizioulas's connection between the Holy Spirit, the person, and worship and comments: "Our being as persons is not given to us complete at birth, but is part of a process, caused by the Holy Spirit, which unfolds through time because we must all participate in it. As we are sanctified we become more human, more responsive and available to God and through God to one another. The worship of God allows us to see others as his creatures, and thus to understand that they are ours because they are first his" (184).

72. Loudovikos, "Person Instead of Grace."

73. Zizioulas, *Communion and Otherness*, 171–77, offers a helpful response to the arguments of L. Turcescu with regard to the question of a "Misreading of the Cappadocians."

the dialogue partners. Zizioulas builds on the arguments already offered by the Cappadocian Fathers in response to such writers as Arius, Sabellius, Eunomius, and those who espoused views that countered a co-equal divine understanding of the three persons of the Trinity.

I argue that this similarity may in itself be viewed as a pointer to the work of the one Holy Spirit. Owen and Zizioulas both focus on the personal and relational nature of the Holy Trinity, the work of the Holy Spirit in drawing people into the communion of the Trinity, the way in which this work has a focus in worship, and the consequent drawing of people into relational personhood. The weight and emphasis of their thinking varies, reflecting to some degree the different traditions from which they come. Owen and Zizioulas both have different writing styles and approaches to theological discourse, with Owen more prolix and voluminous and Zizioulas having a greater focus in articles drawn together in books rather than in sustained pieces of book-length writing.[74]

Reformed and Orthodox Origins

While singling out a theologian from within any one tradition does not necessarily mean that the theologian is fully representative of the diversity within that tradition, Owen and Zizioulas carry with them distinctive Reformed and Orthodox approaches.

The first approach relates to the use of scripture and the way in which this use reflects a view of the Holy Spirit's inspiration of scripture as primary in shaping the knowledge of God. Owen's intensive quoting of scripture reflects the primacy which scripture has within the Reformed tradition. His argument about the personal nature of the Holy Spirit arises out of his attentiveness to the scriptural representation of the Holy Spirit's presence. Zizioulas's more direct focus on the Cappadocian Fathers reflects the role that the tradition of the church plays alongside the scriptures. His argument about the personal nature of the Holy Spirit reflects the debates and controversies within the early councils of the church. However, it is interesting to note the weight that Owen gives to the early Fathers in his theological understanding. And Zizioulas's lesser number of direct references to scripture

---

74. The twenty-four volumes of Owen's collected writings in Gould's *Works* illustrates this, with some of the volumes containing more sustained pieces of writing, as in *Pneumatologia*, and others being collections of shorter pieces and sermons. The five main volumes of Zizioulas's writing indicate his approach to writing, with only one, *Eucharist, Bishop, Church* being a sustained piece of work and the other four—*Being As Communion*; *Communion and Otherness*; *Lectures*; and *The Eucharistic Communion and the World*—being compilations of articles, papers, and lectures.

does not mean a lack of attention to scripture, even while the references to scripture are more visible in the writings of the Cappadocian Fathers, from whom Zizioulas draws heavily, than in Zizioulas's own writings.

A second approach relates to the role of the Holy Spirit in the shaping of ecclesiology. For the Reformed, a key aspect of authority is that of scripture, discerned under the guidance of the Holy Spirit and held within the councils of the church, whether the local congregational meeting or regional or national bodies seeking the Spirit's leading. For the Orthodox, authority is vested in the bishop, an issue to which Zizioulas gives emphasis.[75] Both of these ecclesiological interpretations are influenced by reflection on the nature and activity of the Holy Spirit; both emphasize the significance of the personal relationship in response to the guidance of the Spirit, whether of people meeting together in councils, or of the bishop being a person in special unitive relation with the churches and members of the Diocese.

A third approach relates to the practice of worship, with the Reformed tradition emphasizing the Word and the preaching of the Word on a weekly basis and seeing the significance of the celebration of Holy Communion as emphasized through less frequent celebrations, on a monthly or quarterly basis as in the Church of Scotland, while for the Orthodox, the weekly Eucharist lies at the heart of the church as is seen in Zizioulas's emphasis on the centrality of the Eucharist.[76]

The Interpretation of the Personal Nature of the Holy Spirit

Owen and Zizioulas both emphasize their interpretations of the nature of the Holy Spirit as personal and the consequences of this in terms of worship and the shaping of persons. As outlined above, each of their arguments was developed in response to particular theological challenges to a personal view of the Spirit.

Owen develops his scriptural identification of the work of the Holy Spirit, analyzing the references he sees scripture offering. However, he does this through the lens of the Trinitarian understanding of the early church rather than through a "proof-texting" approach. While his earlier writings have a more Christological focus, it is his later writings which have a more pneumatological orientation. A topic for a different book would be to compare this development in Owen with Zizioulas's critique of the Western church as being too Christological, in order to see whether Owen, centuries

75. Zizioulas, *Eucharist, Bishop, Church* (a work based on Zizioulas's PhD thesis).

76. It is interesting to note that from the Reformed tradition, Calvin lost the battle in Geneva over his advocacy of weekly communion.

before Zizioulas, is offering some counterbalance to Zizioulas's critique. A further topic would be to undertake a more direct cultural and historical analysis of Owen's and Zizioulas's settings in order to compare their ecclesial and political settings and the way these have shaped their thinking. However, this volume is focusing specifically on their theological approaches, and with particular regard to the Holy Spirit.

Zizioulas focuses on the Cappadocian Fathers and what he sees as the personal and relational Trinitarian approach developed in the early church. His more philosophical approach than that of Owen leads to a helpful analysis of Trinitarian doctrine. This philosophical approach, while being different from Owen's more strongly scriptural approach, nevertheless resonates with Owen's Trinitarian understanding. It also helps to counterbalance those aspects of Owen's scriptural interpretation which might seem to project human aspects of personhood onto the Holy Spirit, rather than an understanding of person which is tempered by its rooting in a philosophical-theological approach to the nature of the triune identity. Zizioulas, in his relational interpretation of the triune God, points to personal characteristics which arise out of the nature of God rather than those which are projected onto the nature of God from a human understanding of the person.

One area of difference of interpretation is that of will. Owen has an understanding of the Holy Spirit that reinforces the personal will of the Holy Spirit while Zizioulas moves away from the language of will as offering an approach based on a characteristic of human rather than divine identity. Zizioulas preserves more of a sense of divine mystery in relation to the Trinity while Owen, in response to his understanding of revelation, becomes more specific in his explication of the nature and activity of the Holy Spirit.

Critiques of Owen and Zizioulas

Much recent critical analysis of Trinitarian thinking has focused on the meaning and use of "person" with an extensive debate on "social Trinitarianism," which Zizioulas's understanding of the Trinity is claimed by others to be. Kilby makes one of the most radical critiques, pointing, quite rightly, to the dangers of human projection onto God of personhood. However, her conclusion does not do justice to the development of a biblical understanding or the early church's theological wrestling with the nature of the Trinity:

> The doctrine of the Trinity, I want to suggest, does not need to be seen as a descriptive, first order teaching—there is no need to assume that its main function must be to provide a picture of the divine, a deep understanding of the way God really is. It can

instead be taken as grammatical, as a second order proposition, a rule, or perhaps a set of rules, for how to read the Biblical stories, how to speak about some of the characters we come across in these stories, how to think and talk about the experience of prayer, how to deploy the "vocabulary" of Christianity in an appropriate way.[77]

However, if the doctrine of the Trinity is to become a "second order" proposition, the rich wealth of understanding about God, the three in one and one in three, as the source of creation, salvation, and sanctification, and as the focus of worship, is diminished. Owen and Zizioulas, in raising up the personal nature of the Holy Spirit and focusing on the Holy Spirit's presence in worship, go in a different, and I argue, more helpful, direction from Kilby's interpretation by offering an understanding that begins with who God is in terms of personal and relational identity, and then moves on to how people might relate to God and in that relationship and discover the fullness of human personhood.

CONCLUSIONS

Owen and Zizioulas point to worship as a specific focus for encountering the Holy Spirit. The Holy Spirit draws people into a worshipping relationship with the triune God. In worship the nature of human dependency on God is emphasized, and in this relationship of dependency, God is known. This book is exploring this one particular aspect of the nature and activity of the Holy Spirit. There are a variety of other ways in which the Holy Spirit can be encountered that might be considered, for example, in other realms of personal experience, in the councils of the church, or in the secular world. However, what Owen and Zizioulas helpfully point toward is the need for an interpretative lens in order to recognize the Holy Spirit, whether in personal experience, in councils, or in the wider world. The use of the particular interpretative lens of worship, seeing worship as holding together both the embodiment of the Holy Spirit and drawing people into an encounter with the revelation and mystery of God—an encounter in which people become persons—is a helpful contribution of Owen and Zizioulas to understanding the personal nature and activity of the Holy Spirit.

77. Kilby, "Perichoresis and Projection," 432–45.

6

The Quadrilateral, Part Two

The Holy Spirit Encountered in Worship—
Immediacy, Mediation, and Otherness

INTRODUCTION

The second part of the quadrilateral looks at an understanding of immediacy in relation to the nature and activity of the Holy Spirit, particularly
as embodied in worship.[1] After looking at the significance of personal
relationality as the first part of the quadrilateral, I move to argue that immediacy (despite the, at times, contested and paradoxical nature of this
idea) is an underlying component of personal relationship, in particular in
the context of the relationship with God between worshipper and the one
worshipped. I develop worship thesis four: "The Holy Spirit opens up an immediate encounter with God, mediated within the personal and communal
framework of worship offered in response to the triune God."[2]

---

1. The four interrelated aspects of the quadrilateral are "relational personhood," "immediacy," "truth," and "transformation." These four aspects mutually inform and influence each other, reflecting their common source in the Holy Spirit. Chapter 6 looks at
the way in which, out of the immediate relationship with God encountered in worship,
truth can be conceptualised as personal, and the implications of this for epistemology.

2. From the list of ten theses on worship in chapter 4.

The Holy Spirit is the person of the Holy Trinity who mediates God as Father and Son in the present experience of the person and the community and who, as mediator, is at the same time the immediate presence of God. The Holy Spirit works immediately in the life of a person, yet the knowledge of the Spirit cannot be contained by the limits of that immediate encounter. Immediate and mediated could be seen as mutually exclusive terms but I am referring to them as mutually supportive terms in order to expand an understanding of the nature of the encounter with God. This encounter is immediate but can be seen in the context being mediated both through the prior revelation of the triune God in the received understanding of God from a personal and a church perspective and in the elements which shape an act of worship. In both of these mediated settings, as in the immediacy of encounter, there is a paradox that at one and the same time God is both "other" and "present." In each of these settings there is a discernment which takes place about the balance between revelation from God and the human response to this revelation in terms of the human construction of the elements of worship.

This knowledge of God is not only that discerned by reason but is that which comes of being drawn into a relationship, a relationship with the one whose identity is relational, that is, God the Holy Trinity. I examine some of the parameters of this discussion, looking in particular at what has been seen as the tension between an immediate and a mediated relationship to God. Owen's and Zizioulas's thinking on immediacy is looked at through four categories: "the present moment of personal encounter," "synchronicity," "otherness," and "continuity." This includes a comparison and mutual critique of Owen and Zizioulas in order to highlight the possibilities and problems with the use of immediacy as well as to indicate the boundaries of the notion of immediacy and the way the definition which is being outlined here is held within the framework of the quadrilateral understanding of the Holy Spirit and worship.

Immediacy, Mediation, and Otherness

Immediacy has been, and remains, a contested category in philosophical and theological thinking about the knowledge of God for a range of reasons and from a variety of different directions.[3] These include the question of

3. Much has been written about the thinking of Georg Wilhelm Friedrich Hegel in terms of influencing an understanding about immediacy, particularly in the 1807 work *Phenomenology of Spirit*. In his preface, Hegel writes: "For mediation is nothing beyond self-moving selfsameness, or is reflection into self, the moment of the 'I' which

whether there can be a "natural" immediacy leading to a sense of the presence of God. The dilemma with this approach is that it could be seen to lead to a subjectivist understanding of God—God becoming a projection of human experience rather than the "other." Another issue is about the role of reason and experience in terms of immediacy; whether immediacy in the sense of an encounter with the divine goes beyond rational and experiential analysis. A further issue relates to the need for mediation when it comes to knowing God—whether it be the mediation of God as revealed in Jesus Christ the mediator, or in terms of the mediation of the scriptures or of the church, or of language or of sense perception.

---

is for itself pure negativity or, when reduced to its pure abstraction, simple becoming. The 'I' or becoming in general, this mediation, on account of its simple nature, is just immediacy in the process of becoming and is the immediate itself" (Hegel, *Phenomenology*, 11). Stephen Houlgate, in *Hegel's Phenomenology of Spirit*, looks at a range of ways in which Hegel uses immediacy, as, for example, in self-consciousness and immanence. Gunton in particular, as will be shortly seen, offers a critique of Hegel's view of immediacy. John E. Smith, philosopher of religion, critiques what he sees as Hegel's mystical understanding giving too much weight to the "self" and not enough to the "other." He draws out the balance in knowing God between rational argument and presence: "An individual related to God through the 'must be' argument taken all by itself is left with a sense of something missing. There is necessity and omnipresence, but not presence" (Smith, "In What Sense?" 236). Nicholas Lash further interprets Hegel in a way which points to an immediacy of participation in God: "That is to say: God can only be known in that eternally still movement of utterance and love which he is; known in that movement, not by constructing representations of it, whether these be pictorial, narrative or metaphysical. God is known by participating in that movement which he is" (Lash, *Beginning and the End of "Religion,"* 86). J. Brenton Stearns's "In Mediated Immediacy" looks at a range of models, including mystical and psychological, raising the question of the relation between these models and their epistemological basis as part of attempting to draw out an understanding of immediacy that could apply across different religions. Immediacy and mediation have been looked at from a liturgical perspective, as in Irwin, "Liturgy as Mediated Immediacy," 129–40. John Webster, in *Domain of the Word*, raises issues of illumination and inspiration with regard to the role of the Holy Spirit in the shaping and hearing of scripture, issues which relate to the nature of the immediacy of the activity of the Holy Spirit. Karl Rahner has been critiqued by Paul Molnar as giving a view of mediated immediacy that is too focused on natural theology, rather than on the triune God (see Molnar, "Can We Know God Directly?"). Michael Czapkay Sudduth examines Calvin and subsequent Reformed approaches to immediacy with particular regard to the possibility of "natural" immediacy within the Reformed tradition, asking the question: "More precisely, is man's natural knowledge of God mediated by reasons (other beliefs or knowledge), or is it something in some sense innate or immediate?" (Sudduth, "Prospects for 'Mediate' Natural Theology," 53). Sudduth also refers to "Plantinga's Revision," drawing attention to Plantinga, *Warranted Christian Belief*.

The argument that this chapter takes forward relates to the conceptualizing of immediacy in terms of the activity of the Holy Spirit and worship and to the balance between immediacy, mediation, and otherness. Before looking in more detail at an understanding of immediacy arising out of the writing of Owen and Zizioulas, a brief survey is given of ways in which immediacy has been interpreted.

Anatolios in *Retrieving Nicaea: The Development and Meaning of Trinitarian Doctrine* points to the writing of Athanasius on the immediate and mediating role of both the Spirit and the Son:

> The Spirit, as the actualisation of the content of divine life for us, draws us to the Son and enables us to participate in Christ: "We will become partakers of Christ if we hold fast to the Spirit."[4] Reciprocally, the incarnate Word enables us to receive the Spirit through his own reception of the Spirit in his humanity. . . . Athanasius's positive interpretation of the Trinitarian dynamics of Christian life is that this structure identifies the immediacy of our involvement in the fullness of divine life. If the scriptural narrative represents the Son and Spirit as mediators of divine life, they must both be in full possession of that life in order for their agency to effect the mediation of divine immediacy rather than its mere negation.[5]

The paradoxical nature of the "mediation of divine immediacy" will be explored through the writings of Owen and Zizioulas. This phrase points to the way in which immediacy is rooted in the divine life rather than being solely a subjective human experience. At the same time, immediacy occurs through the mediation of both the Son and the Spirit.

In his history of seventeenth-century England, Nuttall in *Studies in Christian Enthusiasm; Illustrated from early Quakerism* comments on the issues about a possession of the Spirit, which attempted to create a *tabula rasa* in the human mind and experience and led to extraordinary enthusiasm without a moral compass. Nuttall points to the need to hold together the immediate presence of God's Spirit within a mediated framework that is realistic about human limitations:

> The spiritual experience which is behind the abnormalities is the greater thing, and this remains as something we should admire and seek to share. We are still called to the experience of knowing the Spirit of God's presence to guide, bless and sustain,

---

4. Athanasius, *Festal Letter* 3.4. For other instances of the theme of partaking Christ, see 2.5; 5.5.

5. Anatolios, *Retrieving Nicaea*, 148.

turning evil into good, creatively altering situations and making possible for us what would otherwise have been impossible.
Our task is to prove the reality of this experience while fully
acknowledging the conditions, limitations and uncertainties of
our common humanity.[6]

While there is an emphasis on the mediation provided by human experience, it is in the context of acknowledging the immediacy of the Holy Spirit
at work in that experience.

Watkin-Jones, in *The Holy Spirit from Arminius to Wesley*, looks at the
Protestant experience of "assurance" in Owen, Baxter, and Wesley, seeing
this as the immediate work of the Spirit. He quotes John Wesley:

I observed many years ago . . . "by the testimony of the Spirit
I mean an inward impression on the soul, whereby the Spirit
of God immediately and directly witnesses to my spirit that I
am a child of God; that Jesus Christ hath loved me, and given
Himself for me; that all my sins are blotted out, and I, even I, am
reconciled to God." After twenty years' further consideration, I
see no cause to retrace any part of this.[7]

Watkin-Jones also identifies the following three issues: (i) the debate as to
whether this assurance was only available for the elect (as he argues from
Calvin), (ii) the relationship between assurance and a good conscience (here
he points to Donne), and (iii) the greater sense of immediacy in Baxter in
terms of the direct testimony of the Spirit.

Gunton, in *A Brief Theology of Revelation*, opens his book with a section on "The Problems of Immediacy." He writes:

Since Hegel's time, theology has been dominated by quests for
different forms of immediacy, and that, I believe, is one root of
our modern discomfort with questions of a revealed religion.
The [biblical] notion of a revealed religion . . . has been replaced
by different forms of immediacy. These can take forms that either dispense with revelation or appear to have little constitutive

6. Nuttall, *Studies in Christian Enthusiasm*, 88. It is also interesting to note Nuttall's
introductory comment on the need for a renewed emphasis on the Holy Spirit: "The
direction fashionable in much contemporary religious thinking is, in fact, away from
first-hand experience to the acceptance of dogma and tradition on the authority of
the Church. . . . I believe that a recovery of personal religious experience as the center
of our faith is the main thing needed at present in our Christian life; and that a fresh
recognition of the doctrine of the Holy Spirit, as central in our religious thinking, is
the main thing needed at present in our theology" (13).

7. Watkin-Jones, *Holy Spirit from Arminius to Wesley*, 303.

role for it, as in Schleiermacher. But there is also a seeking of what can only be called a revelatory immediacy, a direct apprehension of the content of the faith that will in some way or other serve to identify it beyond question.[8]

Chung, in *Thomas Torrance's Mediations and Revelation*, takes the argument forward. As well as referring to the varied forms which immediacy might take, he raises the issue at this point as to whether biblical criticism leads to another kind of focus on immediacy, revisiting what the scripture is perceived to be saying and reinterpreting this for a contemporary context: "If Gunton's account is acceptable, the nineteenth-century quest of biblical criticism could be read as a form of immediacy as the movement seeks to attain the direct knowing of God independent of tradition."[9]

John Baillie and Karl Barth both bring insights to the specific area of the relation between immediacy and mediation. Baillie's extensive argument about mediated immediacy has been re-examined in Trig Johnson's recent PhD thesis.[10] Baillie, in *Our Knowledge of God*, writes about the "'here and nowness' of revelation." He argues for the knowledge of God being set in the context of the wider tradition of the faith and being such that that which was known of God in the past, for example through the prophets, is also known of God today.[11] Baillie concludes:

> We have to face the fact that we have here to do with an experience of an entirely unique kind, its uniqueness lying precisely in this conjunction of immediacy with mediacy—that is, in the

8. Gunton, *Brief Theology of Revelation*, 1–7.

9. Chung, *Thomas Torrance's Mediations*, xiv.

10. Johnson, "John Baillie's Epistemology." In this thesis, Johnson gives a helpful analysis of the way in which the thinking with regard to mediated immediacy has gone into abeyance since Baillie's original writing and the need for the recovery of Baillie's thinking. Johnson, interestingly—for the purpose of my book—writes in his introduction that "this thesis demonstrates that Baillie's later mediating theology (post-1939) provides a stronger doctrine of the Holy Spirit than that found in Baillie's earlier critical thought" (iv).

11. Baillie, *Our Knowledge of God*. Baillie quotes a rhetorical argument from Rousseau, referred to in a letter to M. de Beaumont, "Is it simple, is it natural, that God should have gone and found Moses in order to speak to Jean Jacques Rousseau?" Baillie goes on to argue: "No it is far from simple, but what right have we to assume that truth is simple? And as to whether it is natural, have we any knowledge of what would be natural in such a region of experience apart from the witness of the experience itself? We have to take experience as we find it—though that apparently was what Rousseau was refusing to do" (185).

fact that God reveals Himself to me only through others who
went before, yet in so doing reveals Himself to me now.[12]

This conjunction of immediacy and mediacy is through the holding together of the experience of those who have gone before as it connects with the
experience of those in the present. Baillie offers a further dimension of the
understanding of immediacy and mediation, which I am arguing is the particular role of the Holy Spirit. There is a continuity with those in whom the
Holy Spirit has been present over the generations. Yet the encounter with
the Holy Spirit in the present goes beyond remembering what has happened
in the past to a moment of unique encounter in the here and now. (Zizioulas, as will be referred to shortly, draws attention to the way in which, in his
eschatological understanding of the Spirit's role, there is a sense in which
the Spirit also draws people from the future to the future.) The mediation
is that of the Spirit, past, present, and future; the Spirit who is encountered
through the mediation of the past, but immediately in the present moment.

Barth comments on immediate and mediated as he develops his understanding of the work and nature of the Holy Spirit in *Church Dogmatics*
in light of the priority which he places on revelation and the revealed Word
of God as the starting point for theology. Barth points to the range of meaning of immediate and mediated, as well as the boundaries of this range:

> According to the Holy Scripture of the Old Testament and New
> Testament, God's revelation always comes to man both imme-
> diately and mediately. Immediately, for whatever mediators or
> media God makes use of, in order to speak to man and to act on
> him, He always remains Himself the subject of this speaking and
> acting. Immediately, for the fact that He does make use of par-
> ticular mediators and media never means a withdrawal by God
> Himself, or a transfer of His properties and activities to the crea-
> tures concerned. But God's revelation comes mediately to man
> in that it actually never does come without creaturely mediators
> or media and it always occurs in a creaturely area and frame-
> work which is fixed in outline and unvarying in appearance.[13]

In these finely balanced few sentences, Barth conveys both the distinctiveness and congruity of immediacy and mediation. While Barth sets his argument in the larger setting of the priority of God's revelation, his emphasis
on God remaining the subject of God's speaking and acting is one which
is developed here in terms of this being the work of the Holy Spirit in the

---

12. Baillie, *Our Knowledge of God*, 185.
13. Barth, *Church Dogmatics*, 1:16.

particularity of worship. However, Barth's emphasis on a framework which is fixed in outline and unvarying in appearance does not entirely do justice to the openness of the Holy Spirit to being present in a range of ways and places, and the variety of the creaturely framework.

Irwin gives a specific focus on the mediated setting of immediacy in the context of worship.[14] He draws out the multivalent nature of the language of the liturgy alongside the centrality of the incorporation into God in the liturgy and how at the end of time there will only be immediacy in God's presence.[15] However, he concludes with a reference to the contrast between the end of all things and the present moment in terms of mediated immediacy:

> Sacraments will and should cease. And then we will meet the Lord face to face. No more mediated immediacy, just immediacy unveiled, unfettered, unencumbered. But in the meantime the tenet of *sacramentality* and the premise of *mediated immediacy* matter a great deal indeed.[16]

Irwin's sacramental perspective will be picked up further in looking at the writing of Zizioulas.

After this brief introduction to issues around immediacy and mediation, I move to look at the writings of Owen and Zizioulas in order to look more deeply into their understanding of immediacy and mediation. I develop the argument through a further examination of the writings of Owen and Zizioulas in order to build on what they write about the nature of

---

14. Irwin, "Liturgy as Mediated Immediacy," 129–40.

15. Irwin writes: "Liturgical language is decidedly and purposefully multivalent. Liturgical terms convey pluriform (many) meanings. Sometimes those meanings are ambiguous. . . . Liturgy and sacraments are like jewels that should be viewed from many and different perspectives and in many and different lights. . . . But I want to argue that something much more important theologically is going on here. The prayers of the Roman liturgy *never* describe who God is without describing how *we are incorporated* into God through the liturgy. I say to my students always check the pronouns and then the verbs. 'Dying you destroyed *our* death, rising you destroyed *our* life.' The memorial acclamations underscore how we are incorporated into the mysteries we are celebrating. They do not describe them as though we were looking at them from afar. The same is true for all the presidential prayers of the Missal. They never describe God or what God has done for us without inviting God to act again among us in the here and now. . . . Liturgy is multi-valent; liturgy recurs. Liturgy matters a great deal. But what is also true is that the goal of the liturgy is that we will not need it anymore. The goal is found in the hymn text 'O Lord at length when sacraments shall cease'" (Irwin, "Liturgy as Mediated Immediacy," 10, 11, 16, 18).

16. Irwin, "Liturgy as Mediated Immediacy," 18.

immediacy, and to highlight issues about the relationship between immediate and mediated encounters with God.

OWEN AND ZIZIOULAS ON
IMMEDIACY AND MEDIATION

Both Owen and Zizioulas write about the immediacy of a relational encounter with the one triune God. Owen writes against a backdrop of English epistemological ferment about the nature of God as trinitarian and the way in which God is known; Zizioulas highlights the significance of relationality in developing a trinitarian understanding of God. The writings of Owen on the Holy Spirit and the significant role he gives to the immediacy of the Holy Spirit in worship are examined, followed by Zizioulas's writing about the Eucharist as the moment of encounter with God. With Owen and Zizioulas, building on the arguments from both the third and fourth centuries of the early church and the seventeenth century in England, I argue against the Holy Spirit as being defined as "the spirit within" or as an "impersonal power" in order to retain an understanding of both the otherness and the personal nature of the Holy Spirit in the life of the one triune God.

Both Owen and Zizioulas develop theological understandings which locate reason's primary role in the development of doctrine, the tradition of the church, and the offering of worship, rather than seeing it as an independent criterion for developing knowledge of God. (This is in contrast, for example, with the attitudes to reason and self-consciousness that would be espoused by Owen's pupil at Oxford, John Locke, and his successors, as outlined in Charles Taylor's *The Sources of the Self* and *A Secular Age*.)[17] I focus on Owen's and Zizioulas's interpretations of immediacy in the context of their accounts of the Holy Spirit in worship in order to redress the balance of what might appear as a more traditional focus on the role of mediation (as for example alluded to by Gunton in *A Brief Theology of Revelation*) whether that mediation be centrally that of Jesus Christ in the setting of scripture, through nature, or particularly through an embodied experience of worship.[18]

17. Taylor, *Sources of the Self*.
18. Gunton, *Brief Theology of Revelation*.

OWEN: IMMEDIACY, MEDIATION, AND OTHERNESS

Introduction

Philip Dixon, in his evocatively titled *Nice and Hot Disputes: The Doctrine of the Trinity in the Seventeenth Century,* introduces his book by writing, "Something happened to the doctrine of the Trinity in the seventeenth century: it ceased being a mystery of faith and became a problem in theology."[19] I argue that this diminishment of the relationship between Trinitarian understanding and Christian practice led to a reduced awareness of the presence of God in worship and a consequent separation between an understanding of that which is mediated and that which is immediate. Dixon argues for the significance of the seventeenth century in the change of the interpretation of the Trinity: "this is not simply *a* key time in the history of Trinitarian doctrine, it is *the* key time as far as the loss of Trinitarian vitality is concerned."[20] He points in particular to the role of Pneumatology in the reduction of the understanding of the Trinity, referring to a fading of the "trinitarian imagination" across the seventeenth century and comments: "Nourishing this loss of imagination was a deep distrust of what we might label 'practical pneumatology'"[21] Not only was the Trinity neglected, but also the doctrine of the Holy Spirit, partly because of the restricted manner in which the Trinity was being thought about and partly through a mistrust of "enthusiastical" approaches, such as were seen in some of the smaller sects in the time of the Commonwealth."[22]

The argument in this book focuses on Owen's holding together of an understanding of the Holy Spirit with an understanding of the practice of worship. The significance of Owen is seen in the way in which, out of his thinking about personal relationality within the Trinity, he sees the immediacy of the Holy Spirit as reflecting the way in which the human person is drawn into the presence of the triune God. This "being drawn" as seen in Owen's understanding of immediacy is, I argue, one part of what Owen offers to bridge the gap between doctrine and worship. Kapic writes: "As we shall see throughout our study, Owen constantly moves from his received theology to experience, then back to theological reflection."[23] Owen continues the tradition, following on from the early Fathers and the Reformers, of those who hold closely together

19. Dixon, *Nice and Hot Disputes*, 1.

20. Dixon, *Nice and Hot Disputes*, 208.

21. Dixon, *Nice and Hot Disputes*, 213.

22. As, for example, referred to above in Nuttall, *Studies in Christian Enthusiasm*.

23. Kapic, *Communion with God*, 22.

theology and reflective practice. Owen's personal understanding of the nature of the Holy Spirit had a correlate in the way he understood the significance of the activity of the Holy Spirit in human experience.

Owen's Understanding of Immediacy in Relation to the Holy Spirit

The significance of immediacy for Owen is highlighted by the extensive use he makes of this word when referring to the Holy Spirit across the range of his writings. Owen refers to the particular work of the Spirit, the "immediate and especial work of the Spirit of God,"[24] "*the immediate revelation* of the Spirit,"[25] the way in which the Spirit is the person of the Trinity who acts in relation to God's "external" works ("for he being the immediate operator of all divine works that outwardly are of God, and they being in themselves all holy, be they of what kind soever, he is called the 'Holy Spirit'"),[26] and the hiddenness of this immediate action of the Spirit ("the immediate actings of the Spirit are the most hidden, curious, and mysterious, as those which contain the perfecting part of the works of God").[27] Owen looks in detail at Old Testament references and compares the coming of the Spirit with God breathing the breath of life into humankind. "So also in the great work of the infusion of the reasonable soul into the body of man, it is said, God 'breathed into his nostrils the breath of life,' Gen 2:7. From hence, I say, it is—namely, from the nature and name of the Holy Spirit—that his immediate actings on the minds of men, in the supernatural communication of divine revelations unto them, is called 'inspiration' or inbreathing."[28] Amongst various examples of what Owen identifies as the work of the Spirit in the Old Testament, he refers to prophecies, dreams, and visions, referring to the way in which these were not as manifest in the New Testament as the Old Testament.[29] The New Testament context places a greater emphasis

24. Owen, *Works*, 3:32.

25. Owen, *Works*, 3:36.

26. Owen, *Works*, 3:57.

27. Owen, *Works*, 3:87.

28. Owen, *Works*, 3:111.

29. "*Dreams* were made use of under the Old Testament to the same purpose, and unto them also I refer all those *visions* which they had in their *sleep*, though not called dreams; and these, in this case, were the immediate operation of the Holy Ghost, as to the divine and infallible impressions they conveyed to the minds of men. Hence, in the promise of the plentiful pouring out of the Spirit, or communication of his gifts, mention is made of dreams: Acts 2:17, 'I will pour out of my Spirit upon all flesh: and your sons and your daughters shall prophesy, and your young men shall see visions, and your old men shall dream dreams.' Not that God intended much to make use of

on the Spirit being given to the whole community of the body of Christ, while the Old Testament focuses more on individual kings and prophets. Owen makes an interesting reference to the work of the Holy Spirit across the political and moral spectrum in the Old Testament: "the next sort of the operations of the Holy Ghost under the Old Testament, whose explanation was designed, is of those whereby he improved, through immediate impressions of his own power, the *natural faculties* and abilities of the minds of men; and these, as was intimated, have respect to things *political, moral, natural*, and *intellectual*."[30]

In chapter 2 of Owen's *Pneumatologia*, "General dispensation of the Holy Spirit with respect unto the new Creation," he summarizes the connection between the personal nature of the Trinity, immediacy, and the link between doctrine and experience that forms the basis of his argument.

> There was no one more glorious mystery brought to light in and by Jesus Christ than that of the holy Trinity, or the subsistence of the three persons in the unity of the same divine nature. And this was done not so much in express propositions or verbal testimonies unto that purpose,—which yet is done also, as by the declaration of the mutual, divine, internal acts of the persons towards one another, and the distinct, immediate, divine, external actings of each person in the work which they did and do perform,—for God revealeth not himself unto us merely doctrinally and dogmatically, but by the declaration of what he doth for us, in us, and towards us, in the accomplishment of "the counsel of his own will"; see Eph 1:4–12. And this revelation is made unto us, not that our minds might be possessed with the notions of it, but that we may know aright how to place our trust in him, how to obey him and live unto him, how to obtain and exercise communion with him, until we come to the enjoyment of him.[31]

I draw out five threads from the range of interpretations of immediacy which Owen makes in order to look at what Owen offers in terms of his understanding of immediacy and some of the pros and cons of the argument: immediacy as the presence of God, immediacy and synchronicity, immediacy and otherness, immediacy and continuity, and immediacy and transformation.

---

this way of dreams and nocturnal visions under the New Testament; but the intention of the words is, to show that there should be a plentiful effusion of that Spirit which acted by these various ways and means then under the Old" (Owen, *Works*, 3:115–16).

30. Owen, *Works*, 3:130.

31. Owen, *Works*, 3:139.

Immediacy as the Presence of God.

Owen argues that it is specifically the work of the Holy Spirit which effects the encounter with God. It is not that the Holy Spirit acts in separation from the other persons of the Trinity, it is that the reference to the person of the Holy Spirit describes God's interaction with the human condition.

> The Holy Ghost . . . is the *immediate, peculiar, efficient cause* of all external divine operations: for God worketh by his Spirit, or in him immediately applies the power and efficacy of the divine excellencies unto their operation; whence the same work is equally the work of each person.[32]

The use of the Aristotelian term "efficient cause" reflects an aspect of Owen's background and influence, that of Scholasticism. These words need to be held alongside other more poetic language in order to reflect the full flavor of Owen's thinking as, for example, in his extensive image of God working in trees and plants, where he emphasizes the need for watering but also that the growth is "*secret* and *imperceptible*."[33] Owen is arguing that it is through the power of the Holy Spirit that God is encountered and therefore known.[34] This power is evidenced through the effect of personal relationality rather than a mechanistic approach such as that of a worker using her tools on an inanimate object. Owen sees human experience as significant but puts this experience as a response to the priority of the Holy Spirit. Human response and human transformation follow on from the prior encounter with God, not only through scripture and tradition, but in the immediacy of present experience of the Holy Spirit.

Immediacy and Synchronicity

One of the dilemmas with the term "immediacy" is that it could be seen so to emphasize the work of the Spirit that there is no room left for a free

---

32. Owen, *Works*, 3:162. Owen continues: "Whereas, therefore, they are the effects of divine power, and that power is essentially the same in each person, the works themselves belong equally unto them: as, if it were possible that three men might see by the same eye, the act of seeing would be but one, and it would be equally the act of all three. But the things we insist on are ascribed eminently unto the Holy Ghost, on the account of the order of his subsistence in the holy Trinity, as he is the Spirit of the Father and the Son; whence, in every divine act, the authority of the Father, the love and wisdom of the Son, with the immediate efficacy and power of the Holy Ghost, are to be considered."

33. Owen, *Works*, 3:396.

34. See chapter 7 for a fuller explication of "knowing God."

human response. The Spirit becomes so powerful that human identity and personhood are reduced to very little. On the other hand, as Owen argued against the enthusiasts, human identity could become so much to the fore that the role of the Spirit is taken out of the equation.[35] Owen identifies the issue as follows:

> But it will be said, "That if not only the *beginning* of grace, sanctification, and holiness be from God, but the *carrying of it on* and the *increase* of it also be from him, and not only so in general, but if all the *actings of grace*, and every act of it, be an immediate effect of the Holy Spirit, then what need is there that we should take any pains in this thing ourselves, or use our own endeavours to grow in grace or holiness, as we are commanded? If God *work all himself in us*, and if without his effectual operation in us *we can do nothing*, there is no place left for our *diligence, duty, or obedience.*" *Ans.* 1. This objection we must expect to meet withal at every turn. Men will not believe there is a consistency between *God's effectual grace* and our *diligent obedience*.[36]

This "consistency" between God's grace and human obedience lies at the heart of Owen's argument about the nature of the relationship between the Holy Spirit and the human person. It is this "consistency" that I am interpreting as synchronicity—the working together of God and the person.

Owen continues with his extended example from plants and trees and their need for watering in order to illustrate the need for both the work of the Holy Spirit and the diligence of the human person in order for human flourishing, by God's grace, to happen. Owen is responding to the argument that in his emphasis on the immediate encounter with the Holy Spirit, the Spirit is so overwhelmingly present that a person has her freedom taken away from her. Rather, there is a moment of synchronicity in which the Spirit and the person are acting in mutual response:

---

35. Owen did not support the "enthusiastical" approach towards the Holy Spirit of some of the writers of his day and indeed was critical of these. He argued for an understanding of the Holy Spirit that was immediate in personal experience, in the setting of worship. Owen's emphasis on an immediate union with God brought him under the accusation of being "enthusiastical," and led to a heated exchange with William Sherlock (see Sherlock, "Discourse," 320–25; Owen, *Works* 2:222–366). Lim comments: "The charge of enthusiasm became a popular anti-Puritan/Dissent invective, used with great effect by the Restoration churchmen" (*Mystery Unveiled*, 199). But Owen himself was more cautious about using this term, and critical of those whose "enthusiastical" approach distanced themselves from the triune God.

36. Owen, *Works*, 3:328, 394.

> He doth not, in our regeneration, possess the mind with any enthusiastical impressions, nor act absolutely upon us as he did in extraordinary prophetical inspirations of old, where the minds and organs of the bodies of men were merely passive instruments, moved by him above their own natural capacity and activity, not only as to the principle of working, but as to the manner of operation; but he works on the minds of men in and by their own natural actings, through an immediate influence and impression of his power: "Create in me a clean heart, O God." He "worketh both to will and to do."[37]

Human freedom is found as the human spirit is open to the divine Spirit, an action that is brought about by the initiative of the Holy Spirit yet responded to by the human spirit.

Immediacy and Otherness

There is a dilemma in thinking about the immediacy of the Holy Spirit in that this immediacy could imply that the fullness of God is wholly present in the immediate moment. But so to imply would limit who God is. Owen holds a balance between the possibility of the encounter with the divine and the mystery of God. He begins in his preface to *Pneumatologia* by setting his writing about the Holy Spirit in the context of the mystery of God:

> Now, all the concernments of the Holy Spirit are an eminent part of the "mystery" or "deep things of God"; for as the knowledge of them doth wholly depend on and is regulated by divine revelation, so are they in their own nature divine and heavenly,—distant and remote from all things that the heart of man, in the mere exercise of its own reason or understanding, can rise up unto.[38]

In Owen's writings, at the moment of immediacy there is a resonance of the apophatic tradition in which the encounter with God is with the one who is unknown, in terms of being beyond human comprehension. The knowledge of God that comes in this moment is not confined to the knowledge of rational understanding but points to the knowledge of personal encounter between the human spirit and the Holy Spirit. Owen's starting point in referring to the mystery of the Holy Spirit leads to many more specific references to immediacy, which are held in the context of mystery.

---

37. Owen, *Works*, 3:268, 319.
38. Owen, *Works*, 3:6.

Immediacy and Continuity

One of the issues with regard to immediacy is that it could appear that the moments of immediacy occur at isolated points and are disconnected from each other. However, for Owen, there is an ongoing process of sanctification. The immediacy of the encounter with God through the Holy Spirit is not just a matter of disconnected moments which happen randomly. The immediate moments of encounter with the holy undergird the growth of the Christian life in holiness. Owen outlines his argument in book 4, chapter 2 of *Pneumatologia*:

> Sanctification is an immediate work of the Spirit of God on the souls of believers, purifying and cleansing of their natures from the pollution and uncleanness of sin, renewing in them the image of God, and thereby enabling them, from a spiritual and habitual principle of grace, to yield obedience unto God, according unto the tenor and terms of the new covenant, by virtue of the life and death of Jesus Christ. Or more briefly: It is the universal renovation of our natures by the Holy Spirit into the image of God, through Jesus Christ.[39]

Owen continues: "But this work of sanctification is *progressive*, and admits of degrees. . . . It is begun at once, and carried on gradually."[40] Owen sees the immediate work of sanctification as ongoing through a person's life, given continuity through the one and the same Holy Spirit at work in the growth of holiness. This work of sanctification is more than an isolated matter of personal self-improvement by each one on his or her own. It takes place through a participation in worship, the point of encounter with God. In worship, in the reading of scripture and the preaching of the Word, the same Word which has been heard and proclaimed over the centuries is opened up for the renewal of God's people.

Immediacy as the Moment of Transformation

Owen makes a further argument with regard to immediacy: that the immediate encounter with the Holy Spirit is an encounter which leads to transformation. Human nature is taken out of separation from God and alienation from the sources of life and restored into a relationship of love and mercy, into the likeness of Christ:

39. Owen, *Works*, 3:316.
40. Owen, *Works*, 3:317.

> There is not any spiritual or *saving good* from first to last com-
> municated unto us, or that we are from and by the grace of God
> made partakers of, but it is revealed to us and bestowed on us
> by the Holy Ghost. He who hath not an immediate and especial
> work of the Spirit of God upon him and towards him did never
> receive any especial love, grace, or mercy, from God. For how
> should he do so? Whatever God works in us and upon us, he
> doth it by his Spirit; he, therefore, who hath no work of the Spirit
> of God upon his heart did never receive either mercy or grace
> from God, for God giveth them not but by his Spirit.[41]

It is this transformation which leads to a renewed ethical life because it
contains within it both the knowledge of moral living and the capacity to
live with generosity as the recipient of God's grace. Owen sees the spiritual
renewal of the person as prior to the moral renewal and yet leading to appropriate ethical activity.

Conclusion

Owen's emphasis on immediacy focuses on the role of the Holy Spirit. Setting the context for the Spirit's activity in worship gives the setting for both
the immediacy of the encounter with God and the mediated nature of this
encounter. Owen addresses issues which have their origins in third- and
fourth-century discussions of the Holy Spirit, but which can also speak in
a twenty-first-century setting. For Owen, the Holy Spirit is not an anony-
mous "universal spirit" discovered in abstraction but has a specific identity
within the triune God. This identity is particularly encountered in present
moments of worship holding together scripture, tradition, and experience.
Owen seeks to draw together doctrine and worship, with doctrine not being purely an argued, rational response, but something located in the mix
of worship and reason. In worship, the Spirit engages the mind, but goes
beyond the mind to engage the emotions and the soul.

One key interpreter of Owen, Kapic, has highlighted Owen's understanding of the Holy Spirit and the significance of both immediacy and mediation. Kapic draws out the following distinction in Owen's understanding
of that which is immediate and that which is mediated:

> Immediately signifies times when the Spirit himself comes with
> intensity, "without the consideration of any other acts or works
> of his, or the interposition of any reasonings, or deductions and

---

41. Owen, *Works*, 3:32.

conclusions."[42] These experiences, which usually arise unex-
pectedly and overwhelmingly, give renewed consideration to
the love of God. On the other hand, the Spirit also works mediately, bringing a fresh sense of God's love through a renewed
consideration of the believer's acceptance as a child of God.
Even so, rational consideration of the promises of God apart
from the Spirit's movement will fail to affect the heart, thus leaving it without joy and peace. Whether immediately or mediately,
the action of the Spirit is the pivotal issue.[43]

However, there is a dilemma with this interpretation and its focus on intensity (a word which Owen does not use, and which was only coined in
the mid seventeenth century) in that it could be seen to reduce the idea of
immediacy to one particular kind of human experience. I argue that Owen
takes a holistic approach, which engages the body, mind, and spirit in a
broad spectrum of ways involving various degrees of what can be referred
to as "intensity."

Owen's thinking about the immediacy of the Holy Spirit is held within
the mediation of all that worship involves—the present moment of personal
relationality, the synchronicity of Spirit and person working together, the
reminder of the "otherness" of God, and the continuity with the history of
faith. Owen holds together the understanding of the triune God in doctrinal
terms with the significance of worship as a primary point of encounter with
the Holy Spirit. I argue that Owen's understanding in the contested area of
immediacy is a positive contribution to any discussion about the relation of
doctrine to encounter with God.

ZIZIOULAS: IMMEDIACY, MEDIATION, AND OTHERNESS

Introduction

The argument I am drawing out of Zizioulas in terms of immediacy arises
out of two aspects of his thinking. The first is about personal relationality
and the immediacy of encounter that personal relationality implies. The
second relates to worship and the presence of God in the Eucharist. In these
two settings, immediacy points both to moments of encounter with God
and also to the way these moments of encounter are mediated by the Spirit

42. Owen, *Works*, 2:252.
43. Kapic, *Communion with God,* 203.

and by the setting of the Eucharist. While the word "immediacy" does not have the frequency of usage in Zizioulas's writings that it does in Owen's, the implication of immediacy is nonetheless present in Zizioulas's thinking and writing. There is one particular passage in Zizioulas's writings where he focuses on immediacy and that is to refer to the divine action in ordination. After a reference to this usage, five points will be drawn out of Zizioulas's thinking in order to refer to the parameters of his thinking as it relates to immediacy: (i) the Eucharist as the central focus of the encounter with God, (ii) immediacy and human freedom (in a comparison with Owen on synchronicity), (iii) immediacy and otherness, (iv) the relation between immediacy and continuity, and (v) immediacy and transformation.

The Immediacy of Divine Action in Ordination

Zizioulas looks at a specific area related to ministry to speak of immediacy and that is the issue of ordination and the divine immediacy in ordination. Zizioulas sees ordination as not only the setting aside of people for specific ministries but the setting apart of the whole people of God.[44] This theological argument with regard to ministry and communion is grounded in three ways: it moves from the priority of Christ in any account of Christian ministry to the way Christology is shaped pneumatologically and finally to the way in which the Spirit is constitutive of the relation between Christ and ministry:

a. There is no ministry in the church other than Christ's ministry.[45]

b. The identification of the church's ministry with that of Christ is possible only if we let our *Christology* be *conditioned pneumatologically.*[46]

c. But by establishing this approach to the relation between the ministry of Christ and that of the church we have done something fundamental to our Pneumatological understanding of ministry: instead of *first* establishing in our minds the scheme "Christ-ministry" and *then* trying to fill this with the work of the Holy Spirit, we have made the Spirit *constitutive of the very relation between Christ and the ministry.*[47]

---

44. A detailed analysis of Zizioulas's views on the nature of ministry and of ordination is a subject for a different book. At this point I am referring to the specific point Zizioulas makes with regard to ordination and immediacy.

45. Zizioulas, *Being as Communion*, 210.

46. Zizioulas, *Being as Communion*, 210.

47. Zizioulas, *Being as Communion*, 212.

He identifies ordination as applying to the whole people of God, through baptism and confirmation.[48] He analyzes the action of ordination as being attributed to God, through prayer.[49] He concludes by summarizing his argument: "This immediacy of divine action in ordination is what safeguards the charismatic nature of the ministry. The same immediacy expresses also the identification of the Church's ministry with that of Christ."[50]

As the church's ministry is a participation in the ministry of Christ, so it is the whole church which participates in this ministry and from which specific ministries emerge.[51] Volf comments on this passage from Zizioulas: "The charismatic character of the office can be secured only by the immediacy of God's actions within the Eucharistic gathering as a pneumatic eschatological event."[52] This example from one very specific area of Zizioulas's thinking with regard to the church's life illustrates the holding together of the immediacy of divine action within the mediation of the work of the Holy Spirit and the worship of the church.

The Eucharist as the Central Focus For the Presence of God

The discussion about ordination and immediacy leads on to the essence of worship for Zizioulas, that is, the Eucharist. It is in the Eucharist that the presence of God is both encountered and embodied. It is this encounter, which takes place in the present moment of the offering of the Eucharist, that I am describing as "immediate." Zizioulas, in building on his understanding of the writing of Basil of Caesarea, highlights the holding together of the revelation of God in the liturgy with the relationality into which

48. "In the first place, it must be stated emphatically, that there is no such a thing as 'non-ordained' persons in the Church. Baptism and especially confirmation (or chrismation) as an inseparable aspect of the mystery of Christian initiation involves a 'laying on of hands.' . . . The East has kept these two aspects (baptism-confirmation) not only inseparably linked with one another but also with what follows, namely the Eucharist" (Zizioulas, *Being as Communion*, 215).

49. "The meaning of all this is that ordination depends essentially on prayer and not simply on an objective transmission of grace. This is to be conceived not in the usual understanding of prayer as assisting us in something we do, but as attributing the very action to God Himself" (Zizioulas, *Being as Communion*, 218).

50. Zizioulas, *Being as Communion*, 219.

51. While Zizioulas in his writing as a whole gives particular weight to the role of the bishop in the church (see, for example, *Eucharist, Bishop, Church*), this aspect of Zizioulas's thinking requires a separate piece of research to that being developed here on immediacy.

52. Volf, *After Our Likeness*, 121.

people are drawn: "The existence of God is revealed to us in the Liturgy as an event of communion."[53] This focus on communion is an ontological category, which is embodied in the Eucharist and draws its meaning from the activity of the Holy Spirit:

> Ecclesiology in the Orthodox tradition has always been deter-mined by the liturgy, the Eucharist; and for this reason, it is the first two aspects of Pneumatology, namely eschatology and communion, that have determined Orthodox ecclesiology. Both eschatology and communion constitute fundamental elements of the Orthodox understanding of the Eucharist. The fact that these two things are also fundamental aspects of Pneumatol-ogy shows that if we want to understand Orthodox ecclesiology properly, and its relation to Pneumatology, it is mainly to these two aspects of Pneumatology that we must turn, namely to es-chatology and communion.[54]

For Zizioulas, worship, as seen in the Eucharist, is the moment of coming to know God. This knowledge of God is not primarily focused in understand-ing but in relationship that is personal, both in terms of the communion of the persons of the Trinity and also in terms of the communion into which the human person is drawn, thus becoming fully who he or she is meant to be, a person in relationship—with God and with other people. Communion and personhood are key ontological categories for Zizioulas.[55] They arise

53. Zizioulas, *Communion and Otherness*, 189.

54. Zizioulas, *Communion and Otherness*, 131.

55. In view of the significance of ontology in Zizioulas's thinking and the ongo-ing debate about his relationship to existentialism, it is worth noting his reference to his own understanding of the term (in chapter 2). Zizioulas writes of ontology as "a word to which various meanings have been given, while for some people it indicates almost nothing at all. In this chapter, we take it to mean the area of philosophy (and theology) in which the question of *being* is raised more or less in the sense in which it was posed for the first time by ancient Greek philosophy, applied here to the specific problem of personal identity. It is all too often assumed that people 'have' personhood rather than 'being' persons, precisely because ontology is not operative enough in our thinking." In his footnote at this point he adds, "This was more or less the sense in which the term *ontology* was employed for the first time in the seventeenth century by authors such as R. Goclenius (*Lexicon Philosophicum* [1613]) and, more explicitly, J. Glauberg (*Metaphysica de Ente* [1656]), who defines it as the part of philosophy which speculates on being *qua* being. The same definition is recovered and employed without change by Ch. Wolff (*Philosophia prima sive ontologia* [1729], esp. paras 1 and 2) who is responsible for the establishment of this term in philosophy. Kant, in his *Critique of Pure Reason* (esp C. III) tried to give the term a different meaning, which however has not prevailed. Heidegger and the modern existentialist philosophers have also em-ployed it with a different meaning in the their attempt to take a critical view of classical

out of his thinking about the Holy Spirit and his understanding that it is the Holy Spirit who constitutes the church in the liturgy.

Zizioulas points to the way in which the Eucharist holds together institutional and charismatic approaches:

> The Eucharist was not the act of a pre-existing Church; it was an event constitutive of the being of the Church, enabling the Church to be. The Eucharist constituted the Church's being. Consequently, the Eucharist had the unique privilege of reuniting in one whole, in one unique experience, the work of Christ and that of the Holy Spirit. It expressed the eschatological vision through historical realities by combining in the ecclesial life the institutional with the charismatic elements.[56]

Zizioulas has been critical of the Western church as being too Christological leading to an over-emphasis on the church as institution rather than the church as Spirit-filled body. He sees an over-emphasis on Christology as leading to too strong an understanding of a church that is rooted in the past revelation of Christ in history. If there is an imbalance between Christology and Pneumatology, the identity of the church can get caught up with a focus on its historical institutional nature rather than be open to the future that is the Spirit's gift. With overtones of the way that seventeenth-century English arguments about the Trinity became a source of debate rather than a lived reality—as well as indicating his difference from what he sees as typical Western views about Christology and the role of revelation—Zizioulas writes:

> Pneumatology is weakened whenever the approach to God is dominated primarily by epistemological concern. If we make *revelation* the decisive notion in theology, Christology dominates pneumatology, since it is Christ who links God and the world ontologically, the Spirit pointing always *beyond* history. A strong pneumatology, therefore, leads to a stronger sense of this "beyond creation" aspect and this to the emergence of meta-historical and eschatological tendencies in theology. It is not accidental, therefore that the Basilian *meta/syn-* doxology is historically linked with all the peculiarities of Eastern theology already mentioned, namely a strong apophaticism in theological epistemology and a Eucharistic, liturgical ethos as opposed to a

---

philosophy, whereas authors such as E. Levinas in our time prefer not to attach to it the traditional metaphysical importance" (Zizioulas, *Communion and Otherness,* 99).

56. Zizioulas, *Being as Communion,* 21.

preoccupation with history and a kerygmatic ethos in theology, which were more prominent in the West.[57]

It is interesting to note Zizioulas's emphasis on the conjunction of the presence of the Holy Spirit in the Eucharist and the way in which the person, in the Eucharist, is drawn into a relationship with the personal God who is both immediately known and yet at the same time unknown. However, I also want to counter what can be seen as Zizioulas's overly "meta-historical" emphasis by arguing that the nature of the encounter with God in the Eucharist is an historical one in that it takes place at specific moments in time and space, and happens through engagement with particular physical elements of bread and wine.[58]

Immediacy and Synchronicity: Human Freedom

The same issue outlined with regard to Owen, in terms of the relationship between the Spirit and the human person, is raised in another way by Zizioulas. The question is whether the Spirit so acts within the human person that human freedom is diminished. Zizioulas places a strong emphasis on the nature of human freedom, a freedom which arises out of the relationship to the triune God but which is a gift, in God's providence, to the person. Zizioulas points to different ways of understanding the Spirit's work:

> The presence and action of the Holy Spirit could be understood as some kind of mechanical or magical intervention of God. For the ancient Greeks, "divine inspiration" was involuntary, manifesting itself through divination and oracles, often without the consent of the individual who was caught up in prophetic rapture. But such an understanding as this would make the authors of the bible and the Fathers of the councils the involuntary tools of the Spirit.[59]

57. Zizioulas, *Communion and Otherness*, 203.

58. Fox refers to the emphasis Zizioulas places on the church as meta-historical, while also pointing to Zizioulas's own self critique: "In practice, however, Zizioulas admits, Orthodox theology very often places such emphasis on the heavenly realities that it runs the risk of disconnecting the Church from the social and ethical implications of life in the world" (Fox, *God as Communion*, 72). She refers in particular to Zizioulas, "Eschatology and History," in Weiser, *Cultures in Dialogue*, 39.

59. Zizioulas, *Lectures*, 10.

Zizioulas responds "The Holy Spirit is the Spirit of freedom, so he does not force himself upon us."[60] He continues by arguing for "the work of the Holy Spirit as an event of communion that centers on a community, and which has a horizontal as well as a vertical dimension" calling this "the ecclesial action of the Holy Spirit" and commenting, "we need to rid ourselves of the belief that the Holy Spirit acts upon us as isolated persons and leaves us as isolated afterwards as before."[61] "This perception that the Spirit takes persons away from community is so widespread that we must reject it emphatically."[62]

The emphasis on the Holy Spirit offering freedom in community arises out of Zizioulas's focus on the Eucharist as the moment in which the Spirit builds communion. The synchronicity comes through the presence of God in the Eucharist, at the same moment drawing people into communion and setting people free. Zizioulas draws out his critique of the understanding of individualism that grows out of the Western Enlightenment, seeing this individualism as needing to be held within the setting of relationality and communion.

Immediacy and Otherness

"Otherness" is one of Zizioulas's key concepts to which he has devoted one of his books, *Communion and Otherness*.[63] The one point I wish to draw out here is in relation to the balance between immediacy and otherness. Zizioulas introduces this work with the question: "Communion and otherness: how can these be reconciled? Are they not mutually exclusive and incompatible with each other?" This is the same question that can be asked with regard to immediacy, with immediacy being a central dimension of communion. Zizioulas continues, as previously referred to: "When the Holy Spirit blows, he creates not good individual Christians, individual 'saints', but an event of communion, which transforms everything the Spirit touches into a *relational* being. In that case the other becomes an ontological part

---

60. Zizioulas, *Lectures*, 10.

61. Zizioulas, *Lectures*, 10.

62. Zizioulas, *Lectures*, 11.

63. Zizioulas, *Communion and Otherness*. A collection of essays looking at the theme from a range of perspectives, including the person, the Trinity, and pneumatology with an extensive development of the nature of otherness in chapter 1, "On Being Other."

of one's own identity. The Spirit de-individualizes and personalizes beings wherever he operates."[64]

Just as communion and otherness are held in a tension that is both paradoxical and creative, so immediacy is held in tension with otherness. The immediate touch of the Spirit, focused in Eucharistic worship, draws together both the real sense of the presence of God and the awareness of the otherness of God. Zizioulas, with his analysis of "otherness," complements his extensive writing on communion.

The Relation between Immediacy and Continuity

A focus on immediacy on its own can lead to a sense of disconnection, in the concentration on the present moment, from the past or the future. Owen addresses this by looking at the ongoing work of sanctification. Zizioulas examines communion and the encounter with God in Eucharistic worship in the setting of the historical understanding of the triune God. Each offering of worship is at one and the same time a unique encounter with God, remembering the past and being drawn into the future. Zizioulas's rooting of his thinking in the writings of the Cappadocian Fathers and the early Ecumenical Councils, with his drawing out of their insights for the present day, points to the sweep of history in which the life of the church is set.[65] To this historical perspective he adds a particular emphasis on the work of the Holy Spirit in drawing people to the future, this eschatological perspective being his second primary emphasis on the Holy Spirit after communion.

Immediacy and Transformation

Zizioulas looks at transformation from an ecclesial standpoint with the immediacy of the Holy Spirit in worship being the starting point for the transformed community. His emphasis on the church as being continually constituted by the Holy Spirit carries with it an understanding of ongoing moments of transformation.

---

64. Zizioulas, *Communion and Otherness*, 6.

65. While throughout Zizioulas's works there are references to the influence of the Fathers and the early church, he draws this influence out in terms of continuity in two particular chapters. See Zizioulas, *Being as Communion*, 171–208; *Communion and Otherness*, 178–205.

Conclusion

In the contested area of immediacy, Zizioulas has a different approach to that of Owen in terms of the central focus he gives to the relationality of communion, communion seen both as the life of the Trinity and as that which is embodied in the liturgy. Papanikolaou draws attention to the wider issue that surrounds that of immediacy, that is, the economic and immanent Trinity, particularly as seen in Zizioulas's *Communion and Otherness,* looking at the way in which Zizioulas emphasizes the holding together of liturgy and theology.[66] Papanikolaou both develops this thinking as well as offering a critique:

> Although Zizioulas cautions against collapsing the immanent Trinity into the economic Trinity, he is clearly arguing for less of an "apophatic" distance between the two realms. . . . Thus, the experience of God in the Eucharist is really that of the "immanent" Trinity, since the Eucharist, as the work of the Holy Spirit constituting the community as the resurrected body of Christ, is a meta-historical or meta-economical work. The Holy Spirit makes present God's immanent life. Based on this strict definition, Zizioulas seems to be emphasizing a distinction between the economic and immanent realms. If, however, one conceives of economy more broadly, as argued above—namely, as God's action in relation to the created realm—then Zizioulas is clearly affirming an identification, though not an exhaustive one, between the *economic* and the *immanent* Trinity. In other words, what one "experiences" of God in history, is who God *is*.[67]

In my use of immediacy as one part of the quadrilateral on the Holy Spirit and worship I seek to look at a particular moment of connection between the economic and immanent understandings of the Trinity. In Zizioulas's particular focus on worship, he gives a helpful re-balancing of the critiques of immediacy, especially those related to a "natural" sense of immediacy in which there is uncertainty about who the "other" might be. In Zizioulas's understanding of communion, there is a clear understanding of the "otherness" of the triune God who is also encountered in the Eucharist.

While it has been argued that Zizioulas is being overly "meta-historical," I argue that the rootedness of his theology in the present reality of the Holy Spirit's presence in the Eucharist opens up a different kind of perspective on history, which is a valuable offering from the Eastern to the

66. Zizioulas, *Communion and Otherness,* 178–205

67. Papanikolaou, "Divine Energies," 384n93.

Western church. The Eucharist is not an ahistorical event. The celebration of the Eucharist is located in particular historical moments within specific communities.

This thinking on immediacy seeks to hold together the two dimensions of the economic and immanent Trinity, with each dimension being distinctive, but interrelated in the immediacy of the activity of the Holy Spirit in worship. The vision of God in worship gives a priority and distinctiveness to the immanent Trinity while affirming the presence of God in the economy.

SIMILARITIES AND DIFFERENCES

While both Owen and Zizioulas place a key emphasis on the nature and activity of the Holy Spirit and the way in which they understand this in relation to the worship offered by the church, their particular approaches travel on different routes, at times more markedly than at others. Immediacy is an area in which there is a greater degree of diversity between the two theologians, in part arising from their different historical and theological backgrounds. Owen wrote more polemically in response to the religious turmoil of the seventeenth century. He took a robust approach to those he saw as being less than fully Trinitarian, to those who by emphasizing a rationalist approach to trinitarian argument he saw as separating the doctrine of the Trinity from worship, to those who diminished the sense of the presence of God in worship by what he saw as an over-emphasis on ritual, and to those with whom he was on the opposing side after the Restoration. His strong emphasis on immediacy, and the significance of the presence of God in worship, flows in part out of his arguments on each of these four fronts. Zizioulas comes from a more settled tradition of the church in what might be seen as a less broken line of succession to the early church.[68] Zizioulas has a concern to respond to some of the modernist and rationalist philosophical trends of the West with a theological narrative that he sees as more faithful to the tradition of the church in terms of a personal approach to God.[69] He

68. Depending on how the division of the Eastern church from the Western church, which culminated in 1054, is interpreted. For more detailed arguments around these events, see Chadwick, *East and West*; Louth, *Introducing Eastern Orthodox Theology*.

69. Reinders, *Receiving the Gift of Friendship*. In chapter 5, he comments on "The Contribution of John D. Zizioulas"—on the way in which Zizioulas's understanding of personhood and freedom is contrary to Western philosophy and, interestingly, refers to Zizioulas's critique of what Zizioulas sees to be a false sense of immediacy, that of the "immediate connection between agency and self-reflexivity" which cuts against human freedom. Reinders goes on to re-iterate Zizioulas's argument for the freedom that flows out of the personal and relational understanding of the Trinity (252–63).

is interested in giving a theological interpretation that can provide a bridge between the Eastern and the Western church and increase ecumenical understanding while being faithful to his own Orthodox tradition. He places an emphasis on worship, in particular the Eucharist, as the central point of encounter with God.

I turn to a comparison of Owen and Zizioulas to see the insights that they offer to an understanding of immediacy in relation to the Holy Spirit. I look at their similarities and their differences and at some of the challenges that are raised. I argue that despite their seemingly large areas of difference, they hold theological threads in common in a way that can contribute to a renewed understanding of the Holy Spirit, particularly in relation to worship. Each of these threads is developed by other writers, but I argue that what is distinctive is the particular combination that is seen in both Owen and Zizioulas in the way in which they draw together the centrality of the Trinity, the nature and activity of the Holy Spirit in the framework of worship, and the consequent renewal in human experience at particular moments and places. Owen and Zizioulas share a sense of the immediacy of the activity of the Holy Spirit in worship alongside the radical otherness of God, and a sense of an epistemological framework which not only takes account of reason, but sees the personal relationship through the Holy Spirit within the Holy Trinity as key to knowing God. While Owen has a more personal understanding of the activity of the Holy Spirit, as described in the work of sanctification in a person's life, Zizioulas's understanding involves a more directly ecclesial approach rooted in the way in which he sees the church as both instituted by Christ and constituted by the Holy Spirit.

The Use of "Immediacy"

While Owen frequently uses immediacy in relation to the Holy Spirit, the word itself is not as prominent in Zizioulas's writings apart from his writing on the immediacy of the Holy Spirit in ordination. However, Zizioulas carries the implication of immediacy in his understanding of communion as embodied in the Eucharist. For both Owen and Zizioulas, the nature of personal relationality within the Trinity and between God and the person undergirds an understanding of immediacy. In this immediacy of encounter, God is both present and other.

The Holy Spirit and Worship

Both Owen and Zizioulas locate the immediacy of the encounter with the Holy Spirit within the setting of worship. In this setting, the Holy Spirit is both encountered immediately, but can also be said to be mediated through the particular shape and nature of the worship that is being offered. It is through the activity of the Holy Spirit, drawing people into worship, that the knowledge of God comes, a knowledge which engages human reason but also draws people into an awareness of God that embraces body, mind and spirit. The different approaches which Owen and Zizioulas take to worship, with Zizioulas's greater emphasis on the Eucharist and Owen's greater emphasis on the Word, read and preached, are held within a shared understanding of the Holy Spirit's activity in worship and provide a shared context for the development of thinking about immediacy.

Immediacy and Otherness

Within the setting of worship, the Holy Spirit is encountered in a way that is immediate to the person and yet in a way which does not limit the otherness and fullness of God. Worship draws together the knowledge of God that comes through scripture and tradition but brings people to an encounter with transcendent otherness that is beyond naming. The way in which Owen and Zizioulas, in their different ways, hold together knowledge of God which is both through an immediate encounter with the Holy Spirit in worship and yet also mediated through the particular framework of worship, is a helpful contribution to the discussion about whether knowledge of God can only be mediated. Similarly, their holding together of an understanding of the otherness of God alongside the way in which God is known through scripture and tradition is a positive contribution to the discussion about worship as a human construction as well as a response to the divine initiative.

The Nature and Activity of the Holy Spirit

Out of a Cappadocian approach to the Trinity, both Owen and Zizioulas emphasize the specific role of the Holy Spirit as personal and relational. The consideration of the personal and relational understanding of the Holy Spirit lays the foundation for an understanding of immediacy in terms of an encounter with God. Owen emphasizes the role of the Holy Spirit in relation to the person in terms of sanctification. Zizioulas focuses on the Holy Spirit drawing people into communion—the communion of the Holy Trinity, the communion in which people become who they are meant to be. Holding together Owen's emphasis on personal sanctification with Zizioulas's emphasis on communion offers a rounded approach to the personal and communal activity of the Holy Spirit, with Zizioulas counterbalancing what could be seen as Owen's leaning towards individuality and Owen counterbalancing what could be seen as Zizioulas's diminishment of personal identity.

Developing an understanding of immediacy raises a range of epistemological considerations. The next chapter will look further at these considerations, with particular reference to the Holy Spirit as leading into truth based on an understanding of truth as relational.

7

The Quadrilateral, Part Three

"The Spirit Will Guide You into All the Truth"

INTRODUCTION

This chapter argues that the knowledge of God that arises out of the encounter with the Holy Spirit in the relationship and activity of worship leads to an emphasis on what I am referring to as "relational truth." This relational understanding of truth involves holding together doctrinal or propositional approaches to truth with a whole-bodied approach to truth, engaging the mind, the heart, the body, and the spirit. Relational truth flows out of the personal relationality of the triune God and stands against a relativizing of truth in which truth becomes the private domain of an individual on his or her own.

John's Gospel describes a specific role of the Holy Spirit in terms of truth: "When the Spirit of truth comes, he will guide you into all the truth; for he will not speak on his own, but will speak whatever he hears, and he will declare to you the things that are to come" (John 16:12 NRSV). But later Pilate asks the unanswered question: "What is truth?" (John 18:38 NRSV). The tension between statements about truth and the questioning of what truth is has continued down the centuries. The nature of truth, whether in a secular or a religious context, is still a contested issue and a range of approaches exist that variously invoke the role of reason, emotion, scripture, tradition, culture, language, science, or psychology, or highlight the differences between Western or Eastern approaches.[1]

The third side of the quadrilateral framework is that, in the midst of the complexities of varied understandings of the nature of truth, there is a particular and specific aspect of truth, the nature of which is relational. It sees truth grounded above all in relationship with God; in the particular relationship(s) in which God is known. I argue that what I identify as "relational truth" arises out of the work of the Holy Spirit, embodied in the relationship and activity of worship. Despite Owen's and Zizioulas's contrasting epistemological frameworks, I note the congruity between these two theologians in their focus on the Holy Spirit in the relationship and activity of worship as giving the principal epistemological framework for knowing God.

I outline Owen's and Zizioulas's arguments that the truth into which the Spirit leads is relational and is particularly uncovered in the relationship of worship and in acts of worship. Theological sources of truth in scripture, tradition, reason, and experience are looked at in order to draw out an understanding of the relationality of truth. This is then offered as a contribution to the wide-ranging discussions of the nature of truth. The variation in approaches of these discussions in the theological arena alone can be seen in the following references. We consider first the critical approach by Clutterbuck to the classic writing of George Lindbeck in which Clutterbuck opens up the difficulty of categorizing theologians:

> Lindbeck's *The Nature of Doctrine* presented a rather crude classification of attitudes to doctrine as "cognitive-propositional" (doctrines refer to external states of affairs in the real world), "experiential-expressive" (doctrines refer to deep experiences of human existence) or as "cultural-linguistic" (doctrines refer to those rules which regulate the grammar of Christian discourse). In practice, it is rarely easy to place a concrete theologian precisely into any one of these categories or say whether

1. The range of views from different theological perspectives are reflected in the following writers: Alston, *Perceiving God*; Anatolios, *Retrieving Nicaea*; Barth, *Church Dogmatics*; Healy, *Thomas Aquinas*; Davis, *Evidential Force*; Gunton et al., *Practice of Theology*; Frei, *Types of Christian Theology*; Janz, *Command of Grace*; Lash, *Beginning and the End of "Religion"*; Lindbeck, *Nature of Doctrine*; Oman, *Natural and the Supernatural*; Pelikan, *On the Growth of Medieval Theology*; Plantinga, *Where the Conflict Really Lies*; Smith, *Reason and God*; Staniloae, *Experience of God*; Torrance, *Belief in Science*; Balthasar as seen in Oakes and Moss, *Cambridge Companion*; Nichols, *Say It Is Pentecost*; Webster, *Barth's Ethics of Reconciliation*; Yandell, *Epistemology of Religious Experience*.

they are more interested in ontological truth or in truth as intra-systematic coherence.[2]

Secondly, consider these opening words from Milbank and Pickstock's book *Truth in Aquinas*:

> One can detect four main attitudes toward truth in contemporary thought. The first is a doubt as to the possibility of truth altogether; the second is a confinement of truth to practice rather than theory; the third, a confinement of truth to theory rather than practice, but a theory so esoteric that only a tiny minority is privy to it; the fourth promotes, in the face of the first attitude, a fideistic affirmation of some religious truth or other.[3]

There is a range of issues about truth arising out of these authors and the other works cited on the previous page. These include the objectivity/subjectivity divide, the relation between modernity and post-modernity and between the discussion about the "meta-narrative" and the "narrative," the role of memory in shaping reason and experience, and the language of "scientific evidentialism." In this chapter, the focus is on Owen and Zizioulas, examining the particular insights they offer in terms of relationality in truth, looking at a comparison between the two theologians and concluding with outcomes from this comparison in order to see the significance that "relationality" can offer to contemporary understandings of the nature of truth.

OWEN AND RELATIONAL TRUTH

I turn to Owen's understanding of the nature of truth, particularly the way in which he understands truth as involving relationality. This understanding builds on the argument already articulated about the personal and relational nature of the Trinity. Owen draws together doctrine and worship in the development of his Trinitarian understanding and sees the relationship of worship into which the Holy Spirit draws the person as a relationship which leads to truth about God, the world, and the human person. The focus of truth lies in knowing God, and out of that knowledge, seeing the truth about creation and the human person. The Holy Spirit guides people into truth, truth which is embodied in worship and which, in this embodiment, embraces the heart and the mind. Truth as the whole-bodied knowledge of God is thus seen as having a relational dimension in contrast to a

---

2. Clutterbuck, "Jürgen Moltmann," 493.

3. Milbank and Pickstock, *Truth in Aquinas*, xi.

solely propositional or doctrinal understanding, or a purely individualistic approach in which the person on his or her own is the sole arbiter of truth.

Theological Sources and Historical Context

In his writing, Owen responds to the contextual challenges of his day, drawing on his interpretation of the Holy Spirit's activity in scripture, tradition, experience, and reason.

The political and social ferment of the seventeenth century was matched by vigorous theological debate. Mortimer, in her extensive look at the challenge of Socinianism in seventeenth-century England, a theological strand against which Owen argued robustly, writes:

> Theological speculation in the 1650s was a dangerous busi-
> ness—and too dangerous to be allowed to grow unchecked. On
> this point there was, and remained, broad consensus. And yet
> the experience of the 1640s and 1650s had shown there was
> also deep controversy over the correct approach to theology, let
> alone the correct lessons to be drawn from the Scripture. Few
> Protestants had ever doubted that their religion was to be found
> in the Scripture, that the Scriptures were in principle open to
> all, and that human reason enlightened by the spirit of God pro-
> vided the best guide to their meaning.[4]

A feature of Owen's writing on the Holy Spirit, is the way in which he identifies the Spirit as engaging with the mind, the will and the heart. For Owen, the Spirit is the dynamic and relational presence of the Holy Trinity. The Spirit's engagement with mind, heart and will gives a response to a common seventeenth-century emphasis on the primacy of reason.

Rehnman points to the way in which different periods and historical circumstances in Owen's life caused him to vary his emphasis on the role of reason in theology, with *Theologoumena* being more heavily weighted against a purely rationalistic approach whereas others of Owen's writings give a more positive role to the role of reason.[5] Rehnman offers an analysis of the development in Owen's writing from his time of ascendency in the

---

4. Mortimer, *Reason and Religion*, 231. Mortimer details the arguments that Owen had with the Socinians alongside the way in which Socinian views fed in to English theological thinking. Interestingly, Mortimer sees Owen as following a path of persuasion rather than enforcement of religious belief.

5. Owen, *Works*, 17:xvii. *Theologoumena* was published in 1661.

Commonwealth period followed by a more wilderness time in the later days of Cromwell and in the Restoration.[6]

Reason and Revelation

Owen writes lucidly about the relationship between reason and the knowledge of God. Reason leads to knowledge of the natural world but cannot in and of itself lead to knowledge of God. Knowledge of God depends on God's self-disclosure to which reason can respond in terms of analyzing the parameters of this self-disclosure. For Owen, reason plays an important role but a role that is consequent upon God's revelation in Jesus Christ through the scriptures and in the power of the Holy Spirit. Rehnman puts the matter succinctly by asking the question: "Can it be coherent to claim, as Owen does, both that philosophical arguments count in favor of faith and that philosophical arguments are not the ground of faith?"[7] On the basis of Owen's writing, Rehnman answers with a well-argued "yes" on the grounds that the evidence over the centuries has not pointed convincingly to philosophical arguments bringing people to faith, but that philosophical arguments can prepare the ground for faith and lead to the strengthening of faith. Rehnman draws together the series of arguments that Owen makes:

> The "use" and "proper place" of philosophical arguments is twofold. "In the first way," they are "considered as previous inducements unto believing," but this "use is not great, nor ever hath been in the church of God." "Hence they were not of old insisted on for the ingenerating of faith." So the first use of philosophical arguments is merely to dispose to rather than to produce faith. "But in the second way," philosophical arguments are used as "concomitant means of strengthening faith in them that do believe." In this way, rational arguments "may be pleaded with good use and purpose" wherever there is occasion from objections, oppositions or temptations." Yet, philosophical arguments are "not demonstrations" but "produce an opinion only, thought in the highest kind of probability, and firm against objections."[8]

6. Rehnman, *Divine Discourse,* 123–28 ("A Contextual Line of Explanation"). Rehnman also points to the debate about the nature of authority in the Reformation churches, with the emphasis on the authority of the scripture offered as an alternative to the authority of tradition and hierarchy in the Roman Catholic Church in chapter 5, "Belief and Evidence," in particular the sections on "The Question of Authority' and "Owen on Authority" (129–35).

7. Rehnman, "John Owen on Faith and Reason," 36.

8. Rehnman, "John Owen on Faith and Reason," 37, quoting Owen, *Works,* 4:71, 4:72, 50.

In his understanding of the role of reason in relation to faith, Owen does not see himself as an "enthusiast." Owen wrote against those who he sees as "enthusiasts" in terms of their disregard of the role of reason. Owen argues that reason itself is the "effect of the infinite reason, understanding and wisdom of God," and so is a gift to be welcomed and to be put to use in the development of human understanding. However, he also keeps a distinction between the capacity of human reason in reflecting on the natural world and reason that follows on from reflection on the enlightenment that the Holy Spirit brings through God's work of grace.[9]

The ways in which the role of reason and the interpretation of scripture are promulgated in relation to the development of the Christian faith and to the knowledge of God vary considerably, both now and in Owen's day.[10]

9. Two decades before the publication of John Locke's (Owen's pupil at Christ Church, Oxford) *The Reasonableness of Christianity* (1695)—a work which highlights the contested nature of reason in English philosophical and theological thinking—Owen wrote in *Pneumatologia*: "But the inquiry in this matter is, what reasonableness appears in the mysteries of our religion when revealed unto our reason, and what ability we have to receive, believe, and obey them as such. The latter part of this inquiry is so fully spoken unto in the ensuing discourses as that I shall not here again insist upon it; the former may in a few words be spoken unto. It cannot be, it is not, that I know of, denied by any that Christian religion is highly reasonable; for it is the effect of the infinite reason, understanding, and wisdom of God. But the question is not, what it is in itself? But what it is in relation to our reason, or how it appears thereunto? And there is no doubt but everything in Christian religion appears highly reasonable unto reason enlightened, or the mind of man affected with that work of grace, in its renovation, which is so expressly ascribed unto the Holy Spirit in the Scripture; for as there is a suitableness between an enlightened mind and spiritual mysteries as revealed, so seeing them in their proper light, it finds by experience their necessity, use, goodness, and benefit, with respect unto our chiefest good and supreme end" (Owen, *Works*, 3:12).

10. The range of these discussions (about the nature of human knowledge of God), is seen in Rehnman's commentary on Owen's Theological Methodology, *Divine Discourse*. In his introduction, Rehnman outlines the theological influences on Owen, from within his Reformed tradition in Europe, from within England, and from the early Fathers, in order to provide the setting for Owen's development of his theological interpretation. Each page in the thirty-one pages of Rehnman's introduction has an extensive list of references to the early Fathers, to Owen's immediate predecessors, and to contemporaries and to subsequent writing on Owen in relation to his particular theological methodology. Rehnman introduces his chapter by writing: "On the one hand, theology rests upon principles and presuppositions, but on the other the prolegomenous discussion grows out of the body of doctrine as a self-conscious justification and formulation of the system. The Christian tradition reveals this intimate connection between the growth of apologetics, hermeneutics, theological method, and prolegomenon" (*Divine Discourse*, 16). In highlighting the wide range of influences on Owen's theological development, Rehnman at the same time highlights the discussions that have unfolded over many centuries with regard to developing an understanding about

Vickers focuses on the increasing role of reason in relation to faith in the seventeenth century, drawing attention to the thinking of William Laud and William Chillingworth. "Laud argued that all clear-thinking and intellectually virtuous people could by reason discern that scripture was the Word of God."[11] Vickers argues that this "cognitive or rational activity of giving assent to propositions," followed by Chillingworth's emphasis on a rational approach to scripture, "effected a subtle but extremely powerful shift in the English Protestant doctrines of God and of salvation—from participation in the Trinity to giving assent to propositions in scripture."[12] Vickers concludes that this approach marginalized the emphasis on the role of the Holy Spirit:

> The appeal to reason meant that the presence and work of the Holy Spirit was no longer needed in the discernment of divine revelation and in the interpretation of scripture. To the degree that assent to clear and intelligible propositions in scripture was all that was needed for salvation, even the work of the Holy Spirit in ecclesial practices such as baptism, worship and the Eucharist was not sufficiently emphasised.[13]

Owen's extensive writing on the Holy Spirit is part of the way he countered what he saw as the emphasis being placed on reason as the primary epistemological starting point for knowing God. Owen was concerned to continue the Calvinist emphasis on the priority of God's initiative in leading people to the knowledge of God rather than seeing the possibility of knowing God as located primarily within the boundaries of human reason.

---

knowledge of God, where this originates, how it is formed and shaped, and how it develops. In Rehnman's book, he deals extensively with Owen's Reformed influences. However, this leads to a slight neglect of the influence of the early Fathers, which, at least in *Pneumatologia*, are more widely referenced by Owen in the development of his thinking with regard to the Holy Spirit (as I have indicated in chapter 3). See Rehnman, *Divine Discourse*, 15–46.

11. Vickers, *Invocation and Assent*, 44. Vickers continues: "In taking this direction Laud laid the groundwork for a new conception of salvation in English Protestantism. Instead of salvation having primarily to do with the invocation of the triune God in repentance, demon exorcism, baptism and the Eucharist, and in worship, thanksgiving and praise, it now had to do with the cognitive or rational activity of giving assent to propositions contained in or deduced from scripture. Salvation was being relocated from the domain of doxology to the domain of epistemology."

12. Vickers, *Invocation and Assent*, 48–56. While Vickers's approach could be argued to over-simplify Laud's thinking, it does also raise the interesting issue of a comparison between Laud and Owen in terms of the role of the Holy Spirit in inspiring scripture.

13. Vickers, *Invocation and Assent*, 57.

Lim highlights Owen's epistemological starting points when he writes of the way in which Owen saw the Incarnation as "logically improbable." Lim continues:

> All of the foregoing statements [which Owen made on the Incarnation] were designed to "fight for" an epistemic space where things beyond reason could be allowed as real. In other words, Owen was committed to the notion of mystery and apophatic theology as undergirding modes to support his Trinitarian theology, as it was also buttressed by rigorous scriptural exegesis and deep awareness of patristic theology. The two strands, apophatic theology and scriptural-patristic exegesis, were not separated in Owen, even though this dialectical tension was in the process of giving way under the enormous pressure of Socinian rationalism and natural religion.[14]

The theological ferment that arose out of the debates engendered by writers such as Faustus Socinus (1539–1604) led to the rise of Unitarian thinking and the formation of Unitarian churches as well as a more general caution across the churches with regard to the use of trinitarian language.[15] As referred to previously, the theological reflection on doctrine of the Trinity was diminished in this period and in the two centuries afterwards, although the expression of God as trinitarian continued to be held within the worshipping life of the English churches. The argument being made about the nature of truth as relational responds to this separation of doctrine and worship in order instead to draw them together.

14. Lim, *Mystery Unveiled*, 201. Lim continues by drawing out the similarities between Owen and Gregory of Nazianzus, highlighting the influence of the Cappadocian Fathers on Owen: "There was a good deal of Trinitarian apophatic spirituality of Gregory of Nazianzus in Owen's liturgical meditations." Lim follows by quoting Owen: "When we bring our *Prayers* to God the Father, and end them in the name of *Jesus Christ*; ye the *Sonne* is no lesse invocated, and worshipped in the beginning then the *Father*, though he be peculiarly mentioned as *mediator* in the close; not as *Sonne* to himself, but as *Mediator* of the whole Trinity, or God in Trinity . . . for the Sonne and the *Holy Ghost* are no lesse worshipped, in our *accesse* to God, then the Father himself. . . . So that when by the distinct dispensation of the *Trinity*, and every Person, by what name soever, of Father, Sonne or Holy Ghost, we invoke him." Lim then comments: "Rather than being theologically imprecise, Owen, and Gregory Nazianzen much more, spoke of the ineffable mystery of the Trinity, for which the best proof is found in one's participation in worship."

15. Mortimer, *Reason and Religion*.

Scriptural Interpretation

An important aspect of Owen's thinking is his ability to hold together scripture alongside the early tradition of the church, reason, and experience, with a focus on the Holy Spirit bringing scripture alive in the life of the Christian. Owen's scriptural focus differs from a biblical literalist interpretation because of his emphasis on understanding scripture in terms of the original context of language and history, and his emphasis on the Holy Spirit not only inspiring scripture when it was first written, but also opening up the reception of scripture in the believer's life.[16] His focus on the personal interpretation of scripture, under the guidance of the Holy Spirit, took Owen into conflict with what he saw as the Roman Catholic understanding of an interpretation of scripture which gave sole authority to the church. For Owen, authoritative interpretations of scripture were fostered by the inspiration of the Holy Spirit in the life of the believer and among the believers gathered together in the local congregation. However, as outlined previously, Owen was also critical of a Quaker interpretation—the Quaker Meeting depending on the illumination of the inner light—which he saw as too subjective and not giving enough weight to the interpretative authority of the Holy Spirit or to tradition.

While Owen's theological approach is deeply rooted in the priority of scripture in shaping knowledge of God, as seen, for example, in the arguments Owen outlines in *The Reason of Faith*,[17] *Pneumatologia* draws out the development of this approach as the relationship between the Holy Spirit and human experience. It is interesting to note that this emphasis on human experience comes as a later development in Owen's writing, rounding out his earlier strongly Christological and doctrinal emphasis within a fuller Trinitarian and Pneumatological relational framework.

16. Howson, recommending that Owen's hermeneutics be taken seriously in the twenty-first-century context, offers an sequence of analysis of Owen's interpretation ("Puritan Hermeneutics," 372–74). Howson draws out twelve points from Owen, starting with a reference to the Holy Spirit as offering illumination to the interpreter, and continuing with a further range of points, including the need to know the original languages, looking at "the analogy of faith" and at the context and purpose of the writers, seeking to understand the scriptures theologically and using commentaries and dictionaries.

17. Owen, *Works*, 4:4–118. This book gives the detailed argument that Owen makes about the role, priority and interpretation of scripture, including the role of the Holy Spirit in opening up the interpretation of scripture.

The Holy Spirit and Truth

The emphasis on relationality in truth is seen in the way in which Owen sees the role of the Holy Spirit as guiding into truth affecting both the mind and the heart. Owen sees the Spirit as both illuminating the mind and refreshing the heart. He writes of the mind:

> Wherefore, in the first place, this anointing with the Holy Ghost is the communication of him unto us with respect unto that gracious work of his in the spiritual, saving illumination of our minds, teaching us to know the truth, and to adhere firmly unto it in love and obedience. This is that which is peculiarly ascribed unto it; and we have no way to know the nature of it but by its effects.[18]

The Spirit is seen as a teacher, a teacher who both imparts the truth (that is, draws people into a relationship with God) and who enables people to continue to live in the truth. Truth is seen both as that which is known and that which enables a particular way of living to take place.

The work of the Holy Spirit affects both the mind and the heart. The role of the Holy Spirit in bringing about a knowledge of God is seen when Owen writes about the work of the Spirit upon the human heart, a theme which he takes up regularly:

> Again, it respects his comforting and refreshing them on whom he is poured. Hence is he said to be poured down from above as rain that descends on the earth: Isa 44:3, "I will pour water upon him that is thirsty, and floods upon the dry ground"— that is, "I will pour my Spirit on thy seed, and my blessing upon thine offspring; and they shall spring up as among the grass, as willows by the water courses," verse 4; see 35:6, 7. He comes upon the dry, parched, barren ground of the hearts of men, with his refreshing, fructifying virtue and blessing, causing them to spring and bring forth fruits in holiness and righteousness to God, Heb 6:7.[19]

Owen points to the preparatory work of scripture and reason in opening the heart and mind to hear the voice of the Spirit in the preface to the arguments he is about to make in *Pneumatologia* about the role of the Holy Spirit in bringing knowledge of God:

18. Owen, *Works*, 4:394.
19. Owen, *Works*, 3:116.

> For although the letter of the Scripture and the sense of the
> propositions are equally exposed to the reason of all mankind,
> yet the real spiritual knowledge of the things themselves is not
> communicated unto any but by the especial operation of the
> Holy Spirit. Nor is any considerable degree of insight into the
> doctrine of the mysteries of them attainable but by a due waiting
> on Him who alone giveth "the Spirit of wisdom and revelation
> in the knowledge of them;' for "the things of God knoweth no
> man but the Spirit of God," and they to whom by him they are
> revealed.[20]

Owen's emphasis on the activity of the Holy Spirit reinforces the sense of the
prevenience of the grace of God acting in the human condition without first
waiting for a response. God is known as God discloses God. People are led
into that disclosure by the Holy Spirit. It is the Spirit who leads people into
a relationship of worship of God. The activity of worship becomes the key
place for growing in the truth that is the knowledge of God.

Truth and Relationality

In Owen's introduction to *Pneumatologia* he places his thinking in the setting of God as the author of truth. "At present, it may suffice to observe,
that God, who in himself is the eternal original spring and fountain of all
truth, is also the only sovereign cause and author of its revelation unto us."[21]
He continues by making the distinction, outlined previously, between the
truth that is known through human reason and truth that is "supernatural,"
that is, to do with God's revelation of God.[22] Owen gives priority to God as
the source of truth and to the way in which truth is known through God's
revelation. In *Pneumatologia*, Owen's emphasis is on the Spirit as the one
who draws people into truth. Truth is thus not only conveyed in the abstraction of propositions but through a relationship. Throughout *Pneumatologia*,
Owen emphasizes the mutual interplay between the Spirit and the person.

20. Owen, *Works*, 3:7.

21. Owen, *Works*, 4:6.

22. Owen, *Works*, 4:6. "And whereas that truth, which originally is one in him, is of
various sorts and kinds, according to the variety of the things which it respects in its
communication unto us, the ways and means of that communication are suited unto
the distinct nature of each truth in particular. So the truth of things natural is made
known from God by the exercise of reason, or the due application of the understanding that is in man unto their investigation; for 'the things of a man knoweth the spirit
of a man that is in him,'" continuing: "But as to things supernatural, the knowledge and
truth of them, the teachings of God are of another nature."

This is not a relationship of equals but it is a relationship which both draws the person into the knowledge of God (within the human limits of that person's understanding) and enables the person to be fully human. It is in this relationship that knowledge of God and knowledge of the person in the human condition emerges.

Kapic, in his commentary on Owen, draws out the divine/human nature of this relationship in terms of communion. He argues that Owen defines communion in three ways: relating "to things and persons," relating to "a state and condition," and relating to "actions"; and he goes on to make the point: "Communion with God cannot be restricted to any one of these, nor can it simply be said to include all of them without qualification."[23] It is in this communion that truth is revealed, firstly the truth about God that is found in knowing God, and consequentially, the truth about the world.[24]

Origins and Originality

Owen's understanding of worship resulted in his opposition to the imposition of the *Book of Common Prayer* (1662).[25] In this opposition can be seen his affirmation both of the origins of the faith and the originality that the Spirit brings in the life of the congregation with the freedom of the congregation to develop its own worship patterns based on scriptural precedents. In the philosophical and religious ferment in which Owen was living, it is not surprising that Owen's theological discourses on the Spirit reflected both a desire for the security of being in continuity with the tradition of faith while also at the same time seeking to let the Spirit renew that faith in new ways in his present moment. In Trueman's biography of Owen he quotes William Sherlock as criticizing Owen's theology for being "novel and innovative." However, Trueman argues that:

---

23. Kapic, *Communion,* 151, quoting Owen, *Works,* 2:7–8.

24. It is noteworthy that it is not only the perspective of communion which draws out the understanding of relationality in Owen's writing. Trueman (in *John Owen and Claims of Truth*) directs attention to a different angle in Owen on relationality, and that is the aspect of "covenant." Owen points extensively to the covenants made between God and a range of Old Testament, particularly in book 1, chapter 4 of *Pneumatologia.* Trueman comments: "For Owen, covenant facilitates articulation of the basically relational nature of theology, it allows for the bridging of the ontological chasm that exists between an infinite, self-existent Creator and a finite, dependent creation; and it picks up terminology that reflects a basic biblical motif" (Trueman, *John Owen,* 67).

25. Owen was happy to use the *Book of Common Prayer,* but not to have it imposed upon a congregation as a regular requirement for worship.

> While Owen's book [*On Communion with God in Three Persons*,
> London, 1657] was innovative in the way that it really did try to
> take seriously the importance of the Trinity for personal piety
> and devotion (and that, one might add, might be a necessary
> innovation, filling in an embarrassing gap in the church's tradi-
> tion), the doctrine of God which Owen applied in the work was
> profoundly and intentionally unoriginal in origin and content.[26]

Owen was unoriginal in holding to the received trinitarian faith of the
church. However, his interpretation of this faith, particularly with the priority given to the Holy Spirit, brought a new focus to trinitarian understanding. There are two strands of thinking in Owen with regard to origins and
originality. One strand of thinking relates to the Holy Spirit's faithfulness in
making present the origins of the faith. The other strand relates to the Holy
Spirit's transformative activity in the present, bringing about renewal and
change. Owen held together the importance of the origins of the Christian
faith, particularly as seen through the lens of scripture and the writings of
the early church, with the originality of the work of the Holy Spirit making
all things new in each generation. The intersection of origins and originality
relates to the activity of the Holy Spirit in bringing the past into the present and, in the present, being transformative in a way which prefigures the
future. This sense of "going back to the origins" is not about an ahistorical
leap into the past, or from the past to the present, leaving to one side the
years that lie between the origins and the present moment; it is about the
continuous revelation of the Spirit in each generation and in each place.
Originality is thus used both in its meaning of going back to the origins, and
in its meaning of the creation of something new.[27]

---

26. Trueman, *John Owen*, 124.

27. In this thinking about origins and originality, there are intriguing parallels
between Owen and the twentieth-century Catholic *ressourcement* movement, which
holds together the significance of going back to the origins of the Christian faith as the
starting point for discovery of the new ways in which the faith is to be interpreted in
the contemporary setting. John Milbank writes that the eventual aim of *ressourcement*
theology was "a renewal of speculative theology in a new mode that would restore
its closeness to the exegetical, mystical and liturgical reading of revealed signs" (see
Milbank, "Henri de Lubac," in Ford and Meurs, *Modern Theologians*, 77). D'Ambrosio
writes of *ressourcement* as a revitalization (D'Ambrosio, "*Ressourcement* Theology").
The *ressourcement* theologians' common instinct was a paradox in theology: in order
to go forward in theology one first had to go backward. Etienne Gilson expressed it
succinctly: "If theological progress is sometimes necessary, it is never possible unless
you go back to the beginning and start over" (*Letters of Étienne Gilson*, 179). What was
necessary then, was a "return to the sources" of tradition. The theological revolution
which the church so desperately needed, had to begin with, in the words of Peguy

ZIZIOULAS AND RELATIONAL TRUTH

Relationality, as noted, provides an underlying theme in Zizioulas's thought as articulated in his use of the language of "communion."[28] For Zizioulas, the nature of truth is rooted in his relational understanding of the triune God. God draws people and creation into relationship with God. Out of this relationship people become who they are meant to be as persons and the creation is drawn towards its eschatological goal. The work of the Holy Spirit is to draw people and creation into this knowledge of and relationship with the triune God. The nature of truth is to know God and, out of this knowing, to know both self and the world, not primarily in an abstract propositional way but in a living relationship out of which propositions and doctrine flow. Zizioulas summarizes this in the following way:

> The relationships that constitute this community and make it this body are the actualisation by the Spirit of the revelation of God in the world. . . . Doctrine acquires its authority from its faithfulness to the truth of the relationship between God and the world.[29]

For Zizioulas, the relational truth into which people are drawn by the Holy Spirit is embodied in the church. This emphasis on the embodiment of an understanding of truth in the relationality into which people are drawn in the church is used by Zizioulas to emphasize the way in which truth is not primarily an individual matter, arising out of self-consciousness, but a relational matter arising out of the awareness of the Holy Spirit's leading and guiding, particularly in the Eucharist. Zizioulas expresses his opinion of this when he continues:

> The truth is revealed and secured, and in this sense becomes infallible, only as we submit to the communion of the Holy Spirit and are incorporated into the body of the Church. God is not

---

"a new and deeper sounding of ancient inexhaustible and common resources." See Péguy, *Oeuvres complètes*, 12:186–92, reproduced in part by Congar, *Vraie*, 602. Hence the term "*ressourcement.*" It is important to note that the ressourcement advocated by these writers was not ultimately a work of scholarship but a work of religious revitalization. Indeed, in their writings the word "source" only secondarily refers to a historical document; the primary meaning they assign to the term is a "fountain-head of dynamic spiritual life which never runs dry."

28. It is also interesting to note Zizioulas's chapter on relational ontology, "Relational Ontology: Insights from Patristic Thought" (Polkinghorne, *Trinity and an Entangled World*, 146–56).

29. Zizioulas, *Lectures*, 13.

known outside the communion of the Spirit and the love created by him.[30]

I turn to examine Zizioulas's arguments for the way God is known and the way in which this relates to an understanding of truth as relational.[31] In looking at the relational nature of truth, Zizioulas sets his understanding within the debates of the early Fathers and explicates the relationship of theology to worship, in particular the Eucharist, to the relationship between scripture and tradition, and to the role of the Spirit leading into truth.

Theological Sources and Historical Context: The Patristic Debate

In his chapter on "Truth and Communion" Zizioulas argues, by referring back to Pontius Pilate's question "What is truth?" that the problems with defining truth over the centuries date back to this unanswered question:

> Christ left Pontius Pilate's question unanswered, and through-out the ages the Church has not answered it with one voice. Our problems today concerning truth appear to stem directly from these different understandings of truth in the course of the Church's history.[32]

He follows this with reference to what he sees as the particular debate in the Patristic period with regard to truth as eternal and truth as historical. He points to the way in which "the Greek mind, for its part, seeks truth in a way which transcends history."[33] The dilemma with this approach, he argues, is that it stands against the New Testament sense of the historicity of Christ. "If, therefore, we want to be faithful to the Christological character of truth, we must affirm the historical character of truth and not despise it for the sake of its 'meaning.'"[34] Zizioulas proceeds to analyze the Greek Patristic Synthesis, pointing to the debates between the writings of Justin, Origen, and Maximus the Confessor, looking at issues raised by what he variously identifies as the "Logos" approach, the Eucharistic approach, the Trinitarian

---

30. Zizioulas, *Lectures*, 16.

31. I draw in particular from chapter 1 in Zizioulas, *Lectures*, "Doctrine as the Teaching of the Church" (1–39), with a focus on the second part of the chapter on "Knowledge of God" (9–39) as well as chapter 2, "The Doctrine of God" (40–82) and Zizioulas's *Being as Communion*, particularly the extensive second chapter on "Truth and Communion" (67–122).

32. Zizioulas, *Being as Communion*, 67.

33. Zizioulas, *Being as Communion*, 68.

34. Zizioulas, *Being as Communion*, 71.

approach, the "Apophatic" approach, the Christological approach, and the approach through the "Eikon."[35] In response to these differing approaches, I draw out some underlying aspects with regard to Zizioulas's thinking about truth focusing on reason, revelation and worship, scripture and tradition, and the understanding of the Holy Spirit in relation to Christ and truth.

Reason, Revelation, and Eucharist

Zizioulas critiques Origen for placing too much emphasis on the "Logos" approach. He sees this emphasis as arising in Origen out of Justin's understanding of truth in a way which was similar to Platonism, with an emphasis on God being known through the mind. Zizioulas identifies the problem that this approach leaves unanswered: "How can we understand the historical Christ to be the truth?"[36] He continues by pointing to the "problem" of revelation in that revelation "always unifies existence, through an idea or a meaning that is singular and comprehensive, forming a connection between created and uncreated rationality" leading to a contradiction between revelation and history.[37] However, this gives insufficient weight to the possibility of revelation occurring in history, particularly in the history of Christ. Zizioulas addresses this issue by pointing to the presence of Christ in the Eucharist.

Zizioulas turns next to the work of Ignatius of Antioch and of Irenaeus in drawing together truth with life. He identifies a key factor in their thinking—their common experience of the church as a Eucharistic community with an emphasis on the "biblical roots of the relationship between the Eucharist and life," the way in which the Eucharist truly is Christ, and the understanding of the Eucharist as being the "life of communion with God, such as exists within the Trinity and is actualized within the members of the Eucharistic community." Thus, he concludes, "knowledge and communion are identical."[38]

This sequence of the argument out of the Patristic Fathers is key for Zizioulas's interpretation of the relationality of truth and the way in which this relationality is set in the context of worship, in particular the worship offered in the Eucharist. He identifies five points about the Eucharist as the "locus of truth": the Eucharist as a "visitation" and "tabernacle" of God in history and creation, the Eucharist not simply offering truth

35. Zizioulas, *Being as Communion*, 72–101.

36. Zizioulas, *Being as Communion*, 77.

37. Zizioulas, *Being as Communion*, 77, 78.

38. Zizioulas, *Being as Communion*, 81.

as a "historical transmission," the way in which credal definitions relate to truth "only in their being doxological acclamations of the worshiping community," and the way in which a Eucharistic concept of truth shows how truth becomes "*freedom.*"[39]

In this sequence, key elements with regard to the nature of truth are identified starting with the re-formulation of the relationship between reason and truth and continuing with the location of truth within the lived experience of a worshipping community. "The Word of God does not dwell in the human mind as rational knowledge or in the human soul as a mystical inner experience but as communion within a community . . . so truth is not something 'expressed' or 'heard,' a propositional or a logical truth; but something which is, i.e., an ontological truth: the community itself becoming the truth." Therefore "truth is not imposed upon us but springs up from our midst."[40] However, before it could be thought that truth merely becomes fragmented by being realized in different ways in different places, Zizioulas points to the danger of truth being "subjugated through being incarnated in history and culture." Truth being embodied by the Spirit in the Eucharist points to the continuity of the one Christ event throughout history.

Scripture and Tradition

In Zizioulas's writings, scripture is intimately linked with his dependence on the early Fathers. His view of the role of scripture in relation to tradition and

39. Zizioulas, *Being as Communion,* 114–22. On the point about credal affirmations and doxological truth (117), there is an interesting parallel to be explored with von Balthasar's emphasis on the role of aesthetics in relation to theology, as pointed to in Kevin Mongrain's article "Von Balthasar's Way." Mongrain writes of countering theology that "means nothing but abstract propositions about God's truth presented to the intellect for its purely cognitive assent," and "locating theology in in its biblical and traditional sense as reflection directly and deeply rooted in the church's life of prayer and spirituality," and goes on to write: "Von Balthasar argues so forcefully for reintegrating beauty into theology because he believes that failing to do so would mean failing to understand and attain the existential disposition and spiritual posture required for knowing God in the only way God can possibly be known, namely, as self-giving love offered in the gift of creation and, ultimately, in the gift of the Incarnation. Attaining this understanding requires a love for creation and a willingness to participate in the Incarnation and the Paschal Mystery with the whole of one's being—heart, will, and mind. Von Balthasar views this understanding as doxology, and he is convinced that it and it alone is the only path to true theology" (Mongrain, "Von Balthasar's Way," 59).

40. Zizioulas, *Being as Communion,* 112.

to the making present of scripture in each age of the church is illustrated at the beginning of *Lectures in Christian Dogmatics* when he writes: "The task of re-stating Scripture and Christian doctrine is termed hermeneutics" and continues, demonstrating his holding together of scripture, tradition, worship, and doctrine:

> All biblical interpretation requires good historical scholarship. Any account of a doctrine is open to challenge until we offer some description of the original historical setting within which it emerged. What was the relationship to Christian worship and discipleship of each doctrine?. . . In the same way, we need to identify the issues that brought about the drafting of a doctrine. We have to decide which textual and philosophical sources the Fathers used, and what experience of worship and the Christian life any particular doctrine represented.[41]

Zizioulas focuses on seeing the scriptural text in the context of the interpretation of the Fathers in their cultural and theological contexts and the consequent re-interpretation that continues in the life of the church. Zizioulas further explicates this emphasis on the Fathers when he writes: "The Fathers of the Church did not remain fixed to the letter of the New Testament." He points to the early Fathers' ongoing re-interpretation in terms of their contemporary context and the significance of this for interpretation in the twentieth and twenty-first centuries:

> The interpretation of Scripture and doctrine also requires that we interpret our own situation. This means that we must analyse contemporary intellectual movements and the challenges thrown up by economic, technological, ecological and other changes.[42]

Zizioulas's position on scripture has been critiqued from within Orthodox theology as Brown illustrates in his chapter in *The Theology of John Zizioulas*.[43] Brown points to the writing of John Behr who argues that for Zizioulas "theology is really philosophy," critiquing Zizioulas for his use of the language of ontology and arguing that Zizioulas is insufficiently

41. Zizioulas, *Lectures*, 3. Zizioulas continues: "Good historical scholarship will present the historical reality without anachronism. It asks a certain range of questions: What challenges did the Church face in each period? How did it do so? What written and oral traditions, Scripture or doctrinal, were available to it?"

42. Zizioulas, *Lectures*, 4.

43. See Brown, "On the Criticism of Being," 63–71.

scriptural.[44] While Behr's views resonate with Owen's more direct approach to scripture, both Owen and Zizioulas look to the role of the Holy Spirit in the understanding of scripture, with Zizioulas using ontology as part of his philosophical framework for interpreting the knowledge of God, but nonetheless giving priority to the partnership of scripture and tradition in coming to know God. However, it is interesting to note the way in which Zizioulas references scripture and the, at times, generalizing way in which the references can happen.

The Holy Spirit and Truth

Zizioulas summarizes the role of the Holy Spirit, identifying the Spirit as the "verifier" of God's presence and enabling Christ to be present in his body the church:

> A new experience of the relationship with God began after Christ's Ascension, with the arrival of this third person, the Holy Spirit. This person verifies the presence of God himself, and with the gifts and demonstrations of power, does what only God can do. . . . Christ now appeared as this fellowship which breaks through the limits given by nature and creates the Church. The Spirit enables each human being to transcend his limits and to reach out to meet the "other," regardless of their natural differences.[45]

Zizioulas elaborates on the nature of the relationship between the Spirit and Christ, developing the understanding of the relation between "eternity" and "history" by pointing to the way in which it is the Spirit who "makes real" the Christ-event in history.[46] So Zizioulas concludes: "If it is truly possible to confess Christ as the truth, this is only because of the Holy Spirit." He continues by emphasizing this: "So we can say without risk of exaggeration that Christ exists only pneumatologically, whether in his distinct personal particularity or in His capacity as the body of the Church and the recapitulation of all things."[47] He continues by arguing: "In the context of a Christology constructed in this pneumatological manner, truth and communion

44. Brown, "On the Criticism of Being," 71. Reference to John Behr, American Eastern Orthodox priest and theologian, Dean of St. Vladimir's Seminary and Professor of Patristics.

45. Zizioulas, *Lectures*, 45.

46. Zizioulas, *Being as Communion*, 111.

47. Zizioulas, *Being as Communion*, 111.

once more become identical . . . truth itself is inevitably and constantly realized in the Spirit, i.e., in a Pentecostal event."[48] Zizioulas seeks to hold together the nature of being itself with the realization of being in history and thus to point to the nature of truth as not only about universal propositions and meanings but also to the concrete realization of truth within specific communities. Truth being found in community points to the way in which the truth of the nature of the person, as person rather than individual, is realized in community.

Zizioulas's Understanding of Relationality in Terms of Knowing God

Zizioulas's underlying approach is that theology starts in the worship of God and in the church's experience of communion with God. Zizioulas argues that the "worship of God, [in particular] the Eucharist and baptism were the immediate origins of Christian teaching." He outlines the ways in which these "took a variety of forms even in the Scriptures."[49] The setting of truth within worship re-orders the approach to what might be seen as the role of propositional affirmations in the creeds. A further consequence of the emphasis on worship is an opening up to mystery in knowing God. Zizioulas writes about the nature of the knowledge of God, arguing that "all knowledge comes with an unavoidable margin of wonder and mystery."[50] If truth is relational rather than only narrowly propositional, and if the underlying relation in which truth is known is relationship with God who is both revealed in the Incarnation and yet mysterious in God's essence, the knowledge of God, which is the source of truth, contains within it both visibility and mystery.[51]

---

48. Zizioulas, *Being as Communion*, 112.

49. Zizioulas, *Lectures*, 1.

50. Zizioulas, *Lectures*, 57.

51. Zizioulas develops his thinking by drawing on the iconological language of the Greek Fathers as seen in the light of primitive apocalyptic theology which he sees as penetrating the Eucharistic liturgies of the East: "This tradition presents truth not as a product of the mind, but as a 'visit' and a 'dwelling' (cf. John 1:14) of an eschatological reality entering history to open it up in a communion-event. This creates a *vision* of truth not as Platonic or mystical contemplation understands it but as picturing a new set of relationships, a new 'world' adopted by the community as its final destiny" (*Being as Communion*, 100). The language of "visit," "dwelling," and "vision" explicates Zizioulas's understanding of truth as arising out of the otherness of God, who is yet present in the midst of the community, particularly in the celebration of the Eucharist.

In Zizioulas's emphasis on relation in terms of truth, rather than truth being about intellectual assent to propositions, he sees himself addressing what he refers to as the "Western problem," which is:

> Regarding revelation as primarily rational or intellectual and the Scriptures and the Church simply as a repository of truths, available as individual units of inert information. In the Orthodox tradition, however, Scripture and the Church are regarded as the testimonies of those prophets and apostles who have experienced the truth of Christ. But truth is not a matter of objective, logical proposals, but of personal relationships between God, man and the world. We do not come to know truth simply through intellectual assent to the proposition that God is triune. It is only when we are drawn into the life of God, which is triune, and through it receive our entire existence and identity, that we have real knowledge.[52]

Zizioulas offers an Eastern Orthodox counter-balance to some of the ways in which Western theological thinking has focused on intellectual issues about the Christian faith. Zizioulas places an emphasis on the distinction between propositional and relational truth with the priority being given to the personal relationship between God, humanity, and the world, and how this relationship engenders knowledge. In his arguments about the relational character of truth, Zizioulas sees himself as countering two emphases.

The first is an emphasis on the discovery of truth as taking place primarily in reason and the mind. Relational truth carries with it the sense of a full-bodied approach and an engagement of the whole person, and thus points to truth as more than what is encountered by reason and the mind alone.

The second emphasis that Zizioulas is countering is about truth as the basis for human autonomy:

> If communion is conceived as something *additional* to being, then we no longer have the same picture. The crucial point lies in the fact that being is *constituted* as communion; only then can truth and communion be mutually identified.[53]

This conviction leads away from a consideration of the individual on his or her own to an understanding of the person as discovered in relationship. Relational truth cuts against individualism. A relational understanding of

---

52. Zizioulas *Lectures in Christian Dogmatics*, 7.

53. Zizioulas, *Being as Communion*, 101.

truth roots truth in openness to the other, either God or the other person (or both).

Zizioulas locates the embodiment of his understanding of relational truth in the setting of the church as the place which makes visible the relational dynamics of the Trinity. This relational dynamism stands as a continual challenge to notions of human autonomy and to the location of truth as solely within the bounds of the individual's understanding and comprehension.[54] Zizioulas continues to develop his understanding of the relational role of the church in explicating an understanding of truth as he writes:

> The Fathers tell us that it is the Spirit's chief work to lead us towards the gathered Church, and not towards an isolating individual experience. . . . Our conclusion is that the revelation of the truth always brings about communion, the particular communion of Christ. Christian doctrine points to this communion and teaches us that this communion is the truth itself.[55]

This communion is brought about by the Holy Spirit and finds its focus in worship, which Zizioulas sees primarily as Eucharistic worship. In the Eucharist, the truth of God becomes visible and embodied, both in the bread and wine and in the gathering of the people, through the power of the Holy Spirit. In this embodiment, God is known in a way that is both mysterious and revealed and which engages the full life of the person, body, mind, and spirit.

Zizioulas points to the particularity of the nature of the relationship with God, which is held "in Christ" and in the body of Christ, with the persons who together make up this body. Zizioulas continues with his emphasis on the relational participation that leads to the knowledge of God:

> We may come to know God only as we love him, and we are known by him only as we are loved by him. Ascetic purification will not reveal God to us, automatically as it were, simply by re-ordering our desires. It is through love realized in communion within the body of Christ, as we come to participate in the relationships that make us this body, that God becomes known to us.[56]

---

54. While the influences of such Western philosophers as Heidegger and Hegel can be seen in Zizioulas's writing, it is also clear that his writing stands as a challenge to that part of the Enlightenment thinking which carried with it a focus on human autonomy.

55. Zizioulas, *Being as Communion*, 12.

56. Zizioulas, *Being as Communion*, 32.

The integration of knowing God with loving God, of personal participation in communion with God in the setting of the communion that is the body of Christ, and the continual interaction between personal and communal that marks all encounter with God, are what together form the basis of Zizioulas's view of the way in which the knowledge of God is manifested as relational truth.

Origins and Originality

It might have been thought that an Eastern Orthodox theologian would emphasize the unchangeability of the faith. However, Zizioulas offers a more nuanced position that arises out of his understanding of the role of the Holy Spirit. While he is clear about the role of the church in establishing the doctrines of the church, he holds this view in the context of a specific Pneumatology:

> The preaching, and teaching, of Christians becomes doctrine when it is confirmed by the Church. Since the Church is a living body, it may set out new statements of its teaching for each generation. The Holy Spirit acted not only in its earliest period, but he acts through every period of the Church, now as much as in what we refer to as the Patristic period. For this reason there is no upper limit to the number of dogmas the Church can affirm in its history. It can make whatever statements are required to preserve the faithfulness of the Church in each age. The Holy Spirit enables Church councils to make, and the whole Church to acknowledge, these re-statements of the Church's teaching.[57]

The ecumenical implications of this understanding are explored further in the final chapter.

OWEN AND ZIZIOULAS: CRITIQUE, CONVERGENCE, AND CONCLUSIONS

The congruence between Owen and Zizioulas that is the focus of this book concerns their emphasis on the role of the Holy Spirit in worship leading to the knowledge of God. In this third part of the quadrilateral framework, the focus is on a shared approach to the nature of truth as being found in a relational understanding of the knowledge of God. This relational understanding is discovered and developed through the encounter with the Holy Spirit

57. Zizioulas, *Lectures*, 6.

in worship, both in the relationship with God that takes place in worship and in the activity of worship that takes place within the human community.

I draw out common themes which shape and inform Owen's and Zizioulas's understanding of the knowledge of God and the way in which this knowledge can be articulated in terms of relational truth. While both Owen and Zizioulas focus on personhood, both in Trinitarian and human terms, one of the differences between the two is the nature of this focus. Owen more determinedly examines personal relation with God in the present moment whereas Zizioulas's writing encompasses a wider horizon in terms of his eschatological understanding of the Holy Spirit drawing all creation into God at the end of time.

The Role of Scripture and Tradition

One of the differences between the thinking of Zizioulas and that of Owen is the balance between tradition and scripture. Whereas Owen's emphasis is on uncovering the original meaning of the text in the context in which it was written and then interpreting this through the ancient church for the contemporary situation, Zizioulas focuses on seeing the text through the use made of it by the early Fathers and consequent re-interpretation in the life of the church. In terms of the nature of their approach to the texts of scripture, Owen throughout his writing quotes many individual verses and explicates these in detail while Zizioulas gives general references to larger sections of scripture, illustrating something of his more generalizing approach to scripture.

Whereas Owen places an emphasis on the role of the Holy Spirit in the inspiration of the text of scripture and then in the reception of the meaning of scripture in the life of the person, Zizioulas argues for an emphasis on the ongoing role of the Holy Spirit in the tradition of the church. Zizioulas contrasts the Eastern and Western understandings of the text:

> The West tends to regard Scripture and doctrine as two distinct sources and tries to arbitrate between what it understands as their rival claims. If we understand that the continuity of the apostolic tradition is the work of the Holy Spirit, there is no problematic relationship between tradition and Scripture, for each serves the other.[58]

While such a broad statement would take more explication in the contemporary dialogue between Eastern and Western churches, particularly those

58. Zizioulas, *Lectures*, 7.

churches of the Reformed tradition, it serves to highlight the different emphases of Owen and Zizioulas while also drawing attention to the need to
give attention to the role of the Holy Spirit in relation to the formation and
understanding of scripture.

The Role of the Holy Spirit

Owen and Zizioulas each have a distinct understanding of the relation between God and the world. Whereas Owen sees the work of the Spirit more
in the fullness of the present moment and the sanctification that takes place
in the person's life, Zizioulas has a particular eschatological focus on the
work of the Spirit drawing the whole of creation into God at the end of time.
Zizioulas supplements Owen's more interior personal approach by focusing
the work of the Spirit in the setting of the church in the world.[59] However,
Zizioulas also makes clear the personal nature of the relationship with God:
"We come to know God through a particular relationship. Cf. 1 Corinthians. Here the Apostle lays out an entire epistemology in which love is the
presupposition of knowledge."[60] This epistemological basis of love is used to
support Zizioulas's emphasis on the difference between truth as intellectual
assent to propositions (on the one hand) and "real knowledge" as being
drawn into the life of God (on the other). It is echoed in Owen's emphasis
on the role of the Holy Spirit bringing the scriptures alive in the whole life
of the person and thus drawing the person into the life of God. I argue that
both Owen and Zizioulas recast epistemology in terms of the knowledge
that comes through the guiding of the Holy Spirit, in the setting of the communion of the Trinity, embodied in the community of the church.

The Role of Worship in Understanding Truth as Relational

Owen and Zizioulas each see the Holy Spirit having a particular role in the
development of the knowledge of God, mediating the origins or sources
of the Christian faith and the present encounter with Christ "making all
things new," held within the setting of the expectation of the end times. For
Owen, the preaching of the Word is about the eternal Word being present,
connecting history to a moment in time in which the attentive listener is
transformed by the Holy Spirit. For Zizioulas, the Eucharist is the act which

---

59. Owen's and Zizioulas's understanding of the transformative role of the Holy
Spirit in relation to the person and to creation are developed in chapter 8.

60. Zizioulas, *Lectures*, 30.

holds history together in an eternal framework. Each celebration, historically rooted, participates in the new creation and prefigures the fullness of
the coming of that new creation. I have argued that Owen's engagement
predominantly with the *mind* and its cognitive processes is helpfully balanced, as referred to previously, by an apophatic approach. Zizioulas, more
directly, holds together the engagement with both the body and the mind
but also has a sense of mystery. When Zizioulas's and Owen's approaches
are held together this leads to the mutual enrichment that is the work of the
Holy Spirit in both the historical setting in which worship takes place and
in the drawing of the human spirit into the mystery of the otherness of God.
When one or the other aspect of worship is neglected, worship can become
overly historically rooted or ahistorical. The work of the Holy Spirit draws
together the historical and the mysterious.

Conclusions: The Holy Spirit Guiding into Relational Truth

Origins and Originality

Both Owen and Zizioulas are faithful to the revelation of God in scripture
and tradition (as variously interpreted above). Both see the need for this
revelation of God to lead to a living knowledge of God in the present. I
interpret this balance as being about origins and originality, that is, having
regard for the originating moments of faith in God's self-disclosure through
the Son at one time in history alongside the work of the Holy Spirit as making present in ever new ways this faith in succeeding generations. I argue
that the relational truth into which the Spirit leads is a mix of consolidation,
change, and openness.

The Role of the Holy Spirit as Guiding Into Truth

This "guiding" carries the implication of "the other" who guides. Developing
an understanding of truth involves a process of being led into the truth. This
understanding counters a view of human autonomy in which the individual
on his or her own is the primary arbiter of truth. As argued previously, the
relationship with the Holy Spirit is one of synchronicity in which both Spirit
and person can be seen as acting together.

"Knowing God" and "Knowing About God"

The significance of defining truth as relational is that it broadens truth claims from being primarily propositional. "Knowing" involves relating—as seen in the difference between "thinking about" God and "knowing" God: God draws us into a relationship and is not known as an "object." The dilemma of intellectual arguments with regard to the knowledge of God is that these take place outside a personal relationship, with the resultant lack of connection to the fullness of God.

The Role of the Self in Knowing

Owen and Zizioulas counter an individualizing autonomy of human knowing as well as placing an emphasis on the way in which the nature of human fulfilment is found in relationality.

Reason, Heart, and Soul in Relational Truth

In their emphasis on the encounter with God through the Holy Spirit in the context of a worshipping relationship, Owen and Zizioulas draw together the whole of human experience in developing their thinking about truth. Reason plays a significant role for both theologians but is held within the setting of truth shaping the whole of life and the whole of life being shaped by the truth that is received from God.[61]

Truth Being Focused in Worship

The holding together of reason, heart, and soul is signified by its embodiment in worship. Worship engages the whole person as is seen, for example, in the focus on the mind in receiving the preached word and the body in receiving the bread and wine. For both Owen and Zizioulas, worship as a relationship with God that draws people into truth is central to their thinking.

---

61. There are resonances of argument with Charry and LaCugna in their connecting a doctrinal understanding with a pastoral approach to the whole of life. See Charry, *By the Renewing of Your Minds*; "Doctrine of God."

Relational Truth is Different from Relativized Truth

Rather than relativizing truth, Owen's and Zizioulas's emphasis on relationality supports their understanding that the role of the Holy Spirit in worship is to hold together the immediacy of the encounter with God and the objectivity of the content of that encounter. This holding together retains the sense of the long history of the faith as well as the "otherness" of God. While truth takes root in the life of the person, it is a truth that connects with the tradition of faith and the understanding that is held within the Christian community rather than by an individual on her own.

Truth as Freeing and Dynamic

Truth as freeing and dynamic is a consequence of the role of the Holy Spirit in leading into truth and will be developed further in the next chapter.

8

The Quadrilateral, Part Four

Worship in the Power of the Holy Spirit—
The Nature of Transformation

INTRODUCTION

I turn to the fourth part of the quadrilateral framework in order to look at the nature of transformation in relation to the Holy Spirit and worship. Transformation relates to and arises out of the three previous aspects of the quadrilateral: personal relationality, immediacy, and truth. Each of these aspects has been looked at through the lens of the Holy Spirit and worship. In this chapter I draw out the transformative nature of the encounter with God in worship through the Holy Spirit. In this relationship, God is known in a way in which the boundaries between the knower and the object of knowledge are transcended. There is a real moment of transformation in which the image and likeness of God is discovered, albeit dimly, in frail human form and the very way we know is thus transformed. This transformation, which is the effect of the Holy Spirit, is both communal and personal in that it both brings the church into being and holds the church in being as well as bringing the human person (held within the transformative relationship between God, the individual person, and other persons) to a place in which the wisdom of God is glimpsed and a holy life is enabled.

A vision of the way in which worship of the living God leads to transformed lives lies at the heart of Christianity and has been written about
from a range of perspectives over the centuries and, increasingly, in contemporary discourse.[1] However, the language of transformation has played
a key but sometimes underdeveloped role in such doctrinal discourse. *The*

---

1. McDonald, "Discerning the Spirit," comments on the way in which Barth is
"profoundly transformational"; Buckley and Yeago, *Knowing the Triune God*, examines
the "liturgy as interpretative lens and knowledge of God"; Higton, in his article "Hans
Frei and David Tracy on the Ordinary and the Extraordinary in Christianity," takes an
interesting look at the two different positions of Frei and Tracy in terms of the ordinary
and the extraordinary in relation to ritual and liturgy; Keith F. Pecklers looks at "the
transformative power of symbol and ritual," referring to what the Eastern Church has
to offer the West, offering the interesting conclusion: "The way in which we worship
is inseparably linked to the way in which we live. Emphasising the fundamental role
of the Holy Spirit in this process of transformation, some liturgists have advocated an
imposition of hands over the liturgical assembly as well as over the gifts of bread and
wine. They suggest this manual addition as an important means of linking the assembly
with the Eucharistic gifts of which it partakes, and of symbolizing its empowerment for
Christian mission in the service of others through sacramental sharing in that ritual
meal" (Pecklers, *Worship*, 189); Eugene Rogers, *After the Spirit*, offers a concluding
comment echoing Zizioulas thinking about particularity: "If every human response to
God is credited to God again in the Spirit, does that not destroy the human person's
distinctive, personal response? Not if the Person of the Spirit is the very principle of distinctiveness in love, in which all human distinctiveness, to be distinctive, participates"
(Rogers, *After the Spirit*, 213); Tanya Yik-pui Au, "Eucharist as a Cultural Critique,"
makes reference to Bellah and his work, calling for a return to the practice of worship
and liturgy, as offering a return to the process of building community; David Torevell,
Liturgy and the Beauty of the Unknown, counters some contemporary liturgical trends:
"Unlike those who argue that relevance and adaptation to cultural norms are integral
to any reinvigoration of liturgy at the present time, the position taken here centers on
an aesthetic understanding of worship which releases a transformative movement of
the self through liturgical form, allowing an endless and unsatiated encounter with the
Unknown. I contend that it is the task of the liturgical Church to offer the embodied
presence of the resurrected Christ to the world, a body once disfigured but restored
to glory, a body of beauty" (Torevell, *Liturgy and the Beauty of the Unknown*, 1); John
Webster, *Domain of the Word*, suggests "we must be changed; and the required change
is not simply an extension of skills already possessed but an entire conversion of interpretative reason so that it is made capable of hearing the words of a book. The Spirit
produces *readers*" (Webster, *Domain of the Word*, 27); Michael Welker, *God the Spirit*,
introduces his challenging book on the Holy Spirit by writing: "This book . . . provides
help in coming to a new perception of God and of God's power serving as a guide
past the mistaken paths of totalistic metaphysics, merely speculative trinitarianism,
abstract mysticism and irrationalism undertaken by conventional understandings of
the Holy Spirit. It likewise serves as a guide past empty formulas and mere silence—be
it meaningful or meaningless. The Holy Spirit is neither an intellectual construct nor a
numinous entity" (Welker, *God the Spirit*, ix).

Practice of Theology, drawing together texts from across the centuries, refers to the significance of transformation:

> Christianity concerns both the acts of God in drawing to himself a people to live in covenant relationship with him, and the call of the individual to respond in faith to the saving work of Christ. Unless these things become a matter of personal experience, transforming one's life and reshaping one's understanding of the world, the Christian gospel is but a dead letter.[2]

Hutter, Charry, and LaCugna helpfully write from different twentieth-century perspectives on the relationship between theology and practice, each including reference to the transforming work of the Holy Spirit.[3]

In the writings of the early Fathers the transforming work of the Holy Spirit is held closely together with the transfiguring presence of the Trinity. For example, Ambrose, in his extensive writing on the Holy Spirit, comments on the relationship between the Spirit and Christ, pointing to the work of being "formed anew" by the Spirit. "Therefore since it is the Lord to Whom we are converted, but the Lord is that Spirit by Whom we are formed anew, who are converted to the Lord, assuredly the Holy Ghost is pointed out, for He Who forms anew receives those who are converted."[4] Basil takes up the theme, referring to "the Lord [who] is now called the Spirit," and using the imagery of light to illustrate the transforming work of the Spirit writes: "For just as objects which lie near brilliant colors are themselves tinted by the brightness which is shed around, so is he who fixes his gaze firmly on the Spirit by the Spirit's glory somehow transfigured into greater splendor, having his heart lighted up, as it were, by some light streaming from the truth of the Spirit."[5] I am arguing that this transfiguration by gazing on the Spirit's glory is an aspect of that which the offering of worship points to as worship takes people into an encounter with God. Basil continues by referring to the particular gifts of life, freedom, and power that are given by the Spirit.

In introducing Didymus's writings on the Holy Spirit, his translators point to Didymus's emphasis on the Spirit as the "undiminished giver" while holding this emphasis within his overall Trinitarian framework. "Didymus places much emphasis on the Spirit being the substance of the gifts he is said to give, emphasizing the unmediated transforming presence of the Spirit. At

---

2. Gunton et al., *Practice of Theology*, 185.

3. Hutter, *Suffering Divine Things*; Charry, *By the Renewing of Your Minds*; LaCugna, *God for Us*.

4. Ambrose, *Selected Works and Letters*, 361. For Ambrose on the Holy Spirit, see *Selected Works and Letters*, 237–383.

5. See Basil, *Letters and Selected Works*, 210.

the same time, this account of the Spirit's presence is placed in the frame-work of Didymus's strong insistence on the inseparability of Father, Son and Spirit." In his extensive work, Didymus points to the outcomes of transformation as freedom, joy, consolation, and becoming children of God.[6]

This chapter develops worship thesis 9 (the immediacy of the encounter leads to personal transformation and to a renewal of vocation)[7] by looking at the previous chapter and the way in which truth leads to a mix of consolation, change, and openness. While transformation is seen as a continuous possibility in the Christian life, this is not to imply that it flows in a straight line. Instead it can happen in what seem like fits and starts. Worship is the particular vehicle for transformation as worship takes people into the relationship with God through the Holy Spirit. It is not possible to tie the Holy Spirit down, only to be open to both what might be expected and what is unexpected from the presence of the Spirit. Then the moral life follows from deep within. This does not imply a separation of inner life and outer life for the same morality flows between both.

McDonald comments on Barth's approach in terms of the unsettled and unpredictable nature of God's presence:

> In the transformation of the human creature into persons who receive and return God's love, the presence of God therefore is never settled, never predictable, but always active and living, free and open. In this way God's presence is never pre-determined or prescribed by the past, but is always directed towards new possibilities in the future. Such a vision of the transforming presence of God, through which believers are drawn up into the inner fellowship of God, in which true personhood is conferred upon them as they are loved by God and love God in return, is a far cry from the limited readings of Barth offered by his critics, be that the linear-communication interpretation voiced by Williams and Torrance or the futureless repetition of pre-determined triune events portrayed by Jenson and Gunton.[8]

OWEN AND ZIZIOULAS ON TRANSFORMATION

Both Owen and Zizioulas, building on previous writings over the centuries, see the work of the Holy Spirit as effective, albeit in different ways, with

---

6. DelCogliano, *Works on the Spirit*.

7. See chapter 4.

8. McDonald, "Discerning the Spirit," 59.

Owen having a more personal focus and Zizioulas a greater ecclesial understanding. Both see worship as key to the encounter with the Holy Spirit out of which transformation takes place. Owen has a focus on the personal life in the Spirit, which he describes as sanctification:

> Sanctification, as here described, is the immediate work of God by his Spirit upon our whole nature, proceeding from the peace made for us by Jesus Christ, whereby, being changed into his likeness, we are kept entirely in peace with God, and are preserved unblamable, or in a state of gracious acceptance with him, according to the terms of the covenant, unto the end.[9]

Zizioulas examines the ecclesial life in the Spirit, looking at the life of the church:

> What I mean by "constitutive" is that these aspects of Pneumatology must qualify the very ontology of the Church. The Spirit is not something that "animates" a Church which already somehow exists. The Spirit makes the Church *be*. Pneumatology does not refer to the well-being but to the very being of the Church. It is not about a dynamism which is added to the essence of the Church. It is the very essence of the Church. The Church is constituted in and through eschatology and communion.[10]

I go deeper into discussion of the transformative role of the Holy Spirit as seen in the work of the Holy Spirit in regeneration and sanctification (in Owen) and in the work of the Holy Spirit as constituting the church (in Zizioulas) as well as the consequent transformation of creation that Zizioulas highlights. The Holy Spirit is seen from both doctrinal and experiential perspectives. I identify the way in which these two different perspectives are held together in worship—in particular the worship offered by the community of the church.

"THE HOLY GHOST AT WORK, POURING OUT OF HIS OIL":[11] OWEN AND THE TRANSFORMATIVE WORK OF THE HOLY SPIRIT

Owen affirmed the transformative nature of the Holy Spirit when he wrote:

---

9. Owen, *Works*, 4:370.

10. Zizioulas, *Being as Communion*, 132.

11. Owen, *Works*, 2:248.

> When we find any of the good truths of the gospel come home
> to our souls with life, vigor and power, giving us gladness of
> heart, transforming us into the image and likeness of it,—the
> Holy Ghost is then at his work, is pouring out of his oil.[12]

The transformation of which Owen writes, offered by the Holy Spirit, is
found both in his doctrinal understanding of the Trinity and in the inner
life of the person. The work of renewal is rooted in an understanding of the
nature of the Trinity as personal and relational, with the consequent connection between doctrine and worship leading to knowledge of God. The
Spirit draws people into the image and likeness of Christ giving people the
strength to live in a Christ-like way. The Spirit both renews the interior life
of the person, bringing joy and gladness and removing fear and anxiety, and
works with the human mind:

> The anointing, then, of believers with the Spirit consists in the
> collation of him upon them to this end, that he may graciously
> instruct them in the truths of the gospel by the saving illu-
> mination of their minds, causing their souls firmly to cleave
> unto them with joy and delight, and transforming them in the
> whole inward man into the image and likeness of it. Hence it
> is called the "anointing of our eyes with eye-salve that we may
> see." Rev 3:18.[13]

Owen puts forward a sequence of transformation which takes place
when the Holy Spirit is encountered and which affects the whole human
person. Reason is engaged and the mind is led into truth:

> This is called the *renovation of our minds*: "Renewed in the spirit
> of your mind," Eph 4:23; which is the same with being "renewed
> in knowledge," Col 3:10. And this renovation of our minds
> hath in it a transforming power to change the whole soul into
> an obediential frame towards God, Rom 12:2. And the work of
> renewing our minds is peculiarly ascribed unto the Holy Spirit:
> Titus 3:5, "The renewing of the Holy Ghost."[14]

The heart is touched by God's love, made capable of receiving love and
enabled to love others. Being led into the truth and love that arise out of
communion with God issues forth in the living out of the faith in daily life.

---

12. Owen, *Works*, 2:249.

13. Owen, *Works*, 4:394.

14. Owen, *Works*, 3:332.

Owen's Historical and Theological Context

Kay comments on the significance of Owen's writings in holding together doctrine and worship: "The conclusion of this work is that Owen comes closer than most other figures in western spirituality to integrating a doctrinally rich Trinitarianism into the heart of a spiritual method. . . . Owen did not derive his system *de novo*, but stands at the end of a long history of spiritual writers who were interested to integrate properly the Christian tradition of God."[15] Kay continues with an examination of different spiritual traditions, concluding with an analysis of three devotional traditions which he identifies as setting the scene for Owen's writing: early Quakerism, the mysticism of late-medieval realism, and sixteenth- and seventeenth-century popularized Protestant scholasticism.[16]

Owen, reflecting on the seventeenth-century state of the church in Britain, wrote in *Pneumatologia*: "God himself expostulates with the church how its faith came to be so weak when it had so great experience of him, or of his power and faithfulness."[17] He sees the encounter with God and the power of God, particularly in regeneration and sanctification, as a reality for the Christian, and yet he sees also the way in which this reality has not been fully manifest in the life of the church.

A key theme of his argument is to maintain that this encounter with God is through the work of the Holy Spirit who makes effective the work of regeneration and sanctification. Owen lamented the apparent denial, in some Christians of his day, of the reality of regeneration and sanctification leading to re-vivification: "Now, no such work [the work of grace leading to revivification] can be wrought in us but by an effectual communication of a principle of spiritual life; and nothing else will deliver us." Owen takes particular issue with those who think only metaphorically of the Christian faith: "Some think to evade the power of this argument by saying that 'all these expressions are metaphorical, and arguings from them are but fulsome metaphors': and it is well if the whole gospel be not a metaphor unto them."[18]

Owen took to task those he saw as assenting intellectually to the doctrines of the church without letting their lives be open to the transforming work of the Holy Spirit. For example, Owen reproves Samuel Parker for views expressed in his "Defence and Continuation of Ecclesiastical Polity"

15. Kay, *Trinitarian Spirituality*, 29.

16. Kay, *Trinitarian Spirituality*, 45.

17. Owen, *Works*, 3:390.

18. Owen, *Works*, 3:329.

(1671).[19] Parker was a fierce opponent of dissenters and a major apologist for the State regulation of religion. Parker and Owen exchanged views in a series of strongly-worded pamphlets. Their exchange reflects the nature of the theological argument between Owen and other religious leaders of his day, particularly in relation to where authority comes from and the nature of the authority of the Holy Spirit.

The Holy Spirit as Transformative

In Owen's thinking, the Holy Spirit is fundamental to receiving the transformative work of God in the present, work which is congruous with the revelation of God since the beginning of time and which continually renews God's people. It is as the Holy Spirit makes evident in the present moment the fullness of God that transformation occurs. Owen emphasizes both the "otherness" of the Holy Spirit, as rooted in the life of the triune God, and the closeness of the Holy Spirit, as experienced in everyday living through the work of regeneration and sanctification. Welker alludes to this present experience of the Spirit when he writes: "We encounter the attested experiences of God's Spirit firmly embedded in life's experiences—of life that is threatened and endangered, and of life that has been delivered and liberated."[20]

Owen's work points to the way in which the source and goal of created life is the divine life, not as an abstract proposition, but transformatively present in the human condition. Owen's rich use of imagery about the Holy Spirit—as, for example, a well of water springing up, pouring out of oil, and tuning an instrument—illustrate the diverse ways of his thinking about the Spirit.

For Owen, the Holy Spirit is the fountainhead of dynamic spiritual life (cf. John 4:16; 7:38, 39):

19. Owen, *Works*, 3:121. Owen writes, with his strength of language reflecting his strength of feeling: "I stand amazed, that whereas these things are so plainly, so fully and frequently declared in the Scriptures, both as to the actings of God and his Holy Spirit in them . . . yet men professing themselves to be Christians and to believe the word of God at least not to be a fable, should dare to cast such opprobrious reproaches on the ways and works of God. The end of these attempts can be no other but to decry all real intercourse between God and the souls of men, leaving only an outside form or shape of religion, not one jot better than atheism. Neither is it only what concerns spiritual desertions, whose nature, causes and remedies are professedly and at large handled by all the casuistical divines . . . but the whole work of the Spirit of God upon the hearts of men, with all the effects produced in them with respect unto sin and grace that some men, by their odious and scurrilous expressions, endeavour to expose to contempt and scorn."

20. Welker, *God the Spirit*, x.

So our Saviour himself declares: "The water that I shall give him shall be in him a well of water springing up into everlasting life." The water here promised is the Holy Spirit, called the "gift of God."... No quality in our minds can be a spring of living water. Besides, all gracious habits are effects of the operation of the Holy Spirit; and therefore they are not the well itself, but belong unto the springing of it up in living water. So is the Spirit in his indwelling distinguished from all his evangelical operations of grace, as the well is distinct from the streams that flow from it. And as it is natural and easy for a spring of living water to bubble up and put forth refreshing streams, so it belongs unto the consolation of believers to know how easy it is unto the Holy Spirit, how ready he is, on the account of his gracious inhabitation, to carry on and perfect the work of grace, holiness and sanctification in them.[21]

The Holy Spirit brings the revitalizing, revivifying work of God to fruition. The purpose of being made new is to be made and re-made in the image and likeness of Christ and brought into communion with God.

The Personal Transforming Power of the Spirit

Owen, in arguing for the personal nature of the Holy Spirit, offers a key contribution to my arguments about the transforming power of the Holy Spirit. The Spirit being personal has an implication for who human beings are as persons. The presence of the Holy Spirit is personal presence. The Spirit is not just an impersonal spirit or a philosophical concept. The nature of the Spirit shapes the transformative work of the Spirit in relation to the development of human personhood.

Transformation arises from such personal relationship and from receiving the qualities of the Spirit into the person. The Spirit imparts such characteristics as wisdom, understanding, will, and power. If people are not in relationship with the Spirit, this work of transformation is hindered. Relationship is key to the work of transformation. The Spirit draws persons into relationship with God in the work of regeneration and sanctification. For Owen, sanctification is a lifelong process built on an intimate and ongoing relationship with the Holy Spirit.

---

21. Owen, *Works*, 4:388.

The Holy Spirit's Transformative Presence in Worship

Owen draws together the Spirit and worship and sees worship as a primary locus for the activity of the Spirit, particularly in the preaching of the Word. Preaching takes past events and teachings as outlined in scripture and, in the re-telling and unpacking of these, re-presents them in the present. The Spirit's power is at work in opening up the Word of God, opening up the human heart, and, through this, transforming the human heart. Owen sees worship as the focal point for the transformative activity of the Holy Spirit. It is in worship that the person is caught up into communion with God and is brought into a reflection of the likeness of Christ. Owen writes: "The Holy Spirit excites the graces of faith and love into frequent acts—morally, by proposing their objects suitably and seasonably unto them, through the ordinances of worship, principally preaching the word."[22] From the communion with God, the person is transformed to live a life full of the fruits of the Spirit, entering into new, loving ways of relating to other people. This transformation is a matter of the mind, the heart, and the will. Owen points to some aspects of human disposition that are required, including "a diligent *intension* of mind, in attendance on the means of grace to understand and receive the things revealed and declared as the mind and will of God. For this end God has given men reason."[23] Lim comments: "Owen was convinced that the theological proof is in the liturgical pudding; that is whatever one's theological discourse, it has to lead to character transformation."[24]

In *A Brief Instruction in the Worship of God*, Owen outlines fifty questions with regard to worship, including two, questions 7 and 10, which refer to the way in which they enable the person to grow in the knowledge of God and be built up in the faith.[25]

---

22. Owen, *Works*, 3:389.

23. Owen, *Works*, 3:230.

24. Lim, *Mystery Unveiled*, 194, commenting further in footnote 119: "That is why Owen publishes a popular treatise on sanctification—*Of the Mortification of Sinne in Believers* (Oxford, 1656)—as a concrete response to both the Quakers and the antinomians."

25. Owen, *Works*, 15:447–530.

> *Question 7*: What are the chief things that we ought to aim at in our observation of the institutions of Christ in the Gospel?
> *Answer*: To sanctifie the name of God (Lev 10:3; Heb 12:28, 29); to own our professed subjection to the Lord Jesus Christ (Deut 26:17; John 24:22; 2 Cor 8:5); to build up our selves in our most holy faith (Eph 4:12–16; Jude 20); to testifie and confirm our mutual love, as we are believers (1 Cor 10:16, 17).

While there are many ways in which the Holy Spirit is transformative (in daily living, in encounters with people, in creation) Owen places a particular emphasis on the transformative encounter with the Holy Spirit in worship. Worship leads to the deliberate consciousness of the otherness of God, it re-tells the story of the Christian faith in order to re-present it in the present (see reference in chapter 7 on origins and originality), it opens up the Word, and through the relationship between preacher, sermon, and people develops the I-thou relationship with God—the thinking about

---

Explication: (in summary) we need always to consider the ends for which God has appointed institutions and worship of God–so that our observance of them may be the obedience of faith. This we ought diligently to enquire into–not only what God requires of us, but wherefore he requires it. (455, 6)

Question 10: How do we in and by them build up ourselves in our most holy faith?

Answer: by the exercise of that communion with God in Christ Jesus, which in their due observation he graciously invites and admits us unto, for the increase of his grace in us and the testification of his love and good will towards us. Gen 17:10; Lev 26:11,12; Prov 9:5, 6; Ezek 26–28; Zach 14:16, 17; Matt 26:27, 28; Rom 6:3.

Explication: The next and principal ends of all instituted worship in respect of believers are the increase of the grace of God in them, their edification in their most holy faith and the testification of the good will of God unto them: Eph 4:11–15; 3:16–18; James 1:21; 1 Peter 2:2. In the celebration of the Gospel ordinances, God in Christ proposeth himself in an intimate manner to the believing soul, as his God and reward. Rev 3:20. (460, 1)

Question 14: May not the church find out, and appoint to be observed, such religious rites as, being adjoined unto the celebration of God's instituted worship, may further the devotion of the worshippers, and render the worship itself in its performance more decent, beautiful and orderly?

Answer: All acceptable devotion in them that worship God, is the effect of faith, which respects the precepts and promises of God alone. And the comeliness and beauty of Gospel worship, consisteth in its relation unto God by Jesus Christ as the merciful high-Priest over his house, with the glorious administration of the Spirit therein.

But . . . "God is a Spirit and will be worshipped in spirit and in truth," John 4:24. And no devotion is acceptable unto him but what proceedeth from and is an effect of faith Heb 11:6. . . . God hath given his ordinances of worship as the touchstone and trial of faith and obedience. . . . God hath appointed that his ordinances of worship shall be as effectual means as to instruct us in the mysteries of his will and mind, so of communicating his love, mercy and grace unto us (Owen, *Works*, 15:467).

which Martin Buber significantly developed in the twentieth century.[26] For Owen, worship plays a central role as the point of encounter with God—waiting in worship upon God, being expectant, and moving from a human to a divine focus. In worship people are being drawn into the life of the Trinity. The Spirit comes to be present in the midst of the complex of activities that form worship—the preacher, the community, the scriptures, the Word, and attentive hearts. The Spirit is transformatively present in a multiplicity of ways. It is in this multiplicity that the Spirit is seen as different dimensions and aspects of the life of the Spirit come to fruition.

Owen sees a particular connection between the work of the Holy Spirit in regeneration and sanctification and the worshipping life of the church, especially through personal piety and public preaching. This connection takes place in prayer and preaching when the human heart is open to wait upon God so the Holy Spirit may enter into the heart and sanctify the person, transforming his or her life to one of holiness. The Holy Spirit makes present the origins of the Christian faith as the Word is preached, at the same time making new the persons and community who hear the Word. The Spirit is present at the intersection of originality, drawing together origins and newness. In sanctification, the Spirit is present in the life of the person, working in the life of the person to renew that person. The Spirit is present in the intersection that I am describing by using the word "synchronicity"—bringing together "otherness" and "interiority" in the encounter with God.

The Scriptural Witness to Transforming Presence

Owen has a scriptural basis for his understanding of the Holy Spirit as transforming presence. Owen sees the Holy Spirit as making visible the origins of faith as rooted within the eternal and timeless triune Godhead as seen within the witness of scripture. He points to the New Testament references to the Spirit at work in the life of Christ and amongst the early believers in forming the church and bringing a variety of gifts to fruition. Owen points to the personal characteristics of the Holy Spirit which are analogous to personal human characteristics and also saw two further aspects of the work of the Spirit in scripture. These relate to the way in which the Spirit is seen both as making possible "extraordinary" works and as enhancing natural human abilities. Both these aspects relate to the active empowering work of the Spirit working in individuals and events in order to transform people and situations. In addition to the New Testament references, Owen makes clear his understanding of the continuity of the work of the Holy Spirit

26. Buber, *I and Thou.*

between Old and New Testaments. The following examples are taken from the Old Testament.

The "Extraordinary" Work of the Spirit

Owen's references to the "extraordinary" works start with Old Testament references to the work of God's Spirit. He refers to three main interconnected areas of this "extraordinary" work: prophecy, the writing of scripture, and miracles, in each case quoting a range of biblical texts in support of his arguments.

(A) PROPHECY

Owen saw that there were two ways to understand prophecy—as either prediction or interpretation, coming through inspiration or "in-breathing." By inspiration men's intellectual faculties were elevated:

> The preparation and elevation of their *intellectual faculties*, their minds and understandings, wherein his revelations were to be received. He prepared them for to receive the impressions he made upon them, and confirmed their memories to retain them. He did not, indeed, so enlighten and raise their minds as to give them a distinct understanding and full comprehension of all the things themselves that were declared unto them; there was more in their inspirations than they could search into the bottom of.[27]

Owen compared this to tuning a musical instrument. He also maintained that the Spirit gave to the prophets infallible assurance: "But in the inspirations of the Holy Spirit, and his actings of the minds of the holy men of old, he gave them infallible assurance that it was himself alone by whom they were acted."[28] This raises the issue of the recognition of this assurance in terms of who recognizes and validates that the Spirit has been at work. The prophets who have come to the fore for future generations have been recognized by the wider community for their prophetic wisdom. There is a connection to be made between the inspired word that is delivered through a prophet and the way that inspired word is received and acted upon by the community.

---

27. Owen, *Works*, 3:132.
28. Owen, *Works*, 3:133.

Owen becomes more specific about the role of the Holy Spirit in prophecy when he writes: "He guided their tongues in the declaration of his revelations, as the mind of a man guideth his hand in writing to express its conceptions."[29]

(b) A Second "Extraordinary" Effect of the Spirit is in the Writing of Scripture

In addition to his thinking about the prophets, he identifies three distinct aspects in relation to the writing of scripture: the inspiration of minds, the suggestions of words, and the guidance of their hands.[30]

(c) A Third "Extraordinary" Effect of the Spirit is in Miracles

Owen quotes a range of references in the Old Testament, including referring to Moses, Joshua, Elijah, and Elisha. He sees each person performing the miracle being an organ of the Holy Spirit.[31]

He also saw the Holy Spirit at work in the Old Testament in other "extraordinary" ways, including voices, dream, and visions. However, Owen did not see the Spirit as only manifesting extraordinary characteristics when touching human lives. He also developed his sense of the Spirit's activity in the everyday natural realm.

The Spirit Enhancing Natural Abilities

Alongside the "extraordinary" work of the Spirit, Owen sees the work of the Spirit as "improving and exalting natural faculties." He quotes in particular the following four areas, developing each one with extensive scriptural references from the Old Testament: "1. In things *political*, as skill for government and rule amongst men; 2. In things *moral*, as fortitude and courage; 3.

29. Owen, *Works*, 3:134, quoting Ps 45:1; Luke 1:70.

30. Owen, *Works*, 3:144.

31. Owen, *Works*, 3:146. The role and understanding of miracles and their place in the life of the church has varied over the centuries, especially since the rise of a range of diverse scientific understandings in more recent centuries. At this point I refer briefly to Owen's reference to miracles as part of his analysis of the "extraordinary" work of the Holy Spirit.

In things *natural*, as increase of bodily strength; 4. In gifts *intellectual*."[32] In referring to "political, moral, natural, intellectual gifts" he reflects the long tradition of natural theology.

It is interesting to note that Owen does not see the role of the Holy Spirit in developing natural faculties as confined to the Jews of the Old Testament times. For example, Owen refers to Cyrus, thus seeing the Spirit of God at work in people of other nations. This line of thinking counterbalances some of Owen's exclusivist emphasis on the work of God as only happening among the elect, with the elect being defined as the Hebrew people and as Christians. Here Owen connects the work of the Spirit more broadly to other peoples.

After this brief survey of Owen's thought, I turn to look at Zizioulas's perspectives, which encompass differing directions to those of Owen's, particular with regard to the role and significance of scriptural interpretation.

ZIZIOULAS AND TRANSFORMATION

Zizioulas sees the nature of transformation as primarily ecclesial and Eucharistic, arising out of the work of the Holy Spirit. However, these ecclesial and Eucharistic dimensions have profound implications for history and creation. Zizioulas writes: "Christian doctrine must hold together the past, historical revelation of Christ and the future advent of Christ in glory, and this union and transformation of past and future is the particular task of the Holy Spirit."[33] A repeated emphasis of Zizioulas is that "the Spirit makes the Church *be*."[34] Throughout this book, attention has been given to the way in which Zizioulas offers a personal and relational understanding of ecclesial identity, given particular embodiment in the Eucharist, through the Holy Spirit. It is the Spirit who gives life to the church and in that giving of life opens the door to the possibility of sharing in God's transformative activity in the world.

The Holy Spirit as Transformative in the Building of Communion

Zizioulas builds on his Trinitarian understanding, not seeing the Spirit in isolation but pointing to the relationship between the Spirit and Christ. Wherever he works, the Holy Spirit brings the communion of Christ. This

32. Owen, *Works*, 3:127.
33. Zizioulas, *Christian Dogmatics*, 10.
34. Zizioulas, *Being as Communion*, 132.

same relationship is then embodied ecclesially. Zizioulas's argument continues to focus on what he sees as the Western issue of over-individualization with a particular consequence of seeing the Holy Spirit in individual transformative terms rather than in relation to the ecclesial community.

> We need to rid ourselves of the belief that the Holy Spirit acts upon us as isolated persons and leaves us as isolated afterwards as before. This perception that the Spirit takes persons away from community is so widespread that we must reject it emphatically. Those who defend this view overlook the fundamental distinction between the action of the Holy Spirit in the Old Testament and in the New Testament. In the Old Testament, the Spirit is given to particular persons, prophets and kings, not to the whole nation. In the New Testament, the Messiah gives the Holy Spirit to the entire people of God.[35]

While this view might give insufficient weight to the relational identity of the people of Israel as a whole, it serves to emphasize the imparting of the Holy Spirit to the whole people of God in the New Testament rather than as speaking only through particular individuals.

Athanasios N. Papathanasiou takes up these themes and points to the influence of Zizioulas when he writes:

> The need for a fertile synthesis of Christology and pneumatology has since been fulfilled, especially by Zizioulas. In his thought, the "economy of the Spirit" is not understood simply as the phase of history following the "economy of the Son" (cf. Lossky, *Mystical Theology of the Eastern Church*); it is the constant breath that makes whatever it touches into an event of communion. The very creation of the world took place "in the Holy Spirit"; the Incarnation of the Son is Spirit-conditioned; and church life has a radically *epicletic* character. This means that the church ceaselessly seeks the action of the Spirit, which is also what makes the body of believers into the church.[36]

This present action of the Spirit, "making the believers into the church," I describe as transformative in terms of bringing people from what they are not to what they are or can be in all their fullness. This transformative work of the Holy Spirit in constituting the church is drawn out by Zizioulas in his understanding of communion, particularly arising out the worship offered

---

35. Zizioulas, *Christian Dogmatics*, 11.

36. See Papathanasiou, "Some Key Themes and Figures," 226.

by the people as seen primarily in the Eucharist. This is building on the central concept that has been explicated in chapter 3:

> The Holy Spirit is associated, among other things, with *koinonia* (2 Cor 13:13) and the entrance of the last days into history (Acts 2:17–18), that is *eschatology*. When the Holy Spirit blows, he creates not good individual Christians, individual "saints," but an event of communion, which transforms everything the Spirit touches into a *relational* being. In that case the other becomes an ontological part of one's own identity. The Spirit de-individu-alizes and personalizes beings wherever he operates.[37]

The transformative work of the Holy Spirit in human life is to change people from individuals to persons, with persons defined by their being in relationship rather than in isolation.

The Holy Spirit as Transformative in Relational Personhood

As outlined through this book, relational personhood is a significant theme for Zizioulas. He defines the relationality of personhood in response to the relationality which he sees within the Trinity and places weight on people "being" persons rather than "having" personhood. He writes:

> What does it mean that someone *is* rather than *has* a person? It is all too often assumed that people "have" personhood rather than "being" persons, precisely because ontology is not opera-tive enough in our thinking. Personhood in this case becomes a quality added, as it were, to being: you first (logically speaking) *are* and then *act* or *behave* as a person.[38]

He points to the way in which personhood is not just a universal category in which persons are, as it were "anonymized" by their participation in a shared identity. Rather personhood has its own particularity as persons discover their own unique identity. However, this unique identity is not that of an isolated individual on his or her own but held with others in the relationality that is the sign of personhood.

Alongside particularity, freedom is a key theme in Zizioulas's un-derstanding of relational personhood. Zizioulas redefines freedom from being an aspect of individuality, in which an individual is free to decide what she wants on her own, to being a gift of the Spirit that is constitutive

---

37. Zizioulas, *Communion and Otherness*, 6.

38. Zizioulas, *Communion and Otherness*, 99.

of personhood. He refers to the Holy Spirit as "the Spirit of freedom" who creates community in which people discover their true freedom.[39] This freedom flows out of the being of God meaning that knowledge of God is offered as gift rather than forced upon people:

> God does not want to be known or be acknowledged by us, unless this takes place in freedom for us too. Knowledge that is imposed on us, in defiance of our liberty, is not person-to-person knowledge, and so is not the knowledge that God wishes for us.[40]

The freedom to which Zizioulas points is not that of isolationism, but of free participation in an identity that is relational and thus frees people from isolation.

This personal relationality into which persons are drawn through the work of the Holy Spirit is embodied in the ecclesial community and, in particular, in the Eucharist.

The Holy Spirit as Transformative in the Eucharist

A particular "embodiment" of the Holy Spirit is seen in the Eucharist. The Eucharist brings together eternity and history in terms of the presence of the eternal God in the specific moments of history when the Eucharist is celebrated. Zizioulas comments:

> The Eucharist is the inaugural event of freedom and the moment in which eschatological reality becomes the actual presence of this assembly brought together by the Holy Spirit. This is the work of the Holy Spirit, which is why the invocation (*epiclesis*) of the Holy Spirit is fundamental. The gifts that bear the body and blood of Christ bring us into increasing participation in that body. This event of person-to-person relationship takes place in the Spirit, between each of us and Christ. These eschatological events are seen, felt and tasted in the gathering of the Church. This gathering is the event in which the Holy Spirit opens us to life together in freedom.[41]

One of the main criticisms of Zizioulas's thought has been that he is too "other-worldly." For example, Folsom, in his PhD thesis comparing MacMurray, Zizioulas, and Barth, comments: "I believe that an over-emphasis

39. Zizioulas, *Christian Dogmatics*, 10, 11.
40. Zizioulas, *Christian Dogmatics*, 28.
41. Zizioulas, *Christian Dogmatics*, 161.

of this eschatological aspect of the Spirit's work results in a church men-
tality that is so eschatological in focus that it ignores the present, biological existence, and neglects the needs of the world." Folsom continues by
pointing to particular movements, "for example, the pietistic movements
in recent church history (fundamentalism, etc.) have been so heavily engaged in eschatology that they denigrate and ignore the very real needs of
their contemporary world." He critiques Zizioulas: "In the place of God who
comes into human history Zizioulas proposes that the church is the vehicle
by which the created order is taken up out of history. Such a proposal seems
to me to neglect the reality of human needs that require concrete resolution
in the biological sphere."[42] However, I argue that Folsom's analysis is insufficient in two areas.

Firstly, he fails to distinguish sufficiently between pietistic movements
and their focus on individuality and an ecclesial understanding of communion from Zizioulas's Orthodox perspective. There is a danger that pietistic
movements can focus inwardly on the living encounter with God to the
extent of seeming to ignore the relationships with other people and with the
world. However, Zizioulas, in his argument about the nature of personal relationality within the ecclesial community, broadens out an inward-looking
individualistic approach with a sense of a wider shared community identity.

Secondly, he does not give sufficient weight to Zizioulas's argument
with regard to the historicity of the Holy Spirit in each celebration of the
Eucharist. The Eucharist is the point in which the Holy Spirit is made manifest in the unique particularity of the persons gathered. In this gathering,
the community is transformed into the likeness of Christ through the power
of the Holy Spirit and filled with God's life, love, power, and freedom. This
"filling" at the heart of the Eucharistic moment, in which individuals are
transformed into persons, has an inevitable consequence for the embodiment of God's life in the world.

Zizioulas outlines his thinking more fully in *The Eucharistic Communion and the World*.[43] He offers six points in interpretation of the relationship between the Eucharist and the world.

- Firstly, he argues for "The Eucharist as Event," both in history and containing "a particular vision of history." The Eucharist is not detached
  from particular times and places but is rooted in local communities.

- Secondly, he continues by pointing to the relationship between
  the gathered people at the Eucharist and the people sent from the

42. Folsom, "Comparative Assessment," 89n153.

43. Zizioulas, *Eucharistic Communion*, 124–31.

Eucharist into the world—"The Eucharist as the Acceptance of Creation." He argues that "the Liturgy is precisely a journey, a parade of the whole world before the altar. Bringing the world as it is with them, the faithful receive a foretaste of paradise, an eschatological glimpse of the world as it will be, and then are called again to 'go in peace' back into the world."

- Thirdly, he points to "The Eucharist as Anthropology," in which understanding "the Liturgy presupposes—and at the same time leads towards—an anthropology that understands humanity to be 'a new creation in Christ.'" The Eucharist is not detached from an anthropological understanding but rather gives a new shape to what is possible for humanity.

- Fourthly, Zizioulas refers to "The Eucharist as Ethics" offering a reinterpretation of an ethical stance. "The Eucharistic vision of the world and society neither permits nor admits an autonomy of ethics or its reduction to absolute legal rules. Rather, it holds that the moral life follows from the *transformation* and *renewal* of humanity in Christ." The starting point for an understanding of ethics is the new life which God has offered in Christ.

- Fifthly, Zizioulas draws attention to the eschatological dimension of the Holy Spirit, seeing, when he writes of "The Eucharist as Eschaton." The eschatological dimension of the Eucharist points to Zizioulas's argument about the Spirit coming from the future to shape the present.

- Sixthly, he refers to "The Eucharist as Hope"—looking at some of the contemporary dilemmas and challenges within the Orthodox tradition and comments that "if the Orthodox Church resolves the contemporary dichotomies in the Eucharist, it will appear *liturgically* as the hope of the world where humanity finds its integrity in communion with God."[44]

In this brief analysis Zizioulas points to the transformative nature of the Eucharist, not only as the place where the Holy Spirit constitutes the body of Christ but also as the offering of worship which takes this transformation into the life of the world. Yannaras echoes some of Zizioulas's thought, as Payne points out:

> [Yannaras] states, "For the Church is not a religion, it is not a school of spirituality, but a place where we are invited to transform our existence into *being as relationship*. We are invited to

44. Zizioulas, *Eucharistic Communion*, 123–31.

a meal, to a banquet—and a banquet is a way of practicing life as communion."[45] In the Eucharistic meal, the gathered people of God are transformed into the reality of the Body of Christ through the action of the Holy Spirit.[46]

The reference to the banquet as the practice of life in communion has implications for an understanding for the practice of relationality during a meal and for the sense of the banquet being a rich feast to which all are equally invited, rich or poor.

The Holy Spirit as Transformative in Culture and Creation

Zizioulas raises a further topic that has implications for the discussion of transformation, that of the connection between the transformation that is embodied in worship and the transformation of the world. His thinking in this area relates to a discussion of culture and creation. He raises this issue as a question in a World Council of Churches paper: "Would it be going too far, if for example the discussion of the Eucharist in documents such as BEM (the WCC Baptism, Eucharist and Ministry text) were to extend to a consideration of the ecological problem?"[47] He argues that "questions such as the meaning of personhood or the ecological problem must be introduced into the theological problematic of, for example, Trinitarian theology, Christology, Pneumatology, or even ecclesiology."[48] He argues in the paper for making stronger links between theology, science, and cultural issues starting from a Faith and Order perspective—not seeing theology as an enclosed area within Faith and Order, but looking at the way in which theological thinking, as for example with regard to worship, is inextricably linked with scientific and cultural issues. The Eucharist then becomes not an otherworldly escape from the world but the starting point for the engagement with the transformation of the world.

In the Orthodox conference on the environment in Halki in 2012, Zizioulas was said to be "the most prominent Orthodox spokesman on environmental issues," with the hope being expressed from the conference that participants would leave with a sense of the spiritual and ethical importance of issues about sustainability.[49] While these issues demand a broader atten-

45. Yannaras, "Church," 24.

46. Payne, "'Relational Ontology' of Christos Yannaras."

47. Zizioulas, "Faith and Order."

48. Zizioulas, "Faith and Order."

49. The "Halki Summit" to convene and discuss global responsibility and

tion in terms of the implications of the link between theology and culture and creation, for which there is not space in this book, I quote them here as an example of the way in which Zizioulas's approach to the transformative aspects of the Holy Spirit and worship leads on into a grappling with the implications of this for the whole of creation.

SIMILARITIES, DIFFERENCES, AND CONCLUSION

As I have argued throughout this volume, Owen and Zizioulas have different perspectives on worship and the Holy Spirit but hold to the key significance of both the Holy Spirit and worship in leading to the encounter with the triune God and the knowledge of God. I argue that it is this encounter and this knowledge that leads to the fourth part of the quadrilateral: transformation. In this area of transformation there are clear differences of understanding, but also intriguing similarities.

Owen focuses on the personal understanding of sanctification, looking in detail as to what this means, while Zizioulas draws attention to the work of the Holy Spirit in forming the ecclesial community and the way in which this leads to wider participation in God's transforming work in the world. Their two different perspectives draw attention to the range of ways in which the Holy Spirit is manifest and to the focus on the Holy Spirit as present in both the transformation of human life and as the builder of the human community, in reflection of the Holy Trinity. Owen and Zizioulas variously point to this transformation as a movement from separation from God and one another to the fullness of life in Christ; from being an individual to the realization of the full potential of human personhood; from doctrine which primarily engages the mind to worship which is full-bodied; and from isolation to community.

In a parallel, Papanikolaou reflects on the connection between revelation and its actualization and the way in which this actualization is the role of the Holy Spirit. "Such a revelation is not a self-revelation unless it is actualized, and this actualization is accomplished in the person of the Holy Spirit, who is the love that unites the Father and the Son." He continues by quoting Bulgakov: "The self-revelation of the Father is not complete until the content that is revealed in the Son is actualized as life by the Holy Spirit." In this sense, the Holy Spirit, for Bulgakov, is the "spirit of truth" and "represents the principle of reality. He transforms the world of ideas into a

environmental sustainability (June 18–20, 2012) under the auspices of Ecumenical Patriarch Bartholomew.

living and real essence."[50] I argue that it is this "actualization of revelation" which the Holy Spirit accomplishes that is at the heart of transformation and which holds together an intellectual engagement with the Christian faith and an offering of worship. I am arguing in this book for the particular significance of Owen's and Zizioulas's view of the reality of the Trinity as relational as well as doctrinal, and of the role of relationality in bringing about transformation. There is a balance between Owen and Zizioulas—between what might seem like an over-individualizing approach in Owen and an approach in Zizioulas that focuses too fully on the ecclesial community. Holding these two approaches together offers a reminder of the breadth of the presence of the Holy Spirit.

Relationality and Transformation

For both Owen and Zizioulas, relationality lies at the heart of transformation. This relationality, springing out of the participation in the relational life of the Trinity, leads to the transformation of the human person. In Owen's language, the person is sanctified, becomes holy, is given life, and thus participates in the new creation brought about by Christ. In Zizioulas's understanding, relationality leads the person to enter into full humanity, a humanity that is found in relationship with God and with other persons.

The power of God to transform lies in the development of the relationship. Zizioulas emphasizes that this relationship is freely entered into rather than imposed upon a person. The relationality into which people are drawn by the Holy Spirit is embodied in worship in which God is known as both other and present. There is an element of mystery in encountering the Holy Spirit which takes people out of themselves in awe and wonder, and an element of closeness as the Spirit is encountered in the present moment. Participation in the mystery and the closeness leads to a transformation which can be both fully experienced in the moment and be part of a long, slow process of personal growth.

Becoming a Person

The relationships that the Holy Spirit brings about lead to full personhood. Owen and Zizioulas emphasize different aspects of this personhood. Owen focuses more on the development of personal attributes such as understanding

---

50. See Papanikolaou, "Contemporary Orthodox Currents on the Trinity," 328–38. Papanikolaou quotes Sergei Bulgakov, *Sophia—The Wisdom of God*.

and wisdom. Zizioulas points to the significance of persons becoming who they are in relationship rather than as individuals on their own. Both Owen and Zizioulas look to the way in which becoming fully a person—becoming who each one is meant to be—arises out of God's freely offered love in Christ.

The transformation that is brought about by participation in the divine life leads to people becoming holy, reflecting the image and likeness of God, not through human striving but through God's gift. The Holy Spirit comes with the gift of restoration to full humanity and to an ultimate sense of freedom as the person becomes who the person is meant to be. The qualities that the Spirit offers are received by the person and within the ecclesial community. People are no longer on their own in endeavoring to live such fullness of life. They are strengthened and undergirded by the Spirit.

Worship at the Heart of Transformation

Owen and Zizioulas both see worship as key to the embodiment of the Holy Spirit's transforming work. For Owen, there is a strong emphasis on preaching and the opening of the Word of God. The read and preached word is the visible connection with Christ, the living Word. In preaching, the "otherness" of God becomes an incarnational reality through the working of the Holy Spirit. There is an intellectual engagement which is held alongside the inspiration of heart and soul, with the Holy Spirit speaking to both mind and heart. For Zizioulas, the emphasis lies on the Eucharist with the epicletic prayer pointing to the reality of the gift of the Holy Spirit in transforming the bread and wine into the body and blood of Christ and the congregation into the people of God. The visibility of Christ's embodiment is seen in both the bread and the wine and the people. Through this visible embodiment, in the power of the Holy Spirit, the church is continually brought into being and people are transformed into the likeness of Christ and enabled to be participants in Christ's work in the world.

While Owen and Zizioulas have different emphases in terms of the way in which the Holy Spirit in worship is visible in preaching and in the Eucharist, there is an underlying similarity, as suggested by Schmemann, the influential Orthodox liturgical scholar. His comment is noteworthy, on what can seem like a polarization between East and West. He points to the possibility of drawing together what might seem like opposing views:

> Western Christians are so accustomed to distinguish[ing] the Word from the sacrament that it may be difficult for them to understand that in the Orthodox perspective the liturgy of the Word is as sacramental as the sacrament is "evangelical." The

> sacrament is a manifestation of the Word. And unless the false
> dichotomy between Word and sacrament is overcome, the true
> meaning of both Word and sacrament, and especially the true
> meaning of Christian "sacramentalism," cannot be grasped in all
> their wonderful implications. The proclamation of the Word is a
> sacramental act par excellence because it is a transforming act.
> It transforms the human words of the Gospel into the Word of
> God and the manifestation of the Kingdom. And it transforms
> the man who hears the Word into a receptacle of the Word and
> a temple of the Spirit.[51]

Worship offers visibility for the Holy Spirit's transformative activity. This transformative work of the Spirit takes place in the moments of visible offering of worship and contributes to the ongoing process of transformation. The regularity of the offering of worship itself points to the developmental aspects of transformation. This is not something that happens in the moment and is then forgotten. Worship contributes to the development of transformation in the person and the church.

Transforming Time

A sub-text of both Owen's and Zizioulas's arguments is that of the transformation of time. In Owen, the focus is more on the immediate moment as the encounter with God; for Zizioulas, there is an understanding of the future breaking into the present and the present being transformed.

The synchronicity of the encounter with the Holy Spirit and people in the present moment of worship leads to a re-formulation of conceptions of time. In each act of worship, eternity breaks into the present. The Spirit acts in history but takes people beyond history. Both past and future indwell the present moment as the door to eternity is opened. Christian history becomes the story of moments of encounter with God with God seen in all God's fullness in a myriad of different ways.

Wolfgang Vondey writes that "a pneumatological approach to time suggests that eschatology is determined not only by the end and the consummation of the present in the future, but also by the perpetuation of the present moment through the power of God unfolding in time in the operation of the Holy Spirit."[52] Owen's emphasis on the importance of specific

---

51. McPartlan, "Who Is the Church?" 275, quoting Schmemann, *For the Life of the World*, 21, 32–33.

52. Vondey, "Holy Spirit and Time," 17.

moments of encounter with the Holy Spirit points to the way in which the Holy Spirit is active in time but is also transforming time.

Zizioulas points to the way in which the Holy Spirit is not distant from the present day but indwells each present moment through the relationship encountered in worship. It is the same Holy Spirit who is present in each place and across each generation.

There is a contrast between Owen's and Zizioulas's view of the present and the future, but there are also congruities. Both the contrasts and the overlaps demonstrate the need to hold both views in balance: when the Holy Spirit is present, there is a new encounter each time; part of the future becoming present. The new encounter then re-makes and re-shapes people and communities. Owen in particular emphasizes that there are not just moments of immediate change but that these moments relate to a gradual process of growth. In this longer process of growth, there is a need to wait, without knowing what might come. While waiting is a human initiative, what comes is the divine response; the Spirit comes when people are open, waiting, and ready.

CONCLUSION

I have looked at the effectual impact of the Holy Spirit in transformation from the writings of Owen and Zizioulas, focusing in particular on the significance of relationality and the way in which relationality leads to transformation.

There has been a focus on the transformation of the whole of life, human life and that of creation. One of the differences is that between Owen's more inward focus on personal transformation and Zizioulas's ecclesial focus with its impetus towards the transformation of creation and culture.

I suggest that the holding together of these two perspectives offers a helpful ecumenical perspective for looking at this particular aspect of the Holy Spirit in relation to worship.

9

The Holy Spirit and Worship

Ecumenical Implications

INTRODUCTION

In this concluding chapter, I build on the arguments that have been made in this book about the relationship between the Holy Spirit and worship and develop the implications for an ecumenical approach to ecclesiology and thus a renewal of the churches' ecumenical journey. This work has drawn together strands from seventeenth-century Reformed tradition and contemporary Orthodox tradition in order to highlight the significance of the encounter with the Holy Spirit that is found in the relationship of worship and, consequently, that is embodied in acts of worship. I take the argument forward by unpacking my worship thesis ten from chapter 4 of this volume:

> Seeing the Holy Spirit in worship as the one who draws us into the encounter with the Trinity opens up the possibility of a renewed ecumenical appreciation of the varieties of possibility of ways of worship, offered to the one divine source.

This book began by looking at the rise of Pentecostalism and the charismatic movement and (as argued by Eugene Rogers and others)[1] the neglect of

1. Rogers, *After the Spirit.*

the Holy Spirit, particularly in historic Western pre- and post-Reformation churches. McPartlan has also argued: "One of the greatest weaknesses generally acknowledged as something longstanding in Western theology is the lack of attention to the work of the Holy Spirit."[2] Bergen, in his analysis of the Holy Spirit in the reports of ecumenical dialogues from 1982 to 2012, writes, referring to the somewhat contentious book by Radner:

> In his provocative book *The End of the Church*, Ephraim Radner advanced the possibility "that the Holy Spirit has taken leave of the divided Church" with the corollaries that a modern ecumenism that correlates divided churches with a diversity of gifts of the Spirit, or a diversity of "unities" with the Spirit's leading, is therefore incoherent.[3]

Bergen continues by pointing to the declared intention of international ecumenical dialogues as seeking to be led by the Holy Spirit:

> While I do not venture to judge whether the Spirit is *actually* doing what the churches say the Spirit is doing, this essay highlights aspects of the churches' self-understandings of the movement toward lived communion, delineates an implicit or operative doctrine of the Holy Spirit in the church, and thereby provides tools by which to assess Radner's challenge that discerning the Spirit amid division is seriously impaired.[4]

In the critique of Radner by Bergen, the point is made about the separation between the Holy Spirit and the "lived communion" that can take place between churches of different traditions and the way this is reflected in international bilateral dialogues. There can be agreement about the doctrine of the Holy Spirit but a resistance to translate that agreement into a willingness to allow the Spirit to be effectual in overcoming the separation of churches. This book has sought to examine the way in which it is possible to draw together an understanding of the activity of the Holy Spirit in acts of worship which are offered differently in different traditions. This is to articulate that it is the same Holy Spirit who is at work in the offering of diverse acts of worship and therefore to draw out the connection between a doctrinal understanding of the Holy Spirit and the necessity of seeing the consequent embodied activity of the Holy Spirit, in worship. There are many ways of understanding and responding to the Holy Spirit. The variety of ways of

2. McPartlan, *Sacrament of Salvation*, 91.

3. Bergen, "Holy Spirit and Lived Communion," 195, quoting Radner, *End of the Church*, 10.

4. Bergen, "Holy Spirit and Lived Communion," 195.

understanding and of responding can at times make it seem as though there are many Holy Spirits. This work has sought to differentiate between understanding and responding in order to point to an affirmation of one Holy Spirit who is manifest in a variety of ways.

This argument has been advanced in order to draw together a doctrinal understanding of the Holy Spirit with the ways in which the Holy Spirit is actually encountered in the setting of acts of worship. I drew attention earlier to the extensive writing on both the Holy Spirit and on worship from a wide range of different perspectives, and yet to the limited attention that has been given to the specific relationship between the Holy Spirit and worship. This book has sought to redress that lack of attention by looking at the writings of Owen and Zizioulas about the Holy Spirit and worship.

This concluding chapter builds on the arguments that have been made previously and offers ecumenical challenges. This is in order to set the argument about the nature and the work of the Holy Spirit, as seen in a relation of worship and embodied in acts of worship, within the theology and life of the church. In taking two radically different theologians from different traditions and eras of the church's life and seeing the convergences that arise out of their thinking, this volume adds a small pointer to the possibility of renewed ecumenical engagement.[5] In focusing on the area of the Holy Spirit and worship, this work points to the theological richness to be found in this area with the aim of setting this approach alongside the more full-bodied experiential approach that has been seen in the gifts that have been found in the last hundred years of particular Pentecostal/charismatic approaches to the Holy Spirit and worship.

While the conclusions about worship and the shape of worship as offered within their particular Christian traditions have differed between these two theologians, it has been interesting to note, from their different perspectives, a convergence with regard to the understanding of the nature and work of the Holy Spirit and the role of the Spirit in drawing people into a worshipping relationship with God.

This convergence has been explored in detail here in what has been identified as a quadrilateral framework, drawing together four aspects of

---

5. Innovative work is being undertaken under the leadership of Professor Paul Murray of Durham University on the Receptive Ecumenism project, and the three international conferences (together with the two books that have been published thus far) that have been held over the past ten years on the theme of "Receptive Ecumenism." Receptive Ecumenism embraces the range of Christian traditions and their contemporary settings across the continents. It provides a broader background to the much smaller argument made in this book in relation to two specific theologians out of two particular traditions of the church.

a proper understanding of the Holy Spirit. While the topic of the Holy Spirit and worship has been approached differently by Owen and Zizioulas, there are similarities in both theologians as outlined in the four sides of the quadrilateral framework. These similarities are offered as a sign of hope and a fruitful starting point for ecumenical conversation, in contrast with the continual dilemma and challenge of churches being unwilling to recognize the Holy Spirit in each other, or to look at the Holy Spirit primarily from a doctrinal perspective without taking the step of examining the manifestation of the Holy Spirit within the particular tradition in a variety of ways including that of worship.

THE HOLY SPIRIT AND WORSHIP: THE QUADRILATERAL FRAMEWORK

I have looked at the work of the English seventeenth-century Reformed theologian, John Owen (variously described as Puritan, Congregationalist, Separatist, or Independent), and the contemporary Eastern Orthodox theologian, John Zizioulas. The works of both of these theologians, and the writings—both positive and negative—about these two theologians, have seen a high level of publication in the last twenty-five years.[6] This volume seeks to supplement the work offered by Reformed theologians such as Colin Gunton in his chapter on Owen and Zizioulas in *Theology through the Theologians*[7] and the significant input of Thomas Torrance to Reformed/ Orthodox dialogue.[8]

The first half of this book examined the shared Trinitarian understanding of both Owen and Zizioulas, their emphasis on the role of the Holy Spirit, and the significance they give to worship as the ground for encountering God. Out of this shared understanding, in the second half of this work I have developed my quadrilateral framework, outlining four overlapping areas in which there is congruity between Owen and Zizioulas: personal relationality, immediacy, truth, and transformation. I have argued that while they have different emphases, it is significant that both draw out these four areas in their understanding of the Holy Spirit and worship. I have also argued that these areas are not each to be taken in isolation but are

6. As noted in the footnotes in previous chapters and in the bibliography.

7. Gunton, *Theology through the Theologians*, 187–205.

8. For example, see Torrance, *Theological Dialogue Between Orthodox and Reformed Churches*. In the 1980s, under Torrance's co-chairing, a number of Reformed-Orthodox dialogues were held, culminating in the *Agreed Statement on the Holy Trinity* in 1991.

intrinsically interconnected with each other. The presence of each of these "sides" of the quadrilateral is important. One side does not stand on its own; all four stand together. The four sides are each of a different order, thus highlighting that they are each coming out of contemplation of the diversity of interpretation of the role and nature of the Holy Spirit and drawing out the way in which the Holy Spirit goes beyond easy characterization. The significant unifying criterion to diverse interpretation is the Holy Spirit, not only in shaping a doctrinal understanding but as a lived and experienced reality.

In chapter 5 I looked at the personal and relational characteristics that arise out of an understanding of the triune God and the way these personal and relational characteristics are embodied in acts of worship. This is seen in terms of the encounter with God that takes place in worship and the way in which this encounter embodies relationality, in two different ways: firstly, of the worshipper with God, and (out of this relationship) of the worshipper with other human persons. The nature of "personal" in ecclesial terms is significant for both Owen and Zizioulas. In Owen's understanding, the gathered membership of the local church is the primary focus for the discernment of the Holy Spirit. For Zizioulas, it is the personal office of the bishop which is the focal point for authoritative discernment of the Spirit. For both Owen and Zizioulas, the significance of becoming fully human flows out of the relational understanding of the triune God, embodying relationality in human personhood.

Chapter 6 examined immediacy, mediation, and otherness, explicating the way in which the Holy Spirit is both immediately present to the human spirit and the human community in the offering of worship and yet also can be seen to be mediated through the particular elements of worship. For both Owen and Zizioulas, the act of worship is central to the reception of the Holy Spirit and the life of the church. The nature of this act of worship differs, with Owen having a stronger focus on the Word of God as unpacked in reading the scriptures and preaching and Zizioulas emphasizing the centrality of the Eucharist. In both of these understandings of worship, the Spirit draws together the presence and the otherness of God, the immediate moment, and the eschatological horizon.

Chapter 7 addressed the area of truth, seeing truth as having a necessarily relational context. Truth is something into which people are led through the work of the Holy Spirit rather than something determined by an individual person on his or her own. The view of truth as not only revealed as propositions or doctrines but embodied in the relationship of worship which the Holy Spirit opens up is key to both Owen and Zizioulas.

Chapter 8 explored the concept of the Holy Spirit as transformational, looking at this area both personally and ecclesially. Owen has a strong emphasis on personal sanctification into which a person can grow through the course of her life. For Zizioulas, the emphasis is on the Spirit constituting the church and, through this work of constitution, offering both freedom and the fullness of human personhood. The church then becomes an "icon" of the kingdom with the transformative work of the Spirit engaging the whole of creation.

OWEN AND ZIZIOULAS ON THE HOLY SPIRIT AND WORSHIP: ECUMENICAL IMPLICATIONS

I have referred to the way in which Owen and Zizioulas differ in terms of their theological approach, their philosophical and historical setting, and their East/West divide. In each chapter, I have looked at the expected differences and then moved forward to look at the unexpected similarities. I turn now to look in particular at the ecumenical implications of their writing. In this topic, it could appear that there are more divergences than congruities arising out of their differing contexts and settings. For example, Zizioulas has been, from 2005 to 2015, the Orthodox co-chair of the international Orthodox/Catholic dialogue with a keen interest in promoting ecumenical dialogue. Owen, on the other hand, could be seen as a schismatic, whose opposition to the 1662 Act of Uniformity led him in to be allied with the Dissenters who were ejected from the Church of England. It is ironic to note that an Act which sought to impose uniformity in terms of worship, authority, and organizational structure led in practice to the entrenchment of diverse Christian traditions in England.

I am drawing out in this book the value of a convergence in thinking about the Holy Spirit and worship from a Reformed and an Orthodox perspective and seeing this convergence as a helpful contribution to wider ecumenical discussions.

From an ecumenical perspective arising out of work between two different Christian traditions, Gunton reflects on the Anglican-Roman Catholic International commission statement on authority and argues for the need for a greater emphasis on the Holy Spirit in dialogues between different traditions:

> What is required, therefore, is a reconsideration of the relation of pneumatology and christology with a consequent reduction of stress on the Church's institution by Christ and a greater emphasis on its constitution by the Spirit. In such a way we may

create fewer self-justifying and historicizing links with the past and give more stress to the necessity for the present particularities of our churchly arrangements to be constituted by the Spirit.[9]

I argue in this volume for renewed attention to be given to the nature and activity of the Holy Spirit, particularly as seen in the offering of worship, and for the fruitfulness of the convergences in this area between a Reformed and an Orthodox theologian. These convergences help to expand an understanding of the Holy Spirit in the relationship of worship by sharing some of the similarities and insights from their different perspectives. In so doing, Owen and Zizioulas offer a deepening of the church's thinking about the Spirit and worship and a challenge to bring this insight to future ecumenical dialogues.

I turn to look at the differing insights that arise with regard to ecumenism out of Owen's and Zizioulas's approaches and the overarching ecumenical orientation that I argue is offered by their congruities of thinking about the Holy Spirit and worship. There are two dimensions to their contribution that I am arguing they make to an ecumenical dialogue. The first is the overt and organizational dimension that is highly visible in Zizioulas through his participation in ecumenical dialogue and his writing on the significance of ecumenism. This dimension is particular to Zizioulas but not found in Owen. The second dimension is that of theological reflection on the faith, drawing out convergences in areas such as Pneumatology and worship that are central to each part of the church, even if articulated and made manifest in a variety of ways. It is here that Owen and Zizioulas, in the congruities that arise out of a comparison of their theological thinking about the Holy Spirit and worship, have insights that are beneficial ecumenically in the twenty-first century. I argue that these congruities draw the church back to foundational aspects of the Christian faith and of the church's life and provide a helpful starting point in ecumenical discussion, before moving on to the specifics of diversity in worship and ecclesial structure between different traditions of the church. These congruities point to the lived reality of the triune God, and the manifestation of this God in the worship life of the church.

I move to look briefly at some wider issues that are raised in the comparison between Owen and Zizioulas.

---

9. Gunton and Hardy, *On Being the Church*, 62.

Owen's Ecumenical Contribution

In addition to Owen's emphasis on the Holy Spirit and worship and the contribution this makes to ecumenical understanding, two further areas arise in terms of ecumenical dialogue.

The first is Owen's reference to the influence of the early Fathers in the thinking that shapes the church. I have already referred to this in looking at the shape of *Pneumatologia* and the weight of references to the early Fathers. Markschies, in his contribution to *Patristic Studies in the Twenty-First Century,* writes of the way in which, in some contemporary Protestant scholarship, the time before the Reformation can be glossed over: "This is mostly due to the prejudice that the history of the Reformation churches began only in the sixteenth century." He continues by making the ecumenical point about the need for the study of the early history of the church and quotes Ritter as follows: "Protestantism needs to be rooted in the pre-Reformation, ancient Christian and medieval tradition and therefore in antiquity itself, because its ability to take part in an ecumenical dialogue is highly dependent on this."[10] Owen's emphasis on the early Fathers helps to root his writings in the longer tradition of the church from a Reformed perspective and opens up the possibility for stronger dialogue with other traditions for whom this tradition is more central to their thinking.

The second relates to an understanding of the church as based in the local and open to the new. Gunton comments on the emphasis in Owen on both "the strong note of the voluntary exercise of membership in the visible church" and on the way in which "the Church is the work of the eschatological Spirit and so there is in Owen an emphasis, derived from the New Testament, on the newness of what is happening."[11] The emphasis on the gathered membership in the local church and the Spirit leading into the new are characteristic of Owen's more congregationalist emphasis from within the Reformed tradition.

Zizioulas's Ecumenical Contribution

The broad nature of Zizioulas's ecumenical approach is illustrated in his work on behalf of the Ecumenical Patriarchate, his involvement with the World Council of Churches, his lecturing in the West, and the impact his writing has had in both Eastern and Western churches. Jillions refers to

---

10. See Bitton-Ashkelony et al., *Patristic Studies*, 367–88. The quote is from Ritter, *Vom Glauben Der Christen*, 22–23.

11. Gunton and Hardy, *On Being the Church,* 72.

the wider ecumenical challenge facing Christianity and quotes Zizioulas's response in his Balamand lecture, urging greater forbearance between the Eastern and Western churches:

> Today there is a tendency among the Orthodox to stress the responsibility of the Western Christians for the evil of division and for the wrongs done to the Orthodox Church by our Western brothers. History is, of course, clear in witnessing to the face of a great deal of aggressiveness against the Orthodox on the part of the West. Deep however in the tragic reality of Christian division lies also an inability of the Orthodox to overcome and rise above the psychology of polemic in a true spirit of forgiveness and love. The second millennium has been in this respect almost an unfortunate period of the Church's history.[12]

Jillions continues by referring to the broader setting of the church in the world and quotes Zizioulas as urging the church to listen to the world as well as to speak to the world. In his Balamand lecture, given at the turn of the twentieth century, Zizioulas reinforces his emphasis on the significance of Pneumatology and the importance of drawing on the church's liturgical life as two of the ways in which the church needs to respond to the changing world in which she is set. Towards the end of his *Lectures in Christian Dogmatics,* Zizioulas outlines the importance and the difficulties of ecumenical reception. He draws attention to the way in which the church has always received—from the Holy Spirit and the world—and the way in which the church exists to give of what she has received. However, he comments: "The form of reception is the most difficult thing to agree upon in our present ecumenical situation."[13]

Issues of ecumenical reception are explored in *Receptive Ecumenism and the Call to Catholic Learning,*[14] including contributions by McPartlan and Louth which reflect both supportively and critically on Zizioulas's Eucharistic ecclesiology.[15] Zizioulas's own sense of the significance of the tradition in which he stands, the need for his own tradition's renewal, and his critique of the World Council of Churches as an ecclesial body is highlighted in his 1995 WCC essay, "The Self-Understanding of the Orthodox . . . and Their Participation in the Ecumenical Movement."[16]

12. See Jillions, "Orthodox Christianity in the West."

13. Zizioulas, *Lectures,* 162.

14. Murray, *Receptive Ecumenism.*

15. See McPartlan, "Catholic Learning and Orthodoxy"; Louth, "Receptive Ecumenism and Catholic Learning."

16. Zizioulas, "Self-Understanding of the Orthodox."

IMPLICATIONS FOR CONTEMPORARY
ECUMENICAL DIALOGUE

This book builds on the spirit of ecumenical rapprochement in drawing together insights from two different theological approaches to the Holy Spirit
and worship in order to develop a pneumatological theology of worship
on the understanding that the Holy Spirit, as giver of truth, is particularly
present at the intersection of different understandings.

While Owen's emphasis on the "newness" of the Spirit's work might
seem remote from an Orthodox understanding, I note Zizioulas's comment
in his WCC essay:

> The Church is a relational entity, and this means several impor-
> tant things. The first is that the Church is not a petrified entity
> transmitted from one generation to another as an archaeologi-
> cal treasure. . . . The Church is only where the Spirit is, and
> where the Spirit is the past relates to the present and the present
> is opened up to the future. All this is implied in what we call Re-
> ception of tradition. What we have inherited from the Fathers,
> be it dogmas, ethos or liturgy, must be received and re-received
> all the time, and in this process the past becomes existentially,
> and not simply mentally or ritually, present.[17]

The "re-receiving" of the Spirit and the openness of the church to the future bears comparison with Owen's understanding of the presence of the
Spirit renewing the church in each place and thus holding together both the
received tradition of the Word and the newness of the present existential
encounter. For both Owen and Zizioulas, the Spirit has a particular focus in
the acts of worship offered in each place with the Spirit being received anew
in each act of worship.

The increased emphasis on the Spirit has been identified in recent
ecumenical discussion. McPartlan writes from a Roman Catholic perspective: "One of the greatest factors in recent ecumenical progress has been a
renewed appreciation of the Spirit's role. Discussion of the Church and particularly of the Eucharist has been enlivened and greatly advanced through
recognizing them as prime works of the Spirit in the world." He highlights
the way in which "Vatican II signalled this renewed awareness in its Decree
on Ecumenism," continues by quoting Pope John Paul II: "only the Holy
Spirit can overcome the divisions still existing between Christians" and
concludes: "The Holy Spirit is here being identified as the one who gathers
the Church, transforms individuals into a community and directs our gaze

17. Zizioulas, "Self-Understanding of the Orthodox," 3, 4.

to a fuller union in the future, all of this activity being focused upon the celebration of the Eucharist."[18]

I referred at the beginning of this chapter to Bergen's article looking at the place of the Holy Spirit in Ecumenical International Dialogues over a twenty year period from 1992 to 2002.[19] He argues that the dialogues offer an "implicit ecumenical pneumatology" in relation to the Spirit's role in areas such as authority, unity, and mission. Among the missing areas on which he comments are those of relationality and of prayer. With regard to relationality, he points to a need for reflection on the way in which dialogues themselves draw people into relation:

> Finally, lived communion entails a communion in love as well as a communion in truth. Here, it is worth noting a deficiency in my preceding study to make a substantial point. Texts are not dialogues; a final report, even an agreed statement, does not capture the relational process by which it came about. Thus, though I have not been comprehensive or exhaustive even in my analysis of the dialogues' explicit discussions of the Spirit's activity in history, there is a dimension of the Spirit's work in dialogue that is not reflected in reports and therefore is not captured in this study. Just as the experience of being apart causes separate traditions to develop their own cultures, patterns of relating, and intellectual frames of reference, so the experience of working together creates new relationships, new understandings, and new realities.[20]

I find it thought-provoking to reflect on whether, if dialogues can focus further on the personal and relational communion of the Holy Trinity through the Holy Spirit, whether this relationality might come more strongly to the fore.

On the topic of prayer, which is connected with the lack of emphasis on worship in the dialogues, Bergen comments that while there are many references to the need for prayer to the Holy Spirit in the dialogues, "the general absence of such prayers" as offered to those who will receive the

---

18. McPartlan, *Sacrament of Salvation*, 91, 92; John Paul II, "Address to Ecumenical Representatives in Poland."

19. "In particular, the dialogues discern the work of the Spirit in the practice of dialogue, wrestle with how the Spirit may have been active in or despite historical moments of division, identify the Spirit with the present work of healing memories, link the Spirit of unity with the church in mission, and reflect on the experience of koinonia/communion and reception of the gifts of the Spirit" (Bergen, "Holy Spirit and Lived Communion," 193).

20. Bergen, "Holy Spirit and Lived Communion," 216

reports, is noteworthy. However, I note that in the Reformed-Orthodox Dialogue, reporting in 1992, just before the period Bergen covers, there are more references to both the Holy Spirit and worship and an emphasis on the centrality of the Holy Spirit and worship within the setting of the Holy Trinity.[21]

I argue that Owen and Zizioulas, in their holding together of the Holy Spirit and worship, make a significant contribution to wider contemporary ecumenical discussion and reflection. The comparison of approaches to an understanding of the presence of the Holy Spirit in worship across the many different contemporary manifestations of the Christian church is a subject worthy of further study.

CONCLUSION

In comparing the writing of two theologians from different traditions, cultures, and periods of history, I have sought to draw out the helpful nature of the unexpected congruities within their thought as an offering to the wider twenty-first-century ecumenical movement. In their focus on the Holy Spirit and worship, Owen and Zizioulas draw together four strands of approach which I have identified in my quadrilateral framework. They have helpfully sought to hold together a trinitarian doctrinal understanding of the nature of the Holy Spirit with the particular outpouring of the Holy Spirit as received in acts of worship. While they represent differing ecclesial views, as seen in Owen's emphasis on the congregation as the primary focus for the receiving of the Holy Spirit and Zizioulas's stress on the significant role of the bishop in holding the tradition of the church and the lived experience of the people together, I argue that their congruity of approach to the presence of the Holy Spirit in worship is a helpful emphasis.

McDonald, at the end of his thesis on Barth and the Holy Spirit, concludes by commenting "the pneumatologist ought to show a proper humility before the Spirit's work."[22] I echo his comment by suggesting that focusing on the Holy Spirit does indeed lead to humility, and to openness, challenging an individualizing sense of the Holy Spirit as "my personal possession." By seeing the doctrine of the Holy Spirit as interpreted through worship, Owen and Zizioulas offer an approach that draws together the head and the heart in the presence of the One who is always both "present" and "other."

21. World Alliance of Reformed Churches, "Agreed Statement."
22. McDonald, "Discerning the Spirit."

Appendix

Contents of Goold's edition of John Owen's Works

This volume uses *The Works of John Owen, DD*, edited by William H. Goold (London: Johnstone and Hunter, 1856) as the primary source for the writings of John Owen.[1] This appendix summarizes the contents of this twenty-four-volume work. It includes some brief explanatory notes at various points that reference the Holy Spirit or have relevance to the topics covered in the discussion here. Capitalization of headings from the Goold edition has been preserved.

VOLUME 1

"Life of Dr. Owen by Revd. A. Thomson."

"A Declaration of the Glorious Mystery of the Person of Christ."

Chapters 1–22.   1–252

"Meditations and Discourses on the Glory of Christ."

Chapters 1–14.   274–418

"Meditations and Discourses Concerning the Glory of Christ, Applied etc."

Chapters 1–2.   418–64

"Two Short Catechisms." [Very short paragraphs in question and answer format.]

Chapters 1–27, including: 464–end

Chapter 3: "Of the Holy Trinity."

Chapter 20: "Of Sanctification."

Chapter 22: "Of the Sacraments of the New Covenant."

---

1. For a comprehensive overview of Owen's works, see Burden, "John Owen."

PART 3

PART 4

VOLUME 10: A DISPLAY OF ARMINIANISM

VOLUME 11: THE DOCTRINE OF THE SAINTS PERSEVERANCE EXPLAINED AND CONFIRMED

VOLUME 12: VINDICIAE EVANGELICAE; OR THE MYSTERY OF THE GOSPEL VINDICATED AND SOCINIANISM EXAMINED

VOLUME 13: THE DUTY OF PASTORS AND PEOPLE DISTINGUISHED

VOLUME 14: ANIMADVERSIONS ON A TREATISE ENTITLED "FIAT LUX" [AGAINST POPERY]

ORATIONES 6

INDICES

Index to the life of Owen.

Index to the notes by the editor.

Index to the works of Owen according to the arrangement of the volumes in the present edition.

Index to the Works of Owen in their alphabetical order—list of Owen's prefaces to works of other authors.

Index to the principal subjects and occasional topics.

Index to the principle words and phrases in other languages cited or explained: i. Hebrew, Chaldee, or Rabbinical, ii. Greek, and iii. Latin.

Index to passages of scripture explained.

Index of references to authors, opinions, councils and sayings.

VOLUME 17: THEOLOGOMENA PANTODAPA 1661 [IN LATIN]

DE NATURE, ORTU, PROGRESSU, ET STUDIO VERAE THEOLGIAE

VOLUME 18: COMMENTARY ON HEBREWS

PRELIMINARY EXCITATIONS

PART 1: CONCERNING THE EPISTLE TO THE HEBREWS

PART 2: CONCERNING THE MESSIAH

PART 3: CONCERNING THE INSTITUTIONS OF THE JEWISH CHURCH REFERRED TO IN THE EPISTLE

VOLUME 19: COMMENTARY ON HEBREWS

EXERCITATIONS ON THE EPISTLE TO THE HEBREWS

PART 4: CONCERNING THE SACERDOTAL OFFICE OF CHRIST

PART 5: CONCERNING A DAY OF SACRED REST

SUMMARY OF OBSERVATIONS DRAWN FROM THE EXPOSITION OF THE EPISTLE

VOLUME 20: AN EXPOSITION OF THE EPISTLE TO THE HEBREWS

VOLUME 21: AN EXPOSITION OF THE EPISTLE TO THE HEBREWS

Chapters 3–5. [Also has a title page "Volume 4."]

VOLUME 22 [CHAPTERS 6–7]

[Also has a title page "Volume 5."]

VOLUME 23 [CHAPTERS 8–10

[Also has a title page "Volume 6.")

VOLUME 24 [CHAPTERS 11–13

[Also has a title page "Volume 7."]

Bibliography

Abba, Raymond. *Principles of Christian Worship*. London: Oxford University Press, 1957.

Afanasiev, Nicholas. *The Church of the Holy Spirit*. Edited by Michael Plekon. Translated by Vitaly Permakov. Notre Dame: University of Notre Dame Press, 2007.

Aldred, Joe. "The Holy Spirit in the Pentecostal Tradition: With Special Reference to Black Pentecostalism." *Churches Together in England*, November 2006. Online. http://www.cte.org.uk/Groups/236237/Home/Resources/Theology/Papers/Holy_Spirit_in/Holy_Spirit_in.aspx.

Allen, David. *The Unfailing Stream: A Charismatic Church History in Outline*. Tonbridge: Sovereign World, 1994.

Allmen, J. J. von. "The Theological Frame of a Liturgical Renewal." *The Church Quarterly* 2 (1969) 11–23.

———. *Worship: Its Theology and Practice*. London: Lutterworth, 1965.

Alston, William P. *Perceiving God: The Epistemology of Religious Experience*. Ithaca, NY: Cornell University Press, 1991.

Ambrose. *Selected Works and Letters*. Vol. 10 of *Nicene and Post-Nicene Fathers*, Series 2. Edited by Philip Schaff. 1886–1889. 14 vols. Reprint, Grand Rapids: Christian Classics Ethereal Library, 2007.

Anatolios, Khaled. *Retrieving Nicaea: The Development and Meaning of Trinitarian Doctrine*. Grand Rapids: Baker Academic, 2011.

Anderson, Alan H., and Walter J. Hollenweger. *Pentecostals after a Century: Global Perspectives on a Movement in Transition*. Sheffield: Sheffield Academic, 1999.

Anzior, U. "A Spirited Humanity: The Trinitarian Ecclesiology of Colin Gunton." *Themelios* 36.1 (2011) 26–41.

Areeplackal, Joseph. *Spirit and Ministries: Perspectives of East and West*. Bangalore: Dharmaram, 1990.

Augustine. *Confessions*. Translated by R. S. Pine-Coffin. London: Penguin, 1961.

———. *De Trinitate*. Vol. 3 of *Nicene and Post-Nicene Fathers*, Series 1. Edited by Philip Schaff. 1886–1889. 14 vols. Reprint, Grand Rapids: Christian Classics Ethereal Library, 2004.

Avis, Paul. "The Ecclesiological Significance of the Liturgy." Unpublished paper. 2014.

Awad, Najib George. "Another Puzzle Is . . . the Holy Spirit: *De Trinitate* as Augustine's Pneumatology." *Scottish Journal of Theology* 65.1 (2011) 1–16.

———. "Personhood as Particularity: John Zizioulas, Colin Gunton, and the Trinitarian Theology of Personhood." *Journal of Reformed Theology* 4 (2010) 1–22.

———. *Persons in Relation: An Essay on the Trinity and Ontology.* Minneapolis: Fortress, 2014.

———. "Pneumatology and the Defence of the Hypostatic Individuation of the Holy Spirit: Examining the Validity of Trinitarian Theology on the Basis of a Comparison and a Scrutiny of Eastern and Western Pneumatological Perspectives." PhD diss., Kings College London, 2007.

Ayres, Lewis. *Augustine and the Trinity.* Cambridge: Cambridge University Press, 2010.

———. *Nicea and Its Legacy: An Approach to Fourth-Century Trinitarian Theology.* Oxford: Oxford University Press, 2004.

Bagchi, David V. N., and David C. Steinmetz, eds. *The Cambridge Companion to Reformation Theology.* Cambridge: Cambridge University Press, 2004.

Baillie, John. *Our Knowledge of God.* Oxford: Oxford University Press, 1939.

Baker, Deane-Peter. "Plantinga's Reformed Epistemology: What's the Question?" *International Journal for Philosophy of Religion* 57.2 (2005) 77–103.

Baker, Jonny, and Doug Gay. *Alternative Worship.* London: SPCK, 2003.

Barcellos, Richard C. *The Family Tree of Reformed Biblical Theology: Geerhardus Vos and John Owen, Their Methods of and Contributions to the Articulation of Redemptive History.* Palmdale, CA: Reformed Baptist Academic, 2010.

Barr, William R., and Rena M. Yocom, eds. *The Church in the Movement of the Spirit.* Grand Rapids: Eerdmans, 1994.

Barth, Karl. *Church Dogmatics.* Edited by G. W. Bromiley and T. F. Torrance. Edinburgh: T&T Clark, 2009.

Basil. *Letters and Selected Works.* Vol. 8 of *Nicene and Post-Nicene Fathers*, Series 2. Edited by Philip Schaff. 1886–1889. 14 vols. Reprint, Grand Rapids: Christian Classics Ethereal Library, 2007.

Battaglia, Vincent P. "An Examination of Karl Rahner's Trinitarian Theology." *Australian eJournal of Theology* 9 (2007) 1–18.

Baum, G. *The Twentieth Century: A Theological Overview.* Maryknoll, NY: Orbis, 1999.

Beeke, Joel R. "John Owen on Assurance." In *The Quest for Full Assurance: The Legacy of Calvin and His Successors*, by Joel R. Beeke, 165–213. Edinburgh: Banner of Truth, 1999. Online. http://johnowen.org/media/beeke_owen_on_assurance.pdf.

Behr, John. "The Trinitarian Theology of St. Basil of Caesarea." *All Saints of North America Orthodox Church*, 1999. Online. http://www.allsaints-stl.org/Trinitarian%20Theology%20of%20St.%20Basil%20of%20Caesarea%20-%20Web%20Version%202008.pdf.

Benoit, J. D. *Liturgical Renewal: Studies in Catholic and Protestant Developments on the Continent.* London: SCM, 1958.

Bentley, Wessel. "Calvin and the Holy Spirit as *fons vitae.*" *Studia Historiae Ecclesiasticae* 35.2 (2009) 77–85. Online. http://www.researchgate.net/publication/239526523_Calvin_and_the_Holy_Spirit_as_fons_vitae.

Bergen, Jeremy M. "The Holy Spirit and Lived Communion from the Perspective of International Bilateral Dialogues." *Journal of Ecumenical Studies* 49.2 (2014) 195.

Berger, Teresa, and Bryan D. Spinks, eds. *The Spirit in Worship—Worship in the Spirit.* Collegeville, MN: Liturgical, 2009.

Berkhof, Hendrikus. *The Doctrine of the Holy Spirit*. London: Epworth, 1964.

Bernstein, Eleanor, ed. *Liturgy and Spirituality in Context: Perspectives on Prayer and Culture*. Collegeville, MN: Order of Saint Benedict, 1990.

Bitton-Ashkelony, Brouria, et al., eds. *Patristic Studies in the Twenty-First Century: Proceedings of an International Conference to Mark the Fiftieth Anniversary of the International Association of Patristic Studies*. Turnhout, Belgium: Brepok, 2015.

Bosch, David. *Transforming Mission*. Maryknoll, NY: Orbis, 1991.

Boulton, Matthew Myer. *God against Religion: Rethinking Christian Theology through Worship*. Grand Rapids: Eerdmans: 2008.

Bozzo, Edward George. "Theology and Religious Experience." *Theological Studies* 31 (1970) 415–36.

Bradley, James E., and Richard A. Muller. *Church History*. Grand Rapids: Eerdmans, 1995.

Bradshaw, Paul F. "Difficulties in Doing Liturgical Theology." *Pacifica* 11 (1998) 181–94.

Bradshaw, Paul F., and Bryan D. Spinks, eds. *Liturgy in Dialogue*. London: SPCK, 1993.

Brauer, Jerald C. "Reflections on the Nature of English Puritanism." *Church History* 20 (1954) 99–108.

Bredin, Eamonn. *Praxis and Praise*. Ireland: Columba, 1994.

Breslauer, Daniel S. "Immediacy and its Limits: A Study in Martin Buber's Thought by Nathan Rotenstreich." *Association of Jewish Studies Review* 19.1 (1994) 104–6.

Bria, Ion. *Liturgy After the Liturgy*. Geneva: World Council of Churches, 1996.

Brierley, Peter. *Christian England: Results of the 1989 English Church Census*. London: Marc Europe, 1991.

———. *Mission-Shaped Church: Church Planting and Fresh Expressions for Church in a Changing Context*. London: Church House, 2004.

———. *Pulling Out of the Nosedive*. London: Christian Research Association, 2006.

———. *The Tide Is Running Out*. London: Christian Research Association, 2000.

———, ed. *Religious Trends*. 7 vols. London: Christian Research Association, 1997–2008.

British Council of Churches. *The Forgotten Trinity: The Report of the BCC Study Commission on Trinitarian Doctrine Today*. London: BCC, 1989.

Brown, Alan. "On the Criticism of *Being as Communion* in Anglophone Orthodox Theology." In *The Theology of John Zizioulas: Personhood and the Church*, edited by Douglas H. Knight, 35–78. Farnham: Ashgate, 2007.

Brown, Callum G. *The Death of Christian Britain*. London: Routledge, 2001.

Brown, James. *Subject and Object in Modern Theology*. Norwich: SCM, 1955.

Buber, Martin. *I and Thou*. New York: Touchstone, 1996.

Buckley, James J., and David S. Yeago. *Knowing the Triune God: The Work of the Spirit in the Practices of the Church*. Grand Rapids: Eerdmans, 2001.

Burden, Mark. "John Owen: Learned Puritan." *Centre for Early Modern Studies, University of Oxford*, 2013. Online. https://earlymodern.web.ox.ac.uk/john-owen-learned-puritan.

Burleigh, J. H. S. "The Doctrine of the Holy Spirit in the Latin Fathers." *Scottish Journal of Theology* 7.2 (1954) 113–22.

Burns, Stephen. *Liturgy: SCM Study Guide*. London: SCM, 2006.

Burns, Stephen, et al. *The Edge of God: New Liturgical Texts and Contexts in Conversation*. London: Epworth, 2008.

Burrell, David. "Reading the Confessions of Augustine: An Exercise in Theological Understanding." *Journal of Religion* 50.4 (1970) 327–51.

Butner, D. Glenn, Jr. "For and Against de Regnon: Trinitarianism East and West." Paper presented at the Sixty-Sixth Annual Meeting of the Evangelical Theological Society, San Diego, CA, November 19–21, 2014.

Caldwell, Philip. *Liturgy as Revelation.* Minneapolis: Fortress, 2014.

Calvin, John. *The Institutes of the Christian Religion.* 1536. Translated by Henry Beveridge. 1845. Grand Rapids: Christian Classics Ethereal Library, 2013.

Cameron, Charles. "An Introduction to 'Theological Anthropology.'" *Evangel* 23.2 (2005) 53–61.

Carr, Wesley. "Towards a Contemporary Theology of the Holy Spirit." *Scottish Journal of Theology* 28.6 (1975) 501–16.

Carson, Claire. "Bodies: Perfect or Broken? Eucharist, Ecumenism, and Eating Disorders." *Contact* 141 (2003) 2–10.

Carson, D. A., ed. *Worship: Adoration and Action.* London: World Evangelical Fellowship, 1993.

Castellano, Daniel J. "The Composition of the Second Eucharistic Prayer." *Repository of Arcane Knowledge,* 2007. Online. http://www.arcaneknowledge.org/catholic/hippolytus.htm.

Chadwick, Henry. *East and West: The Making of a Rift in the Church.* Oxford: Oxford University Press, 2003.

Chan, Simon. *Liturgical Theology: The Church as Worshipping Community.* Westmont, IL: InterVarsity, 2006.

"Charles II, 1662: An Act for the Uniformity of Publique Prayers and Administrac[i]on of Sacraments & Other Rites & Ceremonies and for Establishing the Form of Making Ordaining and Consecrating Bishops Preists and Deacons in the Church of England." In *1628–80,* edited by John Raithby, 364–70. Vol. 5 of *Statutes of the Realm.* N.p.: Great Britain Record Commission, 1819. Online. http://www.british-history.ac.uk/statutes-realm/vol5/pp364-370.

Charry, Ellen T. *By the Renewing of Your Minds: The Pastoral Function of Christian Doctrine.* Oxford: Oxford University Press, 1999.

———. "The Doctrine of God as a Guide for the Emotions." Paper presented at the Society for Christian Theology, October 19, 2012. Online. http://christianpsych.org/media/the_doctrine_of_god.pdf.

Chung, Titus. *Thomas Torrance's Mediations and Revelation.* Farnham: Ashgate, 2011.

Churches Together in Britain and Ireland (CTBI). *The Forgotten Trinity: The BCC Study Commission on Trinitarian Doctrine Today—Report, Study Guide, and a Selection of Papers.* London: CTBI, 2011.

Ciraulo, Jonathon Martin. "Sacraments and Personhood: John Zizioulas's Impasse and a Way Forward." *Heythrop Journal* 53.6 (2012) 993–1004.

Clark, Mary T. "De Trinitate." In *The Cambridge Companion to Augustine,* edited by David Vincent Meconi and Eleonore Stump, 91–102. Cambridge: Cambridge University Press, 2006.

Cleveland, Christopher. "Thomism in John Owen." PhD diss., University of Aberdeen, 2011.

Clutterbuck, Richard. "Jürgen Moltmann as a Doctrinal Theologian: the Nature of Doctrine and the Possibilities for its Development." *Scottish Journal of Theology* 48.4 (1995) 489–505.

Cocksworth, Christopher J., and Jeremy Fletcher. *Spirit and Liturgy.* Cambridge: Grove, 1998.

Coffey, John, and Paul C. H. Lim, eds. *The Cambridge Companion to Puritanism.* Cambridge: Cambridge University Press, 2008.

Colle, Ralph del. "'Person' and 'Being' in John Zizioulas's Trinitarian Theology: Conversations with Thomas Torrance and Thomas Aquinas." *Scottish Journal of Theology* 54.1 (2001) 70–86.

Collins, Paul M. *Trinitarian Theology: West and East.* Oxford: Oxford University Press, 2001.

———. *The Trinity: A Guide for the Perplexed.* Edinburgh: T&T Clark, 2008.

Committee on the Study of the Doctrine of Worship. *The Worship of the Church: A Reformed Theology of Worship.* Pittsburgh: Synod of the Reformed Presbyterian Church of North America, 2004.

Congar, Yves M.-J. *I Believe in the Holy Spirit.* 3 vols. London: Geoffrey Chapman, 1983.

———. *Vraie et fausse réforme dans l'Église.* Paris: Cerf, 1950.

Cook, Michael J. "Revelation as Metaphoric Process." *Theological Studies* 47 (1986) 388–411.

Cooke, Bernard. *Power and the Spirit of God: Toward an Experience-Based Pneumatology.* Oxford: Oxford University Press, 2004.

Cooper, Jarrod. *Glory in the Church: A Fresh Blueprint for Worship in the Twenty-First Century.* Milton Keynes: Authentic, 2003.

Cooper, Tim. *John Owen, Richard Baxter, and the Formation of Nonconformity.* Farnham: Ashgate, 2011.

Cox, Harvey. "A Review of Pentecostal Spirituality: A Passion for the Kingdom by Steven J. Land." *Journal of Reformed Theology* 12.3 (1994) 1–12.

———. *Fire from Heaven: The Rise of Pentecostal Spirituality and the Reshaping of Religion in the Twenty-First Century.* Boston: Da Capo, 2001.

Craig-Wild, Peter. *Tools for Transformation: Making Worship Work.* Edinburgh: Darton Longman Todd, 2002.

Crouse, Robert D. "Atonement and Sacrifice: 'Doctrine and Worship—St. Augustine and the Fathers.'" Paper presented at the Atlantic Theological Conference, Charlottetown, Prince Edward Island, Canada, June 1990.

Cumin, Paul. "Looking for Personal Space in the Theology of John Zizioulas." *International Journal of Systematic Theology* 8.4 (2006) 356–70.

———. "Robert Jensen and the Spirit of It All: Or You (Sometimes) Wonder Where Everything Else Went." *Scottish Journal of Theology* 60.2 (2007) 161–79.

Cunningham, David S., et al., eds. *Ecumenical Theology in Worship, Doctrine, and Life: Essays Presented to Geoffrey Wainwright on his Sixtieth Birthday.* Oxford: Oxford University Press, 1999.

Cunningham, Mary B., and Elizabeth Theokritoff, eds. *The Cambridge Companion to Orthodox Christian Theology.* Cambridge: Cambridge University Press, 2008.

Curry, David. "Let Us Thus Think of the Trinity: Matters Essential and Matters Indifferent in Seventeenth-Century English Theology." Paper presented at the Atlantic Theological Conference, Moncton, New Brunswick, Canada, June 2010. Online. http://christchurchwindsor.ca/wp-content/uploads/documents/CurryonMattersEssentialAndIndifferent.pdf.

D'Ambrosio, Marcellino. "*Ressourcement* Theology, *Aggionamento*, and the Hermeneutics of Tradition." *Communio: International Catholic Review* 18.4 (1991) 530–55.

Daniels, Richard. *The Christology of John Owen*. Grand Rapids: Reformed Heritage, 2004.

David, Kenneth. *Sacrament and Struggle*. Geneva: World Council of Churches, 1994.

Davie, Grace. *Religion in Britain Since 1945*. Oxford: Blackwell, 1994.

Davies, Horton. *Worship and Theology in England*. 5 vols. Princeton: Princeton University Press, 1961–1975.

———. *The Worship of the English Puritans*. London: Dacre, 1948.

Davies, J. G. *Every Day God*. Norwich: SCM, 1973.

Davies, Oliver. "Reading Theologically." Paper presented at Rebecca Hussey's Book Charity Memorial Lecture, Lambeth Palace, London, April 23, 2015.

Davis, James Colin. *Fear, Myth, and History: The Ranters and the Historians*. Cambridge: Cambridge University Press, 1986.

Davis, Leo D. *The First Seven Ecumenical Councils (325–787): Their History and Theology*. Norwich: Liturgical, 1983.

Dawn, Marva. *Reaching Out without Dumbing Down: A Theology of Worship for the Turn-of-the-Century Culture*. Grand Rapids: Eerdmans, 1995.

Dayton, Donald W. *Theological Roots of Pentecostalism*. Peabody, MA: Hendrickson, 1987.

Deddo, R. Gary W. "The Holy Spirit in the Theology of T. F. Torrance." In *The Promise of Trinitarian Theology: Theologians in Dialogue with Thomas F. Torrance*, edited by E. Coyler, 81–114. Lanham, MD: Rowman and Littlefield, 2001.

DelCogliano, Mark. "Basil of Caesarea's Homily On Not Three Gods (CPG 2914): Problems and Solutions." *Sacris Erudiri* 50 (2011) 87–131.

———, ed. *Works on the Spirit: Athanasius the Great and Didymus the Blind*. Yonkers, NY: St. Vladimir's Seminary, 2011.

Dewes, Deborah. "The Incorporation of an Individual into the Liturgical Action of the Church of England." PhD diss., Durham University, 1996.

Dix, Dom Gregory. *The Shape of the Liturgy*. London: Dacre, 1949.

Dixon, Philip. *Nice and Hot Disputes: The Doctrine of the Trinity in the Seventeenth Century*. Edinburgh: T&T Clark, 2003.

Doctrine Commission of the Church of England. *We Believe in the Holy Spirit*. London: Church House, 1991.

Durheim, Benjamin. "The Human as Encounter: Karl Barth's Theological Anthropology and a Barthian Vision of the Common Good." *Lumen et Vita* 1.1 (2011) 1–20.

Earey, Mark. *Liturgical Worship*. London: Church House, 2002.

Edwards, Rob. *Study Guide for John Owen's The Mortification of Sin*. Edinburgh: Banner of Truth, 2008.

Ellis, Christopher. "Gathering Struggles: Creative Tensions in Baptist Worship." *Baptist Quarterly* 42.1 (2007) 4–21.

Emery, Giles, and Matthew Levering, eds. *The Oxford Handbook of the Trinity*. Oxford: Oxford University Press, 2011.

Empereur, James. *Models of Liturgical Theology*. Cambridge: Grove, 1987.

Evans, Eifion. "John Calvin: Theologian of the Holy Spirit." *Reformation and Revival* 10.4 (2001) 83–105.

Fagerberg, David W. *Theologia Prima: What Is Liturgical Theology?* Chicago: Hillenbrand, 2007.

Fairlamb, Horace. *Sanctifying Evidentialism.* Cambridge: Cambridge University Press, 2009.

Farley, Michael A. "What Is 'Biblical' Worship? Biblical Hermeneutics and Evangelical Theologies of Worship." *Journal of the Evangelical Theological Society* 51.3 (2008) 591–613.

Fee, Gordon D. *God's Empowering Presence: The Holy Spirit in the Letters of Paul.* Peabody, MA: Hendrickson, 1994.

Fenwick, John, and Bryan Spinks. *Worship in Transition: The Twentieth-Century Liturgical Movement.* Edinburgh: T&T Clark, 1995.

Ferguson, Sinclair B. *A Heart for God.* Edinburgh: Banner of Truth, 1987.

———. *John Owen on the Christian Life.* Edinburgh: Banner of Truth, 1987.

———. *The Sermon on the Mount.* Edinburgh: Banner of Truth, 1987.

Ferguson, Sinclair B., and David F. Wright. *New Dictionary of Theology.* Leicester: InterVarsity, 1988.

Flanagan, Kieran. *Sociology and Liturgy: Re-Presentations of the Holy.* London: Palgrave MacMillan, 1991.

Fletcher, Jeremy, and Christopher Cocksworth. *Spirit and Liturgy.* Cambridge: Grove, 1998.

Florenksy, Paul. *Iconostasis.* Yonkers, NY: St. Vladimir's Seminary, 1996.

Florovsky, George. "The Limits of the Church." *Church Quarterly Review* 233 (1933) 117–28.

Folsom, Marty. "A Comparative Assessment of the Concept of Freedom in the Anthropologies of John Macmurray, John Zizioulas, and Karl Barth." PhD diss., University of Otago, 1994.

Ford, David F. "Knowledge, Meaning, and the World's Great Challenges." *Scottish Journal of Theology* 57.2 (2004) 182–202.

———. "What Happens in the Eucharist?" *Scottish Journal of Theology* 48.3 (1995) 360–80.

Ford, David F., and Daniel W. Hardy. *Living in Praise.* London: Darton Longman Todd, 2005.

Ford, David F., and Rachel Meurs, eds. *The Modern Theologians.* Oxford: Blackwell, 2005.

Ford, David F., and Graham N. Stanton, eds. *Reading Texts, Seeking Wisdom.* London: SCM, 2003.

Forrester, D. B., and Doug Gay, eds. *Worship and Liturgy in Context: Studies and Case Studies in Theology and Practice.* Norwich: SCM, 2009.

Forsyth, Peter Taylor. *The Church and the Sacraments.* London: Independent, 1916.

Foster, John. *The Nature of Perception.* Oxford: Oxford University Press, 2003.

Fox, Patricia. *God as Communion: John Zizioulas, Elizabeth Johnson, and the Retrieval of the Symbol of the Triune God.* Minnesota: Liturgical, 2001.

Frame, John M. "An Article Reviewing John L. Pollock's *Contemporary Theories of Knowledge.* Totowa, NJ: Rowan and Littlefield, 1986." *Westminster Theological Journal* 52.1 (1990) 131–41.

———. "A Review Article." *Westminster Theological Journal* 39.2 (1977) 328–53.

Franks Davis, Caroline. *The Evidential Force of Religious Experience.* Oxford: Clarendon, 1989.

Frei, Hans W. *Types of Christian Theology*. London: Yale University Press, 1992.

Fresh Expressions. "Starting Our Journey: Where Do I Begin?" 2017. Online. https://freshexpressions.org.uk/starting-our-journey-where-do-i-begin.

Gabriel, Andrew K. *The Lord Is the Spirit: The Holy Spirit and the Divine Attributes*. Cambridge: James Clarke, 2011.

Galgalo, Joseph D. *African Christianity: The Stranger Within*. Limuru: Zapf Chancery, 2012.

George, K. M. *The Silent Roots: Orthodox Perspectives on Christian Spirituality*. Geneva: World Council of Churches, 1994.

Gibson, William, and Robert G. Ingram, eds. *Religious Identities in Britain 1660–1832*. Farnham: Ashgate, 2005.

Giles, Richard. *Creating Uncommon Worship: Transforming the Liturgy of the Eucharist*. Norwich: Canterbury, 2004.

———. *Re-Pitching the Tent: Re-Ordering the Church Building for Worship and Mission in the New Millennium*. Norwich: Canterbury, 1996.

———. *Times and Seasons: Creating Transformative Worship throughout the Year*. Norwich: Canterbury, 2008.

Gill, Jerry H. "Divine Action and Mediated." *Harvard Theological Review* 80.3 (1987) 369–78.

Gilson, Étienne. *Letters of Étienne Gilson to Henri de Lubac*. Translated by Mary Emily Hamilton. San Francisco: Ignatius, 1988.

Gray-Reeves, May, and Michael Perham. *The Hospitality of God: Emerging Worship for a Missional Church*. London: SPCK, 2011.

Green, Robert. *Only Connect: Worship and Liturgy from the Perspective of Pastoral Care*. London: Darton Longman Todd, 1987.

Grenz, Stanley J. *The Social God and the Relational Self*. Louisville, KY: Westminster John Knox, 2001.

Groppe, Elizabeth T. "Creation *Ex Nihilo* and *Ex Amore*: Ontological Freedom in the Theologies of John Zizioulas and Catherine Mowry Lacugna." *Modern Theology* 21.3 (2005) 463–96.

Grumett, David. "Radical Orthodoxy." *Expository Times* 122.6 (2011) 261–70.

Guardini, Romana. *The Spirit of the Liturgy*. 1918. Reprint, Chicago: Biretta, 2014.

Guiver, George. *Pursuing the Mystery: Worship and Daily Life as Presences of God*. London: SPCK, 1996.

———. *Vision upon Vision: Processes of Change and Renewal in Christian Worship*. Norwich: Canterbury, 2009.

Gunton, Colin E. "Augustine, the Trinity, and the Theological Crisis of the West." *Scottish Journal of Theology* 43.1 (1990) 33–58.

———. *Act and Being*. Norwich: SCM, 2002.

———. *A Brief Theology of Revelation*. Edinburgh: T&T Clark, 2005.

———. *Intellect and Action*. Edinburgh: T&T Clark, 2000.

———. *The Promise of Trinitarian Theology*. Edinburgh: T&T Clark, 1991.

———. *Theology Through the Theologians*. Edinburgh: T&T Clark, 1996.

———. "Using and Being Used: Scripture and Systematic Theology." *Theology Today* 47.3 (1990) 248–59.

Gunton, Colin E., et al., eds. *The Practice of Theology: A Reader*. Norwich: SCM, 2001.

Gunton, Colin E., and D. Hardy, eds. *On Being the Church: Essays on the Christian Community*. Edinburgh: T&T Clark, 1989.

Hambrick-Stowe, Charles E. "Review of *God's Caress: The Psychology of Puritan Religious Experience*, by Charles Lloyd Cohen." *Church History* 55.4 (1986) 532–34.

Hanson, Richard P. C. *The Search for the Christian Doctrine of God*. Edinburgh: T&T Clark, 1988.

Hardy, Daniel W. *Finding the Church*. London: SCM, 2001.

———. *God's Ways with the World: Thinking and Practicing Christian Faith*. London: Bloomsbury, 2005.

Harrison, Peter. *"Religion" and the Religions in the English Enlightenment*. Cambridge: Cambridge University Press, 1990.

Hastie, Peter. "The Last Things: Paul Helm Talks to Peter Hastie." *The Briefing* (blog), December 13, 2010. Online. http://matthiasmedia.com/briefing/2010/12/the-last-things-paul-helm-talks-to-peter-hastie.

Healy, Nicholas. "'By the Working of the Holy Spirit': The Crisis of Authority in Christian Churches." *Anglican Theological Review* 88.1 (2006) 5–24.

———. "Karl Barth's Ecclesiology Reconsidered." *Scottish Journal of Theology* 27 (2004) 287–99.

———. *Thomas Aquinas: Theologian of the Christian Life*. Aldershot: Ashgate, 2003.

Hegel, Georg W. F. *Phenomenology of the Spirit*. Translated by A. V. Miller. Oxford: Clarendon, 1977.

Helm, Paul. "Edwards and John Locke on Emotion." *Helm's Deep: Philosophical Theology* (blog), May 27, 2011. Online. http://paulhelmsdeep.blogspot.co.uk/2011_05_01_archive.html.

———. "Review of *Warranted Christian Belief* by Alvin Plantinga." *Mind* 110.440 (2001) 1110–15.

Hendry, George S. *The Holy Spirit in Christian Theology*. London: SCM, 1957.

———. "The Transcendental Method in the Theology of Karl Barth." *Scottish Journal of Theology* 37.2 (1984) 213–27.

Henry, Carl F. H. "Theology and Biblical Authority: A Review Article." *Journal of the Evangelical Theological Society* 19.4 (1976) 315–23.

Heppe, Heinrich. *Reformed Dogmatics*. Translated by G. T. Thompson. London: Wakeman, 1950.

Heron, Alasdair I. C. *The Holy Spirit*. London: Marshall, Morgan, and Scott, 1983.

Heyd, Michael. "The Reaction to Enthusiasm in the Seventeenth Century." *Religion* 15 (1985) 279–89.

Higton, Mike. "Hans Frei and David Tracy on the Ordinary and the Extraordinary in Christianity." *The Journal of Religion* 79.4 (1999) 566–91.

Hollingworth, Richard. *The Holy Ghost on the Bench, Other Spirits At The Bar: Or, The Judgement of the Holy Spirit Upon the Spirits of the Times*. London: J. M., 1656.

Holmes, Stephen R. *The Holy Trinity: Understanding God's Life*. Milton Keynes: Paternoster, 2012.

———. "Listening for the Lex Orandi: The Constructed Theology of Contemporary Worship Events." *Scottish Journal of Theology* 66.2 (2013) 192–208.

Holtam, Nicholas. *The Art of Worship: Paintings, Prayers, and Readings for Meditation*. London: National Gallery, 2011.

Horrell, John Scott. "Toward a Biblical Model of the Social Trinity: Avoiding Equivocation of Nature and Order." *Journal of the Evangelical Theological Society* 47.3 (2004) 399–421.

Horsman, Andrew. "The Shape of the Trinity: Eucharistic Worship and the Doctrine of the Trinity." *Theology* 102.806 (1999) 89–97.

Houlgate, Stephen. *Hegel's Phenomenology of Spirit.* London: Bloomsbury, 2013.

Howard, John Franklin. "Divine Initiative and Human Response: Experiencing God in Worship Through a Structured Ministry Time." DMin diss., Asbury Theological Seminary, 1997.

Howson, Barry H. "The Puritan Hermeneutics of John Owen: A Recommendation." *Westminster Theological Journal* 63.2 (2001) 351–78.

Hughes, Graham. *Worship as Meaning: A Liturgical Theology for Late Modernity.* Cambridge: Cambridge University Press, 2003.

Hughes, Robert D. "Starting Over: The Holy Spirit and Locus of Spiritual Theology." *Anglican Theological Review* 83.3 (2001) 455–72.

Hunsinger, George. *The Eucharist and Ecumenism: Let Us Keep the Feast.* Cambridge: Cambridge University Press, 2008.

Hutter, Reinhard. *Suffering Divine Things: Theology as Church Practice.* Grand Rapids: Eerdmans, 2000.

Irwin, Kevin W. "Liturgy as Mediated Immediacy: Sacramentality and Enacted Works." Paper presented at the Intellectual Tasks of the New Evangelization conference, Catholic University of America, Washington, DC, September 15–17, 2011.

Jagessar, Michael N., and Stephen Burns. *Christian Worship: Post-Colonial Perspectives.* Sheffield: Equinox, 2011.

Janz, Paul D. *The Command of Grace: A New Theological Apologetics.* Edinburgh: T&T Clark, 2009.

Jenson, Robert W. *The Triune Identity.* Philadelphia: Fortress, 1982.

Jesson, Nicholas A. "Lex Orandi, Lex Credendi: Towards a Liturgical Theology." *Ecumenism.net*, November 2001. Online. https://ecumenism.net/archive/jesson_lexorandi.pdf.

Jiang, Tingcui. "A Critical Study on Zizioulas's Ontology of Personhood." PhD diss., Hong Kong Baptist University, 2014.

Jillions, John A. "Orthodox Christianity in the West: the Ecumenical Challenge." In *The Cambridge Companion to Orthodox Christian Theology*, edited by Mary B. Cunningham and Elizabeth Theokritoff, 276–92. Cambridge: Cambridge University Press, 2008.

John Paul II. "Address to Ecumenical Representatives in Poland." *Oss Rom*, July 6, 1987.

Johnson, Trig. "John Baillie's Epistemology of Mediated Immediacy: It's Logic, Importance for Baillie's Mediating Theology, and Promise as a Model of Revelatory Religious Experience." PhD diss., University of Gloucestershire, 2015.

Jones, Alan. "Falling in Love: The Work of the Holy Spirit." *Anglican Theological Review* 83.3 (2001) 375–86.

Jones, Cheslyn, et al., eds. *The Study of Liturgy.* London, SPCK, 1992.

Jones, Keith G., and Parush R. Parushev, eds. *Currents in Baptistic Theology of Worship Today.* Prague: International Baptist Theological Seminary, 2007.

Jones, Paul Dafydd. "Review of the Domain of the Word: Scripture and Theological Reason by John Webster." *Modern Theology* 30.1 (2014) 174–76.

Jowers, Dennis W. "An Exposition and Critique of Karl Rahner's Axiom: 'The Economic Trinity *is* the Immanent Trinity and Vice Versa." *Mid-America Journal of Theology* 15 (2004) 165–200.

Kalaitzidis, Pantelis. "Challenges of Renewal and Reformation Facing the Orthodox Church." *Ecumenical Review* 61 (2009) 136–64.

Kapic, Kelly M. *Communion with God: Relations between the Divine and the Human in the Theology of John Owen.* Grand Rapids: Baker Academic, 2007.

———. *The Divine and the Human in the Theology of John Owen.* Grand Rapids: Baker Academic, 2007.

Kapic, Kelly M., and Mark Jones, eds. *The Ashgate Research Companion to John Owen's Theology.* Farnham: Ashgate, 2015.

Kapic, Kelly M., and Justin Taylor, eds. *Overcoming Sin and Temptation.* Wheaton, IL: Crossway, 2006.

Karageorgi, Paul. "An Examination of the Contribution of John Owen to Trinitarian Theology, with Particular Reference to How Far He Transcended the Western Augustinian Tradition." August 2015. Online. https://www.academia.edu/15243339/An_Examination_of_the_contribution_of_John_Owen_to_Trinitarian_theology_with_particular_reference_to_how_far_he_transcended_the_Western_Augustinian_tradition.

Kärkkäinen, Veli-Matti. *Pneumatology: The Holy Spirit in Ecumenical, International, and Contextual Perspective.* Grand Rapids: Baker Academic, 2002.

Kavanagh, Aidan. *On Liturgical Theology.* Collegeville, MN: Liturgical, 1992.

Kay, Brian. *Trinitarian Spirituality: John Owen and the Doctrine of God in Western Devotion.* Milton Keynes: Paternoster, 2008.

Kay, William K. *Pentecostalism.* London: SCM, 2009.

Kelley, James L. *A Realism of Glory: Lectures on Christology in the Works of Protopresbyter John Romanides.* Rollinsford, NH: Orthodox Research Institute, 2009.

Kelsey, David H. *The Uses of Scripture in Recent Theology.* Augsburg: Fortress, 1975.

Khoo, Lorna Lock-Nah. *Wesleyan Eucharistic Spirituality: Its Nature, Source, and Future.* Adelaide: ATF, 2005.

Kilby, Karen. "Perichoresis and Projection: Problems with Social Doctrines of the Trinity." *New Blackfriars* 81.957 (2000) 432–45.

Knapp, Henry M. "Review of *Divine Discourse*, by Sebastian Rehnman." *Calvin Theological Journal* 38 (2003) 186–88.

———. "Understanding the Mind of God: John Owen and Seventeenth-Century Exegetical Methodology." PhD diss., Calvin Theological Seminary, 2002.

Knight, Douglas H., ed. *The Theology of John Zizioulas: Personhood and the Church.* Farnham: Ashgate, 2007.

Knox, Ronald Arbuthnot. *Enthusiasm: A Chapter in the History of Religion, with Special Reference to the Seventeenth and Eighteenth Centuries.* Oxford: Clarendon, 1950.

Kreider, Alan, and Eleanor Kreider. *Worship and Mission after Christendom.* Exeter: Paternoster, 2009.

Kreitzer, Mark R. "Review of *The Holy Trinity: In Scripture, History, Theology, and Worship*, Robert Letham, Philipsburg, NJ: P&R, 2004." *Global Missiology* 4.5 (2008). Online. http://ojs.globalmissiology.org/index.php/english/article/viewFile/46/131.

Kulp, A. P. "The Trinity, The Holy Spirit, and Worship." PhD diss., Southern Baptist Theological Seminary, 2001.

LaCugna, Catherine Mowry. *God for Us: The Trinity and Christian Life.* New York: Harper Collins, 1993.

————. "Re-Conceiving the Trinity as the Mystery of Salvation." *Scottish Journal of Theology* 38 (1985) 1–23.

LaCugna, Catherine Mowry, and Killian McDonald. "Returning for the 'Far Country': Theses for a Contemporary Trinitarian Theology." *Scottish Journal of Theology* 41.2 (1988) 191–215.

Ladouceur, Paul. "Treasures New and Old: Landmarks of Orthodox Neopatristic Theology." *St. Vladimir's Theological Quarterly* 56.2 (2012) 191–227.

Lamont, William. "Puritanism as History and Historiography." *Past and Present* 44.1 (1969) 133–46.

Lane, Dermot A. *The Experience of God: An Invitation to Do Theology.* Dublin: Veritas, 2003.

Lash, Nicholas. *The Beginning and the End of "Religion."* Cambridge: Cambridge University Press, 1996.

————. *Easter in Ordinary: Reflections on Human Experience and the Knowledge of God.* Norwich: SCM, 1988.

Lathrop, Gordon W. *"Holy People": A Liturgical Ecclesiology.* Augsburg: Fortress, 1999.

————. *Holy Things: A Liturgical Theology.* Augsburg: Fortress Press, 1993.

Lee, Francis. *John Owen Represbyterianized.* Edmonton: Still Waters Revival, 2000.

Letham, Robert. "John Owen's Doctrine of the Trinity in Its Catholic Context and Its Significance for Today." Paper presented at the Fifty-Fifth Westminster Conference, London, December 20, 2006. Online. http://www.johnowen.org/media/letham_owen.pdf.

Lim, Paul C. H. *Mystery Unveiled: The Crisis of the Trinity in Early Modern England.* Oxford: Oxford University Press, 2012.

Lincicum, David. "Economy and Immanence: Karl Rahner's Doctrine of the Trinity." *European Journal of Theology* 14.2 (2005) 111–18.

Lindbeck, George A. *The Nature of Doctrine: Religion and Theology in a Post-Liberal Age.* London: Westminster, 1984.

The Liturgical Commission. *Living the New Creation.* London: Church of England, 2008.

Locke, John. *An Essay Concerning Human Understanding.* Edited by A. D. Woozley. London: William Collins, 1964.

Loewenstein, D. M. John. *Heresy, Literature, and Politics in Early Modern English Culture.* Cambridge: Cambridge University Press, 2006.

Lomax, Tim, and Michael Moynagh. *Liquid Worship.* Cambridge: Grove, 2004.

Londis, J. J. "Mediated Immediacy in the Thought of John E. Smith: A Critique." *Religious Studies* 11.4 (1975) 473–89.

Lopez, Augustus Nocodemus, and Jose Manoel DaConceicao. "Calvin, Theologian of the Holy Spirit: The Holy Spirit and the Word of God." *Scottish Bulletin of Evangelical Theology* 15.1 (1997) 38–49.

Losel, Steffan. "Guidance from the Gaps: The Holy Spirit, Ecclesial Authority, and the Principle of Juxtaposition." *Scottish Journal of Theology* 57.2 (2006) 140–58.

Loudovikos, Nicholas. "Christian Life and Institutional Church." In *The Theology of John Zizioulas: Personhood and the Church*, edited by Douglas H. Knight, 125–32. Farnham: Ashgate, 2007.

————. "Person Instead of Grace and Dictated Otherness: John Zizioulas's Final Theological Position." *Heythrop Journal* 52.4 (2011) 684–99.

Louth, Andrew. *Introducing Eastern Orthodox Theology.* London: SPCK, 2013.

———. "Receptive Ecumenism and Catholic Learning: An Orthodox Perspective." In *Receptive Ecumenism and the Call to Catholic Learning*, edited by Paul D. Murray, 361–72. Oxford: Oxford University Press, 2008.

Ludlow, Morwenna. *Gregory of Nyssa, Ancient and (Post)modern*. Oxford: Oxford University Press, 2007.

MacLaren, Duncan. *Mission Implausible*. Milton Keynes: Paternoster, 2004.

Marvin, Ernest. *Shaping Up: Re-Forming Reformed Worship*. London: United Reformed Church, 2005.

Mavrichi, Ionuţ. "Rev. Dr. Dumitru Staniloae—Background, Context, and Development of an Orthodox Ecclesiological Synthesis." In *ARSA 2012, Proceedings in Advanced Research in Scientific Areas (The First Virtual International Conference, December 3–7, 2012)*, edited by Stefan Badura et al., 1180–85. Zilina, Slovakia: EDIS, 2012. Online. https://ruj.uj.edu.pl/xmlui/bitstream/handle/item/43906/2012_ARSA_747-750.pdf?sequence=1&isAllowed=y.

Maxwell, Jack M. *Worship and Reformed Theology: The Liturgical Lessons of Mercersburg*. Princeton: Pickwick, 1976.

Mayor, Stephen. "The Teaching of John Owen Concerning the Lord's Supper." *Scottish Journal of Theology* 18 (1965) 170–81.

McCall, Tom. "Holy Love and Divine Aseity in the Theology of Jon Zizioulas." *Scottish Journal of Theology* 61.2 (2008) 191–205.

———. *Which Trinity? Whose Monotheism? Philosophical and Systematic Theologians on the Metaphysics of Trinitarian Theology*. Grand Rapids: Eerdmans, 2010.

McDermott, Gerald, ed. *The Oxford Handbook of Evangelical Theology*. Oxford: Oxford University Press, 2010.

McDonald, R. W. "Discerning the Spirit: The Pneumatology in Karl Barth's Church Dogmatics, Vols. I, II, IV." PhD diss., Cambridge University, 2011.

McDonnell, Kilian. *The Other Hand of God: The Holy Spirit as the Universal Touch and Goal*. Collegeville, MN: Liturgical, 2003.

McGrath, Alister E. *The Intellectual Origins of the European Reformation*. Oxford: Blackwell, 1987.

———. *Reformation Thought: An Introduction*. Oxford: Blackwell, 1993.

———. *Thomas Torrance: An Intellectual Biography*. Edinburgh: T&T Clark, 1999.

McGraw, Ryan M. *A Heavenly Directory: Trinitarian Piety, Public Worship, and a Reassessment of John Owen's Theology*. Göttingen: Vandenhoek and Ruprecht, 2014.

McIntyre, John. "The Holy Spirit in Greek Patristic Thought." *Scottish Journal of Theology* 7.4 (1954) 353–75.

———. *The Shape of Pneumatology*. Edinburgh: T&T Clark, 1997.

McPartlan, Paul. "Catholic Learning and Orthodoxy." In *Receptive Ecumenism and the Call to Catholic Learning*, edited by Paul D. Murray, 160–75. Oxford: Oxford University Press, 2008.

———. *The Eucharist Makes the Church: Henri de Lubac and John Zizioulas in Dialogue*. Edinburgh: T&T Clark, 1993.

———. *Sacrament of Salvation: An Introduction to Eucharistic Ecclesiology*. Edinburgh: T&T Clark, 1995.

———. "Who Is the Church? Zizioulas and von Balthasar on the Church's Identity." *Ecclesiology* 4.3 (2008) 271–88.

Medley, Mark S. "God for Us and with Us: The Contribution of Catherine LaCugna's Trinitarian Theology." *Lexington Theological Quarterly* 35.4 (2000) 219–34.

Metzler, Norman. "The Trinity in Contemporary Theology." *Concordia Theological Quarterly* 67.3–4 (2003) 270–87.

Meyendorff, John. "Continuities and Discontinuities in Byzantine Religious Thought." *Dumbarton Oaks Papers* 47 (1993) 69–81.

Meyers, Ruth A. "By Water and the Holy Spirit: Baptism and Confirmation." *Anglican Theological Review* 83.3 (2001) 417–42.

Milbank, John. *The Suspended Middle: Henri de Lubac and the Debate Concerning the Supernatural.* London: SCM, 2005.

Milbank, John, and Catherine Pickstock. *Truth in Aquinas.* London: Routledge, 2001.

Molnar, Paul D. "Can We Know God Directly? Rahner's Solution from Experience." *Theological Studies* 46.2 (1985) 228–61.

———. *Divine Freedom and the Doctrine of the Immanent Trinity.* Edinburgh: T&T Clark, 2002.

———. "The Function of the Immanent Trinity in the Theology of Karl Barth: Implications for Today." *Scottish Journal of Theology* 42 (1989) 367–99.

———. "'Thy Word Is Truth': The Role of Faith in Reading Scripture Theologically with Karl Barth." *Scottish Journal of Theology* 63.1 (2010) 70–92.

———. "Toward a Contemporary Doctrine of the Immanent Trinity: Karl Barth and the Present Discussion." *Scottish Journal of Theology* 49.3 (1996) 311–57.

Mongrain, Kevin. "Von Balthasar's Way from Doxology to Theology." *Theology Today* 64 (2007) 58–70.

Mortimer, Sarah. *Reason and Religion in the English Revolution: The Challenge of Socinianism.* Cambridge: Cambridge University Press, 2010.

Moule, Charles F. D. *The Holy Spirit.* London: Mowbrays, 1978.

Muller, Richard A. *After Calvin: Studies in the Development of a Theological Tradition.* Oxford: Oxford University Press, 2003.

Mullins, Phil. "Religious Meaning in Polanyi's Personal Knowledge." *Polanyiana: The Periodical of Michael Polanyi Liberal Philosophical Association* 2.3–4 (1993) 75–83.

Murray, Paul D., ed. *Receptive Ecumenism and the Call to Catholic Learning.* Oxford: Oxford University Press, 2008.

Murray, Stuart. *Church After Christendom.* Milton Keynes: Paternoster, 2004.

Nataraja, Kim, ed. *Journey to the Heart: Christian Contemplation through the Centuries.* Norwich: Canterbury, 2011.

Nausner, Bernhard. "The Failure of a Laudable Project: Gunton, the Trinity, and Human Self-Understanding." *Scottish Journal of Theology* 62.4 (2009) 403–20.

Newton, Nigel. "Michael Polanyi's Theory of Knowledge, Habermas and Interdisciplinary Research." 2011. Online. http://www.academia.edu/1572387/Michael_Polanyi_s_theory_of_knowledge_Habermas_and_interdisciplinary_research.

Nichols, Aidan. *Say It Is Pentecost: A Guide through Balthasar's Logic.* Edinburgh: T&T Clark 2001.

Ngien, Dennis. *Gifted Response: The Triune God as the Causative Agency of our Responsive Worship.* Milton Keynes: Paternoster, 2008.

Norris, Barry John. "Pneumatology, Existentialism, and Personal Encounter in Contemporary Theologies of Church and Ministry with Particular Reference to John Zizioulas and Martin Buber." PhD diss., King's College London, 1995.

Nuttall, Geoffrey F. *The Holy Spirit and Ourselves.* London: Epworth, 1966.

———. *The Holy Spirit in Puritan Faith and Experience*. Oxford: Blackwell, 1946.

———. *Studies in Christian Enthusiasm Illustrated from Early Quakerism*. Wallingford, PA: Pendle Hill, 1948.

Oakes, Edward T., and David Moss, eds. *Cambridge Companion to Hans Urs von Balthasar*. Cambridge: Cambridge University Press, 2004.

Oden, Thomas C. *Christ and Salvation*. Vol. 2 of *John Wesley's Teachings*. Grand Rapids: Zondervan, 2012.

O'Donnell, Laurence R. "The Holy Spirit's Role in John Owen's 'Covenant of the Mediator' Formulation: A Case Study in Reformed Orthodox Formulations of the *Pactum Salutis*." *Puritan Reformed Journal* 4.1 (2012) 91–115.

Old, Hughes Oliphant. *The Reading and Preaching of the Scriptures in the Worship of the Christian Church*. Grand Rapids: Eerdmans,1998.

———. *Worship Reformed according to Scripture*. Louisville, KY: Westminster John Knox, 2002.

Oliver, Robert W., ed. *John Owen: The Man and His Theology*. Phillipsburg: P&R, 2002.

Oman, John. *The Natural and the Supernatural*. Cambridge: Cambridge University Press, 1931.

Ormerod, Neil. "History and Theology in Dialogue on the Trinity." *Pacifica* 21 (2008) 146–59.

Osborne, Kenan B. *Christian Sacraments in a Postmodern World: A Theology for the Third Millennium*. Mahwah, NJ: Paulist, 2000.

Otto, Rudolf. *The Idea of the Holy*. London: Oxford University Press, 1923.

Owen, John. *The Works of John Owen*. Edited by William H. Goold. 24 vols. London: Johnstone and Hunter, 1856.

Packer, James Innell. "About John Owen." *JohnOwen.org*. Online. http://www.johnowen.org/about.

———. *A Quest for Godliness*. Wheaton, IL: Good News, 1990.

Papanikolaou, Aristotle. *Being with God: Trinity, Apophaticism, and Divine-Human Communion*. Notre Dame: University of Notre Dame Press, 2006.

———. "Contemporary Orthodox Currents on the Trinity." In *The Oxford Handbook of the Trinity*, edited by Giles Emery and Matthew Levering, 328–38. Oxford: Oxford University Press, 2011.

———. "Divine Energies or Divine Personhood: Vladimir Lossky and John Zizioulas on Conceiving the Transcendent and Immanent God." *Modern Theology* 19.3 (2003) 357–85.

———. "Personhood and Its Exponents in Twentieth-Century Orthodox Theology." In *The Cambridge Companion to Orthodox Christian Theology*, edited by Mary B. Cunningham and Elizabeth Theokritoff, 232–45. Cambridge: Cambridge University Press, 2008.

Papathanasiou, Athanasios. "Some Key Themes and Figures in Greek Theological Thought." In *The Cambridge Companion to Orthodox Christian Theology*, edited by Mary B. Cunningham and Elizabeth Theokritoff, 218–31. Cambridge: Cambridge University Press, 2008.

Parry, Robin A. *Worshipping Trinity: Coming Back to the Heart of Worship*. Milton Keynes: Paternoster, 2006.

Payne, Daniel. "The 'Relational Ontology' of Christos Yannaras: The Hesychast Influence on the Understanding of the Person in the Thought of Christos Yannaras." 2015. Online.   https://www.academia.edu/1479462/The_Relational_Ontology_of_

Christos_Yannaras_The_Hesychastic_Influence_on_the_Understanding_of_ the_Person_in_the_Thought_of_Christos_Yannaras.

Payne, Jon D. *John Owen on the Lord's Supper*. Edinburgh: Banner of Truth, 2004.

Pecklers, Keith F. *Worship*. London: Continuum, 2003.

Peels, Rik. "Sin and Human Cognition of God." *Scottish Journal of Theology* 64.4 (2011) 390–410.

Peguy, Charles. *The Portal of the Mystery of Hope*. Edinburgh: T&T Clark, 1996.

Pelikan, Jaroslav. "An Essay on the Development of Christian Doctrine." *Church History* 35.1 (1966) 3–12.

———. *The Growth of Medieval Theology*. Chicago: University of Chicago Press, 1978.

———. *Historical and Theological Guide to Creeds and Confessions of Faith in the Christian Tradition*. New Haven: Yale University Press, 2003.

Pérez, Ángel Cordovilla. "The Trinitarian Concept of Person." In *Re-Thinking Trinitarian Theology*, edited by Robert J. Wozniak and Guilio Maspero, 105–45. Edinburgh: T&T Clark, 2012.

Peters, Ted. *God as Trinity: Relationality and Temporality in Divine Life*. Louisville, KY: Westminster John Knox, 1993.

Petersen, David G. *Engaging with God: A Biblical Theology of Worship*. Downers Grove, IL: InterVarsity, 2002.

Philibert, Paul, ed. *At the Heart of Christian Worship: Liturgical Essays of Yves Congar*. English translation. Collegeville, MN: Liturgical, 2010.

Plantinga, Alvin. *Does God Have a Nature?* Marquette, WI: Marquette University Press, 1980.

———. *Warranted Christian Belief*. Oxford: Oxford University Press, 2000.

———. *Where the Conflict Really Lies: Science, Religion, and Naturalism*. Oxford: Oxford University Press, 2011.

Plekon, Michael P. "'The World as Sacrament' in Alexander Schmemann's Vision." *Logos* 50 (2009) 429–39.

Polanyi, Michael. *Personal Knowledge*. London: Routledge and Kegan Paul, 1958.

———. "Tacit Knowledge: Its Bearing on Some Problems of Philosophy." *Reviews of Modern Physics* 34.4 (1962) 601–16.

Polkinghorne, John, ed. *The Trinity and an Entangled World: Relationality in Physical Science*. Grand Rapids: Eerdmans, 2006.

Pope, Robert, ed. *T&T Clark Companion to Nonconformity*. London: Bloomsbury, 2013.

Power, D. N. "The Synod on the Eucharist and Ecumenism." *Ecumenical Trends* 34 (2005) 12–15.

Quash, Ben. *Found Theology: History, Imagination, and the Holy Spirit*. London: Bloomsbury, 2013.

———. *Hans Urs von Balthasar*. Oxford: Blackwell, 2005.

———. "Revelation." In *The Oxford Handbook of Systematic Theology*, edited by J. B. Webster et al., 325–43. Oxford: Oxford University Press, 2007.

Radde-Gallwitz, Andrew. "The Holy Spirit as Agent, Not Activity: Origen's Argument with Modalism and Its Afterlife in Didymus, Eunomius, and Gregory of Nazianzus." *Vigilliae Christianae* 65.3 (2011) 227–48.

———. *Basil of Caesarea: A Guide to His Life and Doctrine*. Eugene, OR: Cascade, 2012.

Rahner, Karl. *Spiritual Writings*. Maryknoll, NY: Orbis, 2004.

———. *The Trinity*. New York: Herder and Herder, 1970.

Ratzinger, Joseph C. *The Spirit of the Liturgy*. San Francisco: Ignatius, 2000.

Rehnman, Sebastian. *Divine Discourse: The Theological Methodology of John Owen.* Grand Rapids: Baker Academic, 2002.

———. "John Owen on Faith and Reason." In *The Ashgate Research Companion to John Owen's Theology,* edited by K. M. Kapic and M. Jones, 31–48. Farnham: Ashgate, 2015.

———. "Natural Theology and Epistemic Justification." *Heythrop Journal* 51.6 (2010) 1017–22.

———. "Theistic Metaphysics and Biblical Exegesis: Francis Turretin on the Concept of God." *Religious Studies* 38.2 (2002) 167–86.

Reid, Duncan. "Patristics and the Postmodern in the Theology of John Zizioulas." *Pacifica* 22 (2009) 308–16.

Reinders, Hans S. *Receiving the Gift of Friendship: Profound Disability, Theological Anthropology, and Ethics.* Grand Rapids: Eerdmans, 2008.

Rice, Howard L., and James C. Huffstutler. *Reformed Worship,* Louisville, KY: Geneva, 2001.

Richards, Jay W. *The Untamed God: A Philosophical Exploration of Divine Perfection, Simplicity, and Immutability.* Westmont, IL: InterVarsity, 2003.

Robinson, Peter Mark Benjamin. "Towards a Definition of Persons and Relations: With Particular Reference to the Relational Ontology of John Zizioulas." PhD diss., King's College London, 1999.

Rogers, Eugene F. *After the Spirit: A Constructive Pneumatology from Resources outside the Modern West.* Grand Rapids: Eerdmans, 2005.

Ross, Melanie C., and Simon Jones, eds. *The Serious Business of Worship: Essays in Honour of Bryan D. Spinks.* Edinburgh: T&T Clark, 2010.

Rousseau, Philip. *Basil of Caesarea.* Oakland: University of California Press, 1994.

Rowland, Tracey. "Review of *Rethinking Trinitarian Theology: Disputed Questions and Contemporary Issues in Trinitarian Theology,* by Robert J. Wozniak and Giulio Maspero, eds." *Reviews in Religion and Theology* 21.1 (2014) 153–55.

Russell, Norman. "Modern Greek Theologians and the Greek Fathers." *Philosophy and Theology* 18.1 (2006) 77–92.

Schindler, David L. *Heart of the World, Center of the Church: Communio Ecclesiology, Liberalism, and Liberation.* Grand Rapids: Eerdmans, 1996.

Schmemann, Alexander. *The Eucharist.* Yonkers, NY: St. Vladimir's Seminary, 1997.

———. *Introduction to Liturgical Theology.* Translated by A. E. Moorhouse. Yonkers, NY: St. Vladimir's Seminary, 1987.

———. "Liturgy and Eschatology." *Sobornost Incorporating Eastern Churches Review* 7.1 (1985) 6–14.

Schönborn, Christoph, and Hubert Philipp Weber. *The Source of Life: Exploring the Mystery of the Eucharist.* New York: Crossroad, 2007.

Schwobel, Christoph, ed. *Trinitarian Theology Today: Essays on Divine Being and Act.* Edinburgh: T&T Clark, 1995.

Scott, C. E. "Review of Gadamer's *Truth and Method.*" *Anglican Theological Review* 59.1 (1977) 63–78.

———. "Schleiermacher and the Problem of Divine Immediacy." *Religious Studies* 3.1 (1967) 499–512.

Seville, Thomas. "The Theology of John Zizioulas: Personhood and the Church (Aldershot: Ashgate, 2007)." *Ecclesiology* 6.2 (2010) 213–57.

Sherlock, William. *A Defence and Continuation of the Discourse Concerning the Knowledge of Jesus Christ and our Union and Communion with Him, with a Particular Respect to the Doctrine of the Church of England and the Charge of Socinianism and Pelagianism*. London: W. Ketilby, 1678.

———. *A Discourse Concerning the Knowledge of Jesus Christ and Our Union and Communion with Him*. London: W. Kettilby, 1674.

Shishkov, Andrey. "Metropolitan John Zizioulas on Primacy in the Church." *IKZ* 104 (2014) 205–19. Online. https://www.academia.edu/9283818/Metropolitan_John_Zizioulas_on_Primacy_in_the_Church.

Shults, F. LeRon, and Andrea Hollingsworth. *The Holy Spirit*. Grand Rapids: Eerdmans, 2008.

Simpson, C. "Theologia Corporum and the Cappadocian Fathers." *Radical Orthodoxy: Theology, Philosophy, Politics* 1.3 (2013) 469–83.

Slater, Jennifer. "'Direct Experience of God': A Quest for Refinement and Illumination in Christian Faith and Practice." *Studia Historiae Ecclesiasticae* 36s (2010) 273–86.

Smith, Christian. *What Is a Person?* Chicago: Chicago University Press, 2010.

Smith, John E. "In What Sense Can We Speak of Experiencing God." *Journal of Religion* 50.3 (1970) 229–44.

———. *Reason and God*. New Haven: Yale University Press, 1961.

———. "The Tension between Direct Experience and Argument in Religion." *Religious Studies* 17.2 (1981) 487–97.

Smith, James K. A., and Shannon Schutt Nason. "Radical Orthodoxy: A Select Bibliography." Calvin College, 2002. Online. http://citeseer.ist.psu.edu/viewdoc/download;jsessionid=144C46C32EF38C3653DED1610E660789?doi=10.1.1.627.6726&rep=rep1&type=pdf.

Spellman, W. M. *John Locke*. London: MacMillan, 1997.

Spence, Alan. *Incarnation and Inspiration*. Edinburgh: T&T Clark, 2007.

———. "John Owen and Trinitarian Agency." *Scottish Journal of Theology* 43.2 (1990) 157–73.

Spinks, Bryan D. *Freedom or Order: The Eucharistic Liturgy in English Congregationalism, 1645–1980*. Princeton: Pickwick, 1984.

Staniloae, Dumitru. *The Experience of God*. Brookline, MA: Holy Cross, 2012.

Stearns, J. Brenton. "Mediated Immediacy: A Search for Some Models." *International Journal for Philosophy of Religion* 3.4 (1972) 195–211.

Steinmetz, David Curtis. "The Superiority of Pre-Critical Exegesis." *Theology Today* 37.1 (1980) 27–38.

Stover, D. "The Pneumatology of John Owen: A Study of the Role of the Holy Spirit in Relation to the Shape of a Theology." PhD diss., McGill University, 1967.

Stringer, Michael D. "The Lord and Giver of Life: The Person and Work of the Holy Spirit in the Trinitarian Theology of Colin E. Gunton." PhD diss., University of Notre Dame, 2008.

Studebaker, Steven M. "Jonathan Edward's Social *Augustinian* Trinitarianism: An Alternative to a Recent Trend." *Scottish Journal of Theology* 56.3 (2003) 268–85.

Sudduth, Michael Czapkay. "Plantinga's Revision of the Reformed Tradition: Rethinking Our Natural Knowledge of God." *Philosophical Books* 43.2 (2002) 81–90.

———. "The Prospects for 'Mediate' Natural Theology in John Calvin." *Religious Studies* 31.1 (1995) 53–68.

———. "Reformed Epistemology and Christian Apologetics." *Religious Studies* 39.3 (2003) 300–21.

Sutton, John. "Soul and Body." In *The Oxford Handbook of British Philosophy in the Seventeenth Century*, edited by P. R. Antsey, 285–307. Oxford: Oxford University Press, 2013.

Sweeney, Sylvia. "Future Directions in Liturgical Development." *Anglican Theological Review* 95.3 (2013) 517–24.

Taylor, Charles. *Sources of Self: The Making of Modern Identity*. Cambridge, MA: Harvard University Press, 1989.

Templeton, Julian. "The Practice of Calling Upon the Holy Spirit's Help in Reformed Worship." Paper presented to the Area Forum of the Central and North London Area, Thames, North Synod, United Reformed Church, Trinity Church, Mill Hill, London, May 21, 2013. Online. http://www.academia.edu/8664703/The_Practice_of_Calling_upon_the_Holy_Spirits_help_in_Reformed_Worship.

Templeton, Julian, and Keith Riglin. *Reforming Worship: English Reformed Principles and Practice*. Eugene, OR: Wipf and Stock, 2012.

Theodoert, et al. *Historical Writings*. Vol. 2 of *Nicene and Post-Nicene Fathers*, Series 2. Edited by Philip Schaff. 1886–1889. 14 vols. Reprint, Grand Rapids: Christian Classics Ethereal Library, 2007.

Thomas, R. S. "A Comparative Study of First-and Second-Generation Homiletic in the New Testament Church of God." Paper presented at Postgraduate Seminar Series, Spurgeons College, London, May 13, 2015.

Thompson, Bard. *Liturgies of the Western Church*. Philadelphia: Fortress, 1980.

Tibbs, Eve M. "The Challenges and Potential of Orthodox Ecumenical Doctrine." 2003. Online. https://stpaulsirvine.org/wp-content/uploads/2015/06/ecumenical_challenges.pdf

———. "East Meets West: Trinity, Truth, and Communion in John Zizioulas and Colin Gunton." PhD diss., Fuller Theological Seminary, 2005.

Ticciati, Susannah. "Augustine and Grace Ex Nihilo." *Augustinian Studies* 41.2 (2010) 401–22.

Torevell, David. *Liturgy and the Beauty of the Unknown*. Farnham: Ashgate, 2007.

Torpy, Arthur Alan. *The Prevenient Piety of Samuel Wesley Sr*. Washington, DC: Scarecrow, 2009.

Torrance, Iain. "Gadamer, Polanyi, and Ways of Being Closed." *Scottish Journal of Theology* 26.4 (1993) 497–506.

Torrance, James B. "Authority, Scripture, and Tradition." *Evangelical Quarterly* 87.3 (1987) 245–51.

———. *Worship, Community, and the Triune God of Grace*. Milton Keynes: Paternoster, 1996.

Torrance, Thomas F., ed. *Belief in Science and in Christian Life: The Relevance of Michael Polanyi's Thought*. Haddington: Handsel, 1980.

———. *The Christian Doctrine of God: One Being Three Persons*. London: T&T Clark, 2016.

———. *The Christian Frame of Mind*. Haddington: Handsel, 1985

———. "The Doctrine of the Holy Trinity in Gregory Nazianzen and John Calvin." *Sobornost* 12.1 (1990) 7–24.

———. "Michael Polanyi and the Christian Faith—A Personal Report." *Truth and Discovery* 27.2 (2000) 26–33.

————. *The Trinitarian Faith: The Evangelical Theology of the Ancient Catholic Church.* Edinburgh: T&T Clark, 1988.

Trueman, Carl R. *The Claims of Truth: John Owen's Trinitarian Theology.* Milton Keynes: Paternoster, 1998.

————. *John Owen: Reformed Catholic, Renaissance Man.* Farnham: Ashgate, 2007.

Trueman, Carl R., and R. Scott Clark. *Protestant Scholasticism: Essays in Reassessment.* Milton Keynes: Paternoster, 2005.

Underhill, Evelyn. *Worship.* London: Nisbett, 1936.

Vial, Theodore M. "Friedrich Schleiermacher on the Central Place of Worship in Theology." *Harvard Theological Review* 91.1 (1998) 59–73.

Vickers, Jason E. *Invocation and Assent: The Making and Re-Making of Trinitarian Theology.* Grand Rapids: Eerdmans, 2008.

Vischer, Lukas. *Christian Worship in Reformed Churches Past and Present.* Grand Rapids: Eerdmans, 2003.

Vogel, Dwight W., ed. *Primary Sources of Liturgical Theology.* Collegeville, MN: Liturgical, 2000.

Vogel, Jeffrey. "A Little While in the Son of God: Austin Farrer on the Trinitarian Nature of Prayer." *Scottish Journal of Theology* 64.4 (2011) 410–24.

Volf, Miroslav. *After Our Likeness: The Church as the Image of the Trinity.* Grand Rapids: Eerdmans, 1998.

Volf, Miroslav, and Michael Welker, eds. *God's Life in Trinity.* Minneapolis: Fortress, 2006.

Vondey, Wolfgang. *Beyond Pentecostalism: The Crisis of Global Christianity and the Renewal of the Theological Agenda.* Grand Rapids: Eerdmans, 2010.

————. "The Holy Spirit and Time in Contemporary Catholic and Protestant Theology." *Scottish Journal of Theology* 58.4 (2005) 393–409.

Voskressenskaia, Janna. "The 'Other' Person: The Receiving of the Russian Neopatristics in J. Zizioulas's Theology." In *Russian Thought In Europe: Reception, Polemic, and Development*, edited by T. Obolevich et al., 23–36. Kraków: Akademia Ignatianum, 2013.

Wainwright, Geoffrey. *Doxology: The Praise of God in Worship, Doctrine, and Life.* London: Epworth, 1980.

————. *Worship with One Accord.* Oxford: Oxford University Press, 1997.

Wainwright, Geoffrey, and Karen B. Westerfield Tucker, eds. *The Oxford History of Christian Worship.* Oxford: Oxford University Press, 2006.

Walker, Christopher J. *Reason and Religion in Late Seventeenth-Century England: The Politics and Theology of Radical Dissent.* London: I. B. Tauris, 2013.

Ward, Graham, ed. *The Blackwell Companion to Postmodern Theology.* Oxford: Blackwell, 2001.

Ward, Peter. *Liquid Church.* Milton Keynes: Paternoster, 2002.

Ware, Kallistos. *The Orthodox Church.* London: Penguin, 1993.

————. "The Theology of Worship." *Sobornost* 5.10 (1970) 729–36.

Warfield, Benjamin Breckinridge. *Calvin and Calvinism.* Grand Rapids: Baker Academic, 1981.

Warrington, Keith. *Pentecostal Theology: A Theology of Encounter.* Edinburgh: T&T Clark, 2008.

Watkin-Jones, Howard. *The Holy Spirit from Arminius to Wesley: A Study of Christian Teaching Concerning the Holy Spirit and His Place in the Trinity in the Seventeenth and Eighteenth Centuries*. London: Epworth, 1929.

Webb, Mark. "Religious Experience." *Stanford Encyclopedia of Philosophy*, December 13, 2017. Edited by Edward N. Zalta. Online. http://plato.stanford.edu/entries/religious-experience.

Webster, John. *Barth's Ethics of Reconciliation*. Cambridge: Cambridge University Press, 1995.

———. *The Domain of the Word: Scripture and Theological Reason*. Edinburgh: T&T Clark, 2012.

Webster, John B., et al., eds. *The Oxford Handbook of Systematic Theology*. Oxford: Oxford University Press, 2007.

Weinandy, Thomas. "Zizioulas: The Trinity and Ecumenism." *New Blackfriars* 83.979 (2002) 407–15.

Weiser, T., ed. *Cultures in Dialogue: Documents from a Symposium in Honour of Philip A. Potter*. Geneva: World Council of Churches, 1985.

Welker, Michael. *God the Spirit*. Minneapolis: Fortress, 1994.

Wildman, Wesley J. "An Introduction to Relational Ontology." In *The Trinity and an Entangled World: Relationality in Physical Science*, edited by John Polkinghorne, 55–73. Grand Rapids: Eerdmans, 2006.

White, James F. *Introduction to Christian Worship*. Nashville: Abingdon, 2001.

———. *Protestant Worship: Tradition in Transition*. Louisville, KY: Westminster John Knox, 1989

———. "Writing the History of English Worship: The Achievement of Horton Davies." *Church History* 47.4 (1978) 434–40.

White, Susan J. *Groundwork of Christian Worship*. London: Epworth, 1997.

———. *The Spirit of Worship: The Liturgical Tradition*. Maryknoll, NY: Orbis, 1999.

Wiley, Tatha. *Original Sin*. Mahwah, NJ: Paulist, 2002.

Wilks, J. G. F. "The Trinitarian Ontology of John Zizioulas." *Vox Evangelica* 25 (1995) 63–88.

Willard, J. "Alston's Epistemology of Religious Belief and the Problem of Religious Diversity." *Religious Studies* 37.1 (2001) 49–74.

———. "Plantinga's Epistemology of Religious Belief and the Problem of Religious Diversity." *Heythrop Journal* 44.3 (2003) 275–93.

Willey, Basil. *The Seventeenth-Century Background: Studies in the Thought of the Age in Relation to Poetry and Religion*. London: Chatto and Windus, 1934.

Witvliet, John D. "The Trinitarian DNA of Christian Worship: Perennial Themes in Recent Theological Literature." *Colloquium Journal* 2 (2005) 1–22.

Woolverton, John F. "Hans W. Frei in Context: A Theological and Historical Memoir." *Anglican Theological Review* 79.3 (1997) 377–589.

World Alliance of Reformed Churches. "Agreed Statement on the Holy Trinity: Orthodox-Reformed Dialogue." Kappel-am-Albis, Switzerland, March 1992.

World Council of Churches. *Christian Perspectives on Theological Anthropology*. Geneva: World Council of Churches, 2010.

———. *Together Towards Life: Mission and Evangelism in Changing Landscapes*. Geneva: World Council of Churches, 2012.

Wozniak, Robert J., and Guilio Maspero, eds. *Rethinking Trinitarian Theology: Disputed Questions and Contemporary Issues in Trinitarian Theology*. Edinburgh: T&T Clark, 2012.

Wright, J. R. "Holy Spirit in Holy Church: From Experience to Doctrine." *Anglican Theological Review* 83.3 (2001) 443–54.

Wybrew, Hugh. "A Western Appreciation of Orthodox Worship." *Theology Today* 61.1 (2004) 41–52.

Yandell, Keith E. *The Epistemology of Religious Experience*. Cambridge: Cambridge University Press, 1994.

Yannaras, Christos. "The Church: A Mode of Being That Can Conquer Death." *Sourozh* 49 (1992) 24.

Yik-pui Au, T. "The Eucharist as Cultural Critique: A Construction Based on the Eucharistic Theology of John D. Zizioulas." *International Journal of Orthodox Theology* 3.2 (2012) 53–88.

Yong, Amos. *Beyond the Impasse: Towards a Pneumatological Theology of Religion*. Milton Keynes: Authentic, 2003.

———. *The Missiological Spirit: Christian Mission Theology in the Third Millennium Global Context*. Eugene, OR: Cascade, 2014.

———. *Spirit of Love: A Trinitarian Theology of Grace*. Waco, TX: Baylor University Press, 2012.

———. *The Spirit Poured Out on All Flesh: Pentecostalism and the Possibility of Global Theology*. Grand Rapids: Baker Academic, 2005.

———. *Who Is the Holy Spirit? A Walk with the Apostles*. Brewster, MS: Paraclete, 2011.

Zemler-Cizewski, Wanda. "'The Lord, the Giver of Life': A Reflection on the Theology of the Holy Spirit in the Twelfth Century." *Anglican Theological Review* 83.3 (2001) 547–56.

Zizioulas, J. D. *Being as Communion*. Yonkers, NY: St. Vladimir's Seminary, 1985.

———. "Come, Holy Spirit, Sanctify Our Lives!" Greek Orthodox Archdiocese of America, 2015.

———. *Communion and Otherness*. Edinburgh: T&T Clark, 2006.

———. "The Doctrine of God the Trinity Today: Suggestions for an Ecumenical Study." In *The Forgotten Trinity 3: A Selection of Papers Presented to the BCC Study Commission on Trinitarian Doctrine Today*, edited by Alasdair I. C. Heron, 19–32. London: British Council of Churches, 1991.

———. *Eucharist, Bishop, Church: The Unity of the Church in the Divine Eucharist and the Bishop During the First Three Centuries*. Brookline, MA: Holy Cross, 2001.

———. *Eucharistic Communion and the World*. Edinburgh: T&T Clark, 2011.

———. "Faith and Order: Yesterday, Today, and Tomorrow." Paper prepared for Faith and Order consultation with Younger Theologians, Turku, Finland, August 11, 1995. Online. https://www.oikoumene.org/en/resources/documents/commissions/faith-and-order/xii-essays/faith-and-order-yesterday-today-and-tomorrow.

———. "Humanity and Nature: Learning from the Indigenous." Paper given at Sixth Ecological Symposium on the Amazon River, Amazonia, May 23, 2012.

———. *Lectures in Christian Dogmatics*. Edinburgh: T&T Clark, 2008.

———. *The One and the Many: Studies on God, Man, the Church and the World Today*. Alhambra, CA: Sebastian, 2010.

———. *Remembering the Future*. London: Bloomsbury Academic, 2013.

———. "The Self Understanding of the Orthodox and their Participation in the Ecumenical Movement." In *The Ecumenical Movement, the Churches, and the World Council of Churches: An Orthodox Contribution to the Reflection Process on "The Common Understanding and Vision of the WCC,"* edited by G. Lemopoulos, 46. Geneva: World Council of Churches-Syndesmos, 1996.

———. "The Teaching of the Second Ecumenical Council on the Holy Spirit in Historical and Ecumenical Perspective." *Credo in Spiritum Sanctum, Teologia e filosofia* 6.1 (1993) 38–53.

Index

abstract principle in nature, Spirit as, 116

"abstract structural models," of Zizioulas, 22

acceptance of creation, Eucharist as, 216–17

Act of Uniformity of 1662, 90, 90n21–91n21, 229

activities, of the Spirit referenced by Owen, 123–24

"activity" and "being" in God, balance between, 36–37, 36n33–37n33

activity of God, in the Eucharist, 100

actualization of revelation, 219, 220

Afanasiev, Nicholas, 99

After the Spirit (Rogers), 5, 107, 199n1

Agreed Statement on the Holy Trinity, 227n8

Aldred, Joe, 8–9, 11

Allmen, J. J. von, 108

Ambrose, 200

American Methodism, growth of, 67

American Pentecostalism, development of, 67

Anatolios, Khaled, 85–86, 130, 143

An Answer unto Two Questions: With Twelve Arguments against Any Conformity to Worship Not of Divine Institution (Owen), 94

anthropology, Eucharist as, 217

"anthroposensitive theology," of Owen, 61n18

anti-trinitarian writing and thinking, prevalent in the seventeenth century, 27

apocalyptic theology, 189n51

the "Apophatic" approach, 185

Areeplackal, Joseph, 21

Arian controversy, 29n6

art, as "presence," 132

"assurance," Protestant experience of, 144

Athanasius, 143

Au, Tanya Yik-pui, 199n1

Augustine, Zizioulas's critique of, 127–28

Augustinian understanding of the Spirit, 34

authority
    of the Holy Spirit for Puritans, 16–17
    of the local congregation to interpret scripture, 31
    in Reformation churches, 174n6
    Roman Catholic understanding of, 178
    vested in the bishop for the Orthodox, 137

Awad, Najib George, 49, 113–14

Ayres, Lewis, 42

Azusa Street revival, 9

involving being drawn by the Holy
Spirit into a relationship with
the One, 134
as the key point of encounter with
the Holy Spirit for both Owen
and Zizioulas, 80
as key to the encounter with the
Holy Spirit, 202
leading to the counsciousness of
the otherness of God, 208
leading to transformed lives, 199
lived reality of the Trinity
encountered in, 34–39
nature and content of for Owen
and Zizioulas, 106
nature and understanding of in
Owen and Zizioulas, 86–107
new ways of approaching, 84
next and principal ends of all
instituted, 208n25
not necessarily seen as an
encounter with the living,
transforming God, 3
offered corporately carrying a dual
significance, 115
offering visibility for the Holy
Spirit's transformative activity,
222
opening up a relationship with the
divine, 56
origins in the divine rather than
the human, 95
Owen
and, 88–95
having a stronger focus in the
preaching of the Word, 82
holding together his thinking
about God within the
setting of, 36
as the place in which each person
finds himself or herself as
person, 101
practice of in the Reformed
tradition, 137
reclaiming the holiness of God in,
3–5
relationship

with the Holy Spirit, 86–107,
224–35
with theology for Zizioulas, 46
as response to God's initiative
rather than initiated by human
activity, 88
as a response to the work of the
Holy Spirit, 108
role of in understanding truth
as relational for Owen and
Zizioulas, 194–95
as seen in the Eucharist for
Zizioulas, 42, 160
services, Owen's lack of specificity
in outlining the nature and
content of, 95
significance of for Owen and
Zizioulas, 83–111
similarities and differences
between Owen and Zizioulas,
102–7
similarities of Owen and Zizioulas
in regard to, 103–5
sources and settings for Owen and
Zizioulas, 102–3
study of as a site of the Spirit's
presence and work remains
marginal, 54
thesis nine, 201
thesis ten, 224
truth being focused in, 196
twenty-first-century approaches
to, 4
understanding of the priority
of undergirding Zizioulas's
writing, 97
writers focused on the opening up
of the history and development
of, 84
Zizioulas
context and approach to,
96–102
focus on centered on the
Eucharist, 82
seeing primarily as Eucharistic
worship, 191
understanding of the link with
theology, 22

Lightning Source UK Ltd.
Milton Keynes UK
UKHW020937190121
377295UK00005B/107

9 781725 261112